Language and Justice

Bringing together cutting-edge research at the intersection of language, communication and legal practice, this volume challenges established processes and explores key questions arising from real cases, practices or sites of contention, where tackling linguistic issues can help enhance access to justice. Directly addressing areas of genuine professional and institutional concern, the collection provides novel and groundbreaking insights into the multiple communication-related challenges the justice system and legal professionals have to navigate on a daily basis. The volume engages with a wide range of legal areas, including criminal law, family law, civil law, immigration, international law and legal education. It has an international scope, with relevance across both adversarial and inquisitorial legal systems, international legal institutions and multilingual jurisdictions. Collectively, the chapters highlight the immense benefits and opportunities which arise when legal and applied linguistic scholarship are harnessed together, especially for scrutinising the accountability, transparency and accessibility of the justice system.

TATIANA GRIESHOFER is Professor of Language and Law with an interdisciplinary research profile across socio-legal studies, administrative law and applied linguistics. Drawing on mixed methods approaches, her work explores access to justice pathways across criminal, civil and family proceedings.

KATE HAWORTH is Visiting Senior Research Fellow at the Aston Institute for Forensic Linguistics, of which she is a founding member. Prior to her academic career, she was a practising barrister. She has been an active researcher in the field of investigative interviewing for over twenty years.

Language and Justice

Communication in Legal Practice

Edited by

Tatiana Grieshofer

Birmingham City University

Kate Haworth

Aston University

CAMBRIDGE
UNIVERSITY PRESS

CAMBRIDGE
UNIVERSITY PRESS

Shaftesbury Road, Cambridge CB2 8EA, United Kingdom

One Liberty Plaza, 20th Floor, New York, NY 10006, USA

477 Williamstown Road, Port Melbourne, VIC 3207, Australia

314–321, 3rd Floor, Plot 3, Splendor Forum, Jasola District Centre, New Delhi – 110025, India

103 Penang Road, #05–06/07, Visioncrest Commercial, Singapore 238467

Cambridge University Press is part of Cambridge University Press & Assessment, a department of the University of Cambridge.

We share the University's mission to contribute to society through the pursuit of education, learning and research at the highest international levels of excellence.

www.cambridge.org
Information on this title: www.cambridge.org/9781009540957

DOI: 10.1017/9781009540988

When citing this work, please include a reference to the DOI 10.1017/9781009540988

First published 2026

A catalogue record for this publication is available from the British Library

A Cataloging-in-Publication data record for this book is available from the Library of Congress

ISBN 978-1-009-54095-7 Hardback

To Eddie and Klaus

TG

To Natalie and Aidy

KH

Contents

Part II Communication and Legal Profession

Figures

Tables

Contributors

ELENA BARRETT Doctoral Researcher, Department of Language and Communication Studies, University of Jyväskylä, Finland.

NADJA CAPUS Professor of Criminal Law and Criminal Procedure, Faculty of Law, University of Neuchâtel, Switzerland.

DEBBIE COOPER Associate Research Fellow, School of Law, University of Nottingham, United Kingdom.

MALCOLM COULTHARD Emeritus Professor, Aston Institute for Forensic Linguistics, Aston University, United Kingdom.

SIGURD D'HONDT Professor of Applied Linguistics, Department of Language and Communication Studies, University of Jyväskylä, Finland.

JONATHAN DOAK Professor of Criminal Justice, Nottingham Law School, Nottingham Trent University, United Kingdom.

FABIO FERRAZ DE ALMEIDA Lecturer in Criminology, University of Lincoln, United Kingdom.

MEL GREENLEE Retired Staff Attorney, California Appellate Project, United States.

CORNELIA GRIEBEL Lecturer in Legal Translation, Faculty of Translation Studies, Linguistics, and Cultural Studies, University of Mainz, Germany.

TATIANA GRIESHOFER Professor of Language and Law, Birmingham City University, United Kingdom.

KATE HAWORTH Visiting Senior Research Fellow, Aston Institute for Forensic Linguistics, Aston University, United Kingdom.

CHRIS HEFFER Reader, Centre for Language and Communication Research, School of English, Communication and Philosophy, Cardiff University, United Kingdom.

FRANZISKA HOHL ZÜRCHER Post-doctoral Researcher in Sociology, Faculty of Law, University of Neuchâtel, Switzerland.

John Jackson Emeritus Professor of Comparative Criminal Law and Procedure, School of Law, University of Nottingham, United Kingdom.

Miranda Lai Associate Professor in Translating and Interpreting, School of Global, Urban and Social Studies, Royal Melbourne Institute of Technology, Australia.

Janny H. C. Leung Professor of Linguistics, School of English, University of Hong Kong, Hong Kong.

Eva N. S. Ng Associate Professor, Translation Programme, School of Chinese, University of Hong Kong, Hong Kong.

Judith Reynolds Lecturer in Intercultural Communication, School of Education, Communication and Language Sciences, Newcastle University, United Kingdom.

Michele Ruyters Professor, Associate Dean, Criminology and Justice Studies, School of Global, Urban and Social Studies, Royal Melbourne Institute of Technology, Australia.

Candida Saunders Assistant Professor in Law, School of Law, University of Nottingham, United Kingdom.

Laura Smith-Khan Senior Lecturer, School of Law, University of New England, Australia.

Gregory Stratton Senior Lecturer, Criminology and Justice Studies, School of Global, Urban and Social Studies, Royal Melbourne Institute of Technology, Australia.

L. Alexander Walker III Academic Fellow, Columbia Law School, Columbia University, United States.

David Wright Associate Professor in Linguistics, School of Arts and Humanities, Nottingham Trent University, United Kingdom.

1 Introduction

The Role of Language in Law and Justice

Tatiana Grieshofer and Kate Haworth

1.1 The Purpose of This Collection

This edited collection is inspired by recent developments in research at the intersection of language, communication and legal practice. It aims not simply to compile examples of such research, but to create a methodological and analytical pathway for aligning linguistic understanding with legal practice. What we hope stands out in the collection is a focus on applying linguistic theories, frameworks and methods to diverse areas of legal practice with the aim of enhancing access to justice and due process. Our aspiration is that readers across a broad range of related disciplines, interests and professions which share that aim will take away inspiration for methodological, analytical and practice-related innovations.

The collection presents the state-of-the-art research in applied linguistics directly relevant to procedural and administrative law and practice, with an emphasis on how legal procedure is constructed, negotiated and implemented through language. The focus is, therefore, very firmly on the *applicability* of linguistic theory and methodology to the context of legal practice. The work represented in this volume involves data from real-life cases and legal contexts, providing novel and often groundbreaking insights into the multiple communication-related challenges the justice system and its constituent institutions have to navigate on a daily basis. It showcases methodological approaches from linguistics which can enrich legal reforms and procedural change, ensuring that such developments are evidence-based in terms of being grounded in a sound understanding of how language and communication actually work in the practical, and often messy, reality of day-to-day legal practice.

The chapters do not simply shed light on an issue identified, but reach further to explore its impact on court participants and their access-to-justice journey, as well as on legal professionals and their role in delivering justice. It is no coincidence that quite a number of the contributing authors (or authorial teams) have direct legal experience or qualifications alongside their academic linguistic credentials. This ties in with the intention of this volume to advance research at the interface of language and law towards a more truly interdisciplinary enterprise, rather than a cross-disciplinary one, by which we mean an integration of concepts and approaches from both academic disciplines, not merely a mutual understanding undertaken from a (respectful) distance. Although research on the interface between language and law has advanced considerably over the last decade or more, the legal context has still tended to be no more than a backdrop for many language and law scholars. What we advocate in this collection, however, is a move towards much greater integration of legal and procedural aspects with linguistic analysis or methodology, ensuring both maximal relevance and enhanced likelihood of professional uptake. If we wish to instigate procedural change, we stand a far higher chance of success if that procedure and its institutional rationale are appropriately accounted for at the outset of our research agenda.

Within that specific remit and purpose, the collection embraces a broad conceptualisation of 'communication' and 'legal practice', with the intention of showcasing the breadth and range of opportunities available in this space. It engages with a wide range of legal areas, including criminal law, family law, civil law, immigration, international law and legal education. It has an international scope, with relevance across both adversarial and inquisitorial legal systems, international legal institutions and multilingual jurisdictions. The chapters cover a unique and impressive range of legal contexts, encompassing the full trajectory of the legal system from initial training programmes for professional participants to judicial decision-making and appeals. It thereby involves a wide cast of institutional participants, including lawyers, the judiciary, vulnerable witnesses, non-native speakers, interpreters, court users, police officers and administrative staff.

At the same time, the volume covers different aspects of communication in its widest sense: interpersonal and institutional; written and spoken; interactive and monologic; monolingual and multilingual; and communication across different stages of the legal process. In so doing it draws on a diverse range of methodologies and includes a wide spectrum of data types, from the perhaps more familiar, such as courtroom trial interaction (Wright et al., Ferraz de Almeida & Barrett, D'hondt) and written judgments (Ng, Leung), to the rarely accessible and therefore far less studied, such as lawyer–client interactions (Reynolds) and covert surveillance (Ruyters et al.).

An accountable and fair justice system with decision-making based on accurate evidence is an ultimate goal for social justice and democratic governance. Given that this edited collection presents a new and more nuanced treatment of linguistic research applicable to legal practice, we hope that it is used as a point of reference and springboard for further scholarship and procedural developments in theory and practice.

1.2 Why Language and Justice?

It is widely established that language is an inherent part of law (e.g., Tiersma 1999, Gibbons 2003, Durant & Leung 2016). The significance of language and communication in performative, public-facing legal settings such as the courtroom is equally widely recognised (e.g., Atkinson & Drew 1979, Cotterill 2003, Heffer 2005). This collection highlights another overarching area where language and communication play a significant, yet so far less explored, role – their role in the procedural dimension of the justice system. The justice system viewed from the perspective of applied linguistics frameworks consists of a complex network of interconnected professional and institutional discursive practices which are largely predefined by procedure rules, practice directions and professional conventions; further, it is reliant on interlocutors developing specialised discursive competence in order to navigate it successfully and thereby maintain its institutional and social functions.

Importantly, *justice* as a concept has a broader remit than *law*: it encompasses the system; the process; courts and affiliated institutions (police, social services); the judiciary and legal professionals; administrative support (e.g., transcription services); and the public interacting with the system (e.g., defendants, witnesses, litigants). Exploring the role that state-of-the-art linguistic theories, concepts and methods can play in examining the day-to-day functioning of *justice* presents a novel and much-needed research avenue. The unique input linguistics can provide, as illustrated throughout the chapters in this volume, includes the scrutiny of how justice is administered, negotiated and enacted through language use, interaction and communication.

This collection encompasses a range of interaction types along the journey of accessing and delivering justice:

- communication between legal professionals and lay participants (e.g., jury instructions, Chapter 9; legal advisor–client consultations, Chapters 14 and 15),
- evidence processing practices (e.g., handling interpreted surveillance data, Chapter 4; transcription of evidential recordings, Chapters 5 and 6),
- interactive case management (e.g., checking comprehension of defendants' rights, Chapter 3; judicial assessments of language proficiency, Chapter 7),
- case narrativisation practices (e.g., lay parties' voice projection in court, Chapter 2; eliciting evidence from vulnerable witnesses in cross-examination, Chapter 10; judicial interventions in witness examination, Chapter 11),
- legal discursive practices as part of broader socio-political agendas (e.g., interpreter provision for jurors in bilingual legal contexts, Chapter 8; the negotiation of legitimacy in international criminal law, Chapter 12; official language rights in court, Chapter 13).

The secondary title – *Communication in Legal Practice* – clarifies the scope of this work by tying communicative processes directly to legal professional practice. Importantly, as indicated by the list of chapter descriptions, this entails a wide variety of communicative processes: communication through different stages of legal proceedings in and out of court; communication processes involved in elicitation, evidence collection, case presentation and reporting; communication at the heart of decision-making; communication as part of professional development and intervention choices. We seek to highlight that the focus is on communicative aspects which are part and parcel of legal practice, be it from the perspective of the judiciary or lawyers or from the institutional perspective of procedural rules. There are two factors which help us ensure this.

Firstly, the topics selected by the authors all arose directly from real legal cases, practices or sites of contention where linguistic topics surfaced. So the relevance to legal practice is secured through the direct link to areas of genuine professional and institutional concern. Secondly, from the methodological perspective, the collection demonstrates how linguistic theories and principles can complement more traditional legal doctrinal analysis and socio-legal empirical analyses and be successfully integrated with such approaches. The chapters therefore offer valuable new perspectives for legal professionals when considering procedural reforms or evaluating the accountability, transparency and accessibility of the justice system.

1.3 Structure of the Volume

1.3.1 Legal Process and Legal Profession

The collection is organised around two themes which are at the heart of communication and legal practice: legal process and legal profession. This structure turns the focus to linguistic insights which can have a direct impact on what happens in courts and in agencies and institutions across the wider justice system. In an effort to highlight the applicability of linguistically informed research to legal practice, the collection steers away from the more conventional themes commonly used across existing publications in language and law – themes defined by linguistic topics or communicative events (e.g., multilingualism, interpreting and translation, courtroom discourse, police interview discourse). Promoting the focus on legal process and profession allows the collection to prioritise research questions and topics which arise in legal practice on a day-to-day basis and thus directly affect those who are embedded in institutional practices (e.g., lawyers, judges, police investigators, interpreters) and those who rely on the system to deliver justice (e.g., litigants, witnesses, defendants). This practical, problem-solving focus results in many chapters drawing on multiple datasets and combined analytical approaches, which only emphasises the complexity of issues pursued and the variety of linguistic applications relevant to legal practice.

An additional advantage the chosen structure presents is an opportunity to highlight the continuity between law, language and the wider socio-political agendas with which law interacts through linguistic framing and wider discursive practices. It foregrounds topics which have received a lot of attention in legal literature and research, but so far largely to the exclusion of in-depth linguistic input. Such topics include access to justice and due process for self-represented parties (Grieshofer, Greenlee); vulnerable witnesses (Wright et al.) and defendants (Greenlee, Ruyters et al., Ng); out-of-court legal advice (Reynolds, Smith-Khan); criminal evidentiary rules (Capus et al., Haworth, Walker); court procedure rules (Grieshofer, Ferraz de Almeida & Barrett, Wright et al.); public legal education (Grieshofer, Heffer & Coulthard); legal reasoning (Leung, D'hondt). As a result, the collection creates organic cross-overs between linguistic and legal research agendas, increasing the visibility and relevance of what has perhaps traditionally been viewed as purely linguistic research.

The two themes of legal *process* and legal *profession* are, of course, strongly interconnected, so the division here into separate Parts is inevitably an artificial one. The distinction we seek to make is between (Part I) communicative aspects which can be categorised as relating to the underlying structures, frameworks and procedures of justice as an institution – or more accurately, a series of institutions; and (Part II) the communicative roles, practices and choices of individuals whose professional responsibility is to navigate and uphold that system.

In Part I, the focus on *process* enables this section to highlight common issues with evidence production procedures and to explore opportunities for enhancing procedural fairness and access to justice for those interacting with the justice system. Embedded in these procedural steps are language-related themes, which include communicative challenges during legal–lay interactions (Greenlee, Grieshofer); linguistic disadvantage due to the use of nonstandard language varieties or non-native language use (Walker, Ruyters et al., Ng, Capus et al.); and invisible agency over a suspect's own voice as presented in evidence (Capus et al., Haworth, Walker). Collectively, the chapters reflect on common misconceptions about language deeply enshrined into everyday legal processes.

Part II builds on Part I by emphasising that the legal *profession* is part of the institutional equilibrium and its communicative practices are defined by established legal processes and procedures. The focus here turns to professional practices and the discursive choices legal professionals make, either as part of institutionally accepted procedural boundaries or as part of individual choices due to procedural or institutional flexibility. The socio-cultural and socio-political dimensions equally feature strongly as part of legal professional culture. The themes thus mirror many of the core themes from Part I, with the focus shifting to institutional roles which legal professionals perform when communicating with lay audiences and decisions they make when guided by legal processes, procedures and professional practices. As a result, we revisit the linguistically driven themes of legal–lay communication (Heffer & Coulthard, Wright et al., Reynolds, Smith-Khan) and linguistic disadvantage, vulnerability and language rights (Leung, Wright et al., Reynolds, Smith-Khan); and procedurally driven themes of pre-court evidence construction (Reynolds), court procedures (Heffer & Coulthard, Ferraz de Almeida & Barrett, D'hondt) and due process (Leung, Ferraz de Almeida & Barrett).

We will now turn to a detailed consideration of the contributions of each chapter.

1.3.2 Part I: Communication and Legal Process

Grieshofer initiates Part I by focusing on the core feature of adversarial legal systems, the principle of orality (the right to be heard in a public hearing) and its procedural, legal and discursive function in the justice process. Chapter 2 challenges how orality is understood as a theoretical and systemic principle and how it is implemented in civil legal practice by examining distinct court procedures linked to orality across private family proceedings and small claims cases in England and Wales. A common scene across county and family courts is parties who have to represent themselves due to financial constraints and lack of legal aid funding, and so these 'high volume' types of proceedings impact high numbers of citizens, whose court experiences shape their trust in the justice system (and likelihood of compliance with court orders), only increasing the expectations from the principle of orality. Conceptualising orality as a communicative process and establishing its communicative stages and aims enable the chapter to scrutinise orality in pre-court stages and court hearings and identify procedural measures that weaken court users' access to procedural fairness. Further drawing on the linguistic concepts of voice projection, elicitation and narrativisation, the chapter illustrates the impact of specific procedure rules on the extent to which court users are enabled to present their stories in a legally relevant way. Grieshofer concludes that it is important to consider communicative practices, including evidence elicitation practices, as part of court procedure rules and, more broadly, the systemic design of the justice system to ensure the effectiveness of lay court users' legal participation.

In another example of a legal–lay communicative context, in Chapter 3 Greenlee explores discursive practices in Faretta waivers in capital trials in

California, US. Faretta waivers apply to cases where the defendant wishes to renounce their right to an attorney and to self-represent, and the chapter examines procedural steps carried out by courts to check the defendants' comprehension of the consequent risks. Drawing on lexico-grammatical analysis of the wording used in Faretta waiver forms, and discursive analysis of the court hearings where judges discuss defendants' wishes as expressed on those forms, the chapter raises serious concerns as to whether the typical populace in capital cases would comprehend the wording or consequences of self-representation. Although the procedure is designed to safeguard defendants on their access to justice journey, the process is rendered ineffective by lack of attention to linguistic detail. Greenlee puts forward a strong argument in favour of reforming the language of the process in order to meaningfully explore defendants' comprehension and motivation for self-representation, drawing parallels to positive changes introduced with the help of linguistic input in Miranda warnings and jury instructions.

In Chapter 4, Capus et al. explore communication-related challenges in a different type of context, namely police covert surveillance investigations involving multilingual communication, focusing on the role that 'intercept interpreters/translators' play in the process. Using data from Switzerland, the chapter takes us through several procedural stages of evidence processing, in which intercept interpreters/translators have to perform several challenging communicative and institutional roles: listen and make judgements on the meaning of intercepted communication intentionally or circumstantially rendered ambiguous to anyone not party to the interaction; collaborate with police investigators to assist in deciphering the meaning of the original communication; and produce translated written records which may be used as evidence in court. The chapter highlights that although intercept interpreters/translators thus play an active role in supporting police investigations, the resulting versions of the intercept reports do not explicitly acknowledge their input or presence in the process. Further, the authors demonstrate how the original interactions undergo several recontextualisations, shifting the mode, language, authorship and audience design. The chapter argues that clarifying the institutional boundaries of the roles of intercept interpreters/translators will introduce a much-needed transparency to the process, and even simple steps such as explicit identification of the translated extracts in legal files will be beneficial for upholding due process and the rights of suspects and defendants.

In Chapter 5, Haworth equally challenges evidence production practices in criminal proceedings by focusing on what happens in England and Wales to mandatory audio recordings of police-suspect interviews. The chapter draws on both interview data and focus groups with practitioners to examine how the choices made by police transcribers turn them into active participants in the official written record, yet, as with Chapter 4's interpreters/translators, they are largely invisible in the criminal justice process. The chapter draws our attention to the paradox between, on the one hand, the robust training police interviewers undergo and the stringent legal protections around interviewing suspects and, on the other hand, the ad hoc linguistic choices transcribers are free to make when producing the evidential record of that interview interaction, which can distort the original meaning or intentions of interlocutors. To illustrate the risks involved, the discussion focuses on three practices of transcribers: summarising stretches of talk instead of producing a verbatim transcript; summarising procedural preliminaries at the start of the interview (such as delivery of the caution, and conveying rights around legal representation); and omission of markers of emotion. This highlights that, despite the many legal and procedural safeguards around the audio/video recording of police-suspect interviews, the administrative process of conversion to a written record can unintentionally undermine those efforts. However, the chapter also illustrates how linguistic input into addressing underlying misunderstandings about language and the conveyance of meaning has the potential to make a vital contribution to improving the quality of criminal evidence.

Walker (Chapter 6) further probes the practice of evidential transcript production by evaluating the comparative accuracy of verbatim transcription of Black and Standard American English by private transcription companies used by US courts. Drawing on experimental methods, and including both human and AI-generated transcripts, the chapter demonstrates significant shortcomings in verbatim transcription of male speakers of Black American English, a demographic which is substantially over-represented in the US justice system. The chapter illustrates that the resulting transcripts display significant meaning-changing alterations due to the lack of understanding of dialectal and cultural differences in phonetics, grammar, vocabulary and cultural realities (e.g., typical names), leading to evidentially serious mistakes such as adding non-existent people to the scene. The lower accuracy scores for Black English transcription are contrasted against the common legal practice of relying on verbatim transcripts as an official and finite record, leading to miscarriages of justice in a series of previous US court cases in which Black English speakers were misunderstood or misquoted. The author advocates for better training in non-standard varieties of English for transcribers (both machine and human); legal consideration of the admissibility of such potentially unreliable evidence; and increased awareness among legal professionals about distinctions between Black and Standard American English, so that expert input is sought when Black English is used as evidence in the criminal justice process, in order to affirm accuracy and avoid injustice.

Shifting the focus from interdialectal comprehension to interlingual comprehension, Chapter 7 focuses on judicial assessments of English language proficiency in Australian criminal cases involving the admissibility of police interviews conducted with suspects whose first language was not English. Drawing on judgments in cases where there was no interpreter at the police interview stage, but language was subsequently raised as an issue at trial, Ruyters et al. critique judges' methods for assessing defendants' linguistic proficiency at interview. The chapter considers a series of such cases in which the police interview was either accepted into evidence or rejected, mapping these judicial evaluations against recommended standards for assessing whether a person needs an interpreter in court proceedings. This analysis illustrates inconsistencies in approach across the two contexts and also from case to case. The authors raise concerns about the potential for injustice, especially given the significant role of police interview evidence admitted at trial. They note that expert linguistic evaluation is rarely sought, and that judges tend to be overconfident in the quality of their own 'common sense' assessments, which the authors attribute to 'judicial exceptionalism'. The chapter thus encourages the adoption of expert language competence assessments and application of the existing standards for assessing language ability for court proceedings when determining admissibility of interview evidence, in order to improve accuracy and consistency in judicial decision-making.

The theme of due process for non-native speakers is continued in Chapter 8 by Ng, who probes into the contentious issue of providing interpreting for jurors in the multilingual jurisdiction of Hong Kong, where due to its colonial past English is firmly established as an official language of court proceedings, despite most of the population being speakers of Cantonese. The chapter argues that interpreting for jurors is essential in a jurisdiction where around 90% of the population are essentially excluded from serving as jurors due to being non-English speakers or having limited English proficiency. This linguistic exclusion brings the educational, ethnic and socio-economic divide into the courtroom, inhibiting the democratic function which the lay participation of jurors in the justice system is designed to fulfil. Drawing on consecutive appeals of a court case which involved the provision of simultaneous interpreting to jurors during the trial (which had the potential to set a significant precedent for the provision of interpreting for jurors in Hong Kong), the chapter reflects on the misconceptions among the legal profession about comprehension issues in multilingual settings and discusses the challenges and opportunities interpreting for jurors raises. The author advocates that to ensure the defendant's right to a fair trial, it is important to provide interpretation for jurors both to ensure their comprehension of court proceedings and increase the representativeness of juries; the chapter also encourages the adoption of a fully electronic system of simultaneous interpretation to ensure that the original and interpreted versions are recorded so that the accuracy and adequacy of interpretation can be assessed.

1.3.3 Part II: Communication and Legal Profession

Part II begins with a return to the themes of juror comprehension and legal-lay communication, as Heffer and Coulthard turn the focus to judicial discursive practices in conveying the criminal standard of proof to juries in England and Wales (Chapter 9). They argue that the ordinary word 'sure' has become a technical legal term, which therefore cannot serve the intended purpose of communicating the correct legal meaning clearly to jury members. Applying linguistic theories around comprehension and the conveyance of meaning to critique court judgments, case law and professional practice manuals, and drawing on their own involvement as linguistic experts in a Court of Appeal case on this issue, they identify a series of legal discursive practices which give rise to this position. The authors aim to increase awareness among legal practitioners that simply transplanting ordinary language into a legal context in order to perform a specific institutional task is not the solution to conveying technical legal meaning since this will inevitably imbue those words with a new and different meaning. The chapter comes to the conclusion that to aid the jury with understanding and accurately applying the criminal standard of proof, a template explanation should be formulated which explains this fundamental legal concept in terms which can be understood by all.

Professional discursive practices when interacting with lay people are further explored in Chapter 10 by Wright et al., who turn their attention to the signposting of topics in the cross-examination of vulnerable witnesses. The starting point for the chapter is recent professional guidance encouraging advocates to explicitly signal topics and topic shifts to vulnerable witnesses in order to reduce potential confusion or distress; itself a recognition of the interactional power held by a cross-examiner. Drawing on transcripts of 56 cross-examinations from six Crown Court Centres in the UK and Ireland, the chapter uses a corpus-assisted approach to analyse the trial discourse, in particular applying the linguistic concept of 'metadiscourse' to evaluate how advocates are implementing this guidance in practice. The authors identify the most common lexical bundles used by counsel to signpost topics, finding that they are indeed used more frequently for vulnerable witnesses; however, through detailed analysis of cross-examination sequences, the chapter identifies a series of 'interactional problems' which can arise as an unintended consequence. The chapter's insight into how such communicative strategies actually function interactionally will hopefully lead to more nuanced guidance and recommendations for professional practice.

Moving the theme of professional courtroom discursive practices onto the global stage, in Chapter 11 Ferraz de Almeida and Barrett turn their attention to judicial interventions in the International Criminal Court (ICC). The procedural amalgamation of the ICC's international jurisdiction, which combines elements of adversarial and inquisitorial legal systems, makes the judge's role procedurally more flexible, erasing clear distinctions between the roles of truth-finder and referee. Drawing on verbatim transcripts from the witness examination stages of the trial of Dominic Ongwen (a commander of the Ugandan rebel movement convicted of war crimes and crimes against humanity), the authors explore how the judge manages the interactional challenge that this 'unstable amalgamation' presents. Through turn-by-turn analysis of the judge's questioning practices during witness examinations, the authors show how the judge uses the wide discretion afforded to him by the ICC's procedural rules to shift his participation status through, for example, moving into the questioner role in objection sequences and reformulating questions himself. The chapter demonstrates how detailed linguistic analysis of actual instances of courtroom communication can illuminate our understanding of how the ICC's attempt to blend distinct legal cultures gives rise to challenges and opportunities, especially for practitioners.

In Chapter 12 D'hondt also explores the ICC context, highlighting that it is through linguistically mediated practices that international criminal proceedings are enacted simultaneously as part of the legal process and the wider global socio-political context. Drawing on the concept of contingency in post-structuralist discourse theory and linguistic anthropological work on intertextuality, the author shows that semiotic and substantive aspects are intertwined in the process of discourse production, leading to the discourse of legal proceedings entering into a dialogue with socio-political realities. Analysis of examples from trial hearings and judgments showcases how discursive practices such as the entextualisation of witness testimony and recontextualisation in judgments, and the preferential framing of legal argumentation in accordance with a fitting socio-political agenda, are used to support legal decisions. The author contends that it is time to accept the fact that ICC cases are inevitably interconnected with political agendas, but that this 'radical contingency' should be actively utilised rather than resisted. The chapter demonstrates how a deeper understanding of the discourse of ICC hearings can contribute to this endeavour.

Continuing the theme of the socio-political positioning of courtroom discourse, in Chapter 13 Leung explores the political dimensions of official language rights in multilingual jurisdictions, focusing specifically on the right to use a particular language in legal proceedings. The author examines the varying ways in which judges have chosen to deal with contestations over language rights in court, drawing on cases from Northern Ireland, Brittany, Canada, South Africa, New Zealand, and Hong Kong, among others. The discussion documents the different paths taken when legislating linguistic hierarchies, ranging from jurisdictions where minority languages have managed to gain official recognition by challenging established language practices, to multilingual jurisdictions without formally enforceable language rights for non-priority languages, to those where the choice between official languages is highly politicised. The chapter argues that the socio-political function of recognising official languages in a country's constitution or legislation should be fully acknowledged to avoid unnecessary contestations, such as when proficiency in the majority language leads to excluding bilingual speakers from exercising their rights in the minority language. The author advocates for the importance of judges upholding official language rights in court, bringing benefits which extend well beyond the symbolic.

In another example of applying linguistic ethnography to an underexplored legal discursive context, in Chapter 14 Reynolds sheds new light on the communicative processes which lead to the production of witness statements used as evidence in immigration visa application and appeal cases. Detailed analysis of the interaction between an immigration lawyer and their client, mediated through an interpreter, illustrates how the resulting written statement is co-constructed collaboratively between these three participants, each of which makes an essential contribution to producing the final text. Given that witness statements in this context are about personal circumstances interlaced with cultural references, the analysis demonstrates that the question/answer narrative co-construction of the client's account involves cultural as well as linguistic mediation to ensure the statement is authentic, credible and communicated in a manner which will be legally persuasive to immigration tribunal members. Focusing in particular on metacommunication, the chapter highlights the importance of the communicative work undertaken by the lawyer, especially in building mutual trust and understanding in working towards the institutional goal. Overall, the chapter makes an important contribution towards understanding that co-construction of linguistic evidence by members of legal and related professions can be a positive and supportive enterprise, bridging cultural, linguistic and legal-lay misunderstandings.

Building on the theme of intercultural communication in immigration settings, in Chapter 15 Smith-Khan considers the vocational training of future immigration advisers in Australia, focusing on how they navigate (mis)understanding in simulated client consultations. Using a range of ethnographic methods, including observing training workshops and conducting interviews with participants, the chapter explores the various linguistic and extralinguistic factors which cause misunderstandings in these simulated interactional situations. Arguing that misunderstandings are common in naturally occurring interactions, especially if they cover complex topics and involve interactants with little shared knowledge, varying linguistic proficiency or differing cultural backgrounds, the author highlights that it is erroneous to automatically lay the blame at the door of L2 status or 'culture'. Instead, the chapter demonstrates that the misunderstandings are often perpetuated due to the interactional choices made by the trainees, especially due to the challenges of managing multiple competing discursive priorities such as establishing the facts, providing advice and constructing their own professional identity. The chapter makes a compelling case for how linguistic input can assist practitioners in learning how to manage these complex and dynamic professional contexts better, through enhanced awareness of the interactional sociolinguistic factors at play.

1.4 Future Directions

We hope that this collection highlights the immense benefits and opportunities which arise when legal and applied linguistic scholarship are harnessed together to work towards their common goal, namely serving the interests of justice. This may be in the sense of legal justice, or social justice more broadly; what this collection also hopes to underscore is that there cannot be one without the other.

We hope this volume will further the direction towards more truly interdisciplinary legal-linguistic work, while recognising that it is still only a tentative step along that path. The key to future progress in this area is collaboration, by which we mean a truly meaningful symbiotic partnership, leading to greater depth of collective knowledge, mutual understanding and cross-pollination. Such synergies thereby become more than the sum of their parts, creating something genuinely novel; more than simply an extension or application of what already existed. It was sensing the nascent shoots of such a new space emerging that led us to start work on this volume; we hope that readers will join the endeavour to help it flourish.

If we may be permitted to offer advice, we suggest that several aspects must be incorporated in order for this venture to be successful. Firstly, methodological rigour must always be central. This is of course true of any valid research, but the stakes involved in legal contexts demand the highest standards and the soundest foundations – epistemologically, methodologically and ethically. The pursuit of practical solutions to real-world problems can never be at the expense of sound research principles. Yet epistemological clashes can often arise when bringing disparate academic worlds together; established practice, which may seem non-negotiable in one area may not translate well into a different context (see, e.g., Jol & Stommel 2016 on informed consent and police interview research data). We argue that this should always be acknowledged and addressed head-on rather than ignored; the necessity of finding the common ground can lead to deeper insight into our own work as well as each other's.

Secondly, in order to provide genuinely useful and workable practical solutions, practitioners (in other words, those who will ultimately have the task of implementing recommendations and outcomes) must be an integral part of the research process, beyond performing a merely functional role as gatekeepers of institutional and data access. Research 'impact' should never be a one-way process, whereby academic findings are bestowed upon recipients as the conclusion to a project; 'application' must mean more than simply telling people what our research has discovered (including through publications such as this). While practice should benefit from being informed by research, research is also better when informed by practice. Applied research will be most relevant, and successful, when it involves collaboration both within and beyond academic boundaries. We therefore advocate building practitioner input directly into the research process wherever possible, from as early a stage as practicable. Again, we hope that this volume contributes to opening more lines of communication across several boundaries: language and law; legal and lay; theory and application; research and practice.

We are acutely aware that boundaries still remain; we are equally conscious of the risk of inadvertently reinforcing some of them through the limitations of this volume. For example, this collection is clearly anglocentric, in the sense of being written in English and with English-medium contexts as its primary focus, even when directly addressing issues of linguistic diversity and privilege. Although this arguably reflects the scope and focus of the majority of current research in this area, it is not an aspect which sits comfortably with us or our intentions. However, we equally hope that the variety of methodological approaches, research contexts, and analytical foci across the collection will inspire further research and collaboration globally, with all the mutual benefits that will bring.

If we are to have achieved one thing with this volume, we hope that it is to have demonstrated the immense potential for incorporating linguistic insights into the legal process across a wide range of institutional and professional contexts and the benefits this can bring on all sides. This can involve finding solutions to areas which are known to require reform, as well as identifying problems which are not yet fully recognised within the legal system. In particular, this collection highlights that many currently unresolved issues appear to stem from common misunderstandings with respect to language theory and language-in-action. But just as linguists cannot be expected to have a full understanding of legal practice, nor can legal professionals be expected to have specialist knowledge of language and communication, even if it is the primary tool of their profession. The onus therefore falls on all of us to work together constructively towards workable, evidence-based solutions. We look forward to seeing what comes next.

References

Atkinson, J. M. and Drew, P. (1979). *Order in Court: The Organisation of Verbal Interaction in Judicial Settings*. London: Macmillan.

Cotterill, J. (2003). *Language and Power in Court: A Linguistic Analysis of the O.J. Simpson Trial*. London: Palgrave.

Durant, A. and Leung, J. H. C. (2016). *Language and Law: A Resource Book for Students*. London: Routledge.

Gibbons, J. (2003). *Forensic Linguistics: An Introduction to Language in the Legal System*. London: Blackwell.

Heffer, C. (2005). *The Language of Jury Trial: A Corpus-Aided Analysis of Legal-Lay Discourse*. Basingstoke: Springer.

Jol, G. and Stommel, W. (2016). 'Ethical considerations of secondary data use: What about informed consent?' *Dutch Journal of Applied Linguistics*, 5:2, 180–195.

Tiersma, P. M. (1999). *Legal Language*. Chicago: University of Chicago Press.

Part I

Communication and Legal Process

2 The Principle of Orality in County and Family Courts

Tatiana Grieshofer

2.1 Introduction

The principle of orality is a key feature of legal systems rooted in adversarialism and is often considered a beacon of transparency and procedural justice (Ainsworth 2015), but there are also debates challenging many of the factors related to its implementation (e.g., criticism of cross-examination – Gibbons 2003). The issues are especially prevalent in family and county courts across England and Wales, the lower courts which deal with legal matters related to family life (e.g., divorce or dissolution of civil partnership, adoption cases) and civil disputes (e.g., personal injury cases, disputes between landlords and tenants, financial disputes between businesses or citizens). Across these first-instance courts, possibly the most common legal proceedings are private family proceedings (ending a marriage or civil partnership, resolving who children live with or have contact with, settling post-separation finances) and small claims cases (financial disputes up to £10,000). A shared characteristic of these proceedings is that many of the parties appear without a legal representative (e.g., *Family Court Statistics Quarterly: October–December* 2024), which makes it difficult for them to argue their case effectively without the relevant legal or procedural knowledge. But even legally represented parties often feel they are not heard due to procedural restrictions on the timing and scope of their narratives (Hunter et al. 2020, cf. Grieshofer 2024). Focusing on high-volume proceedings in county and family courts with a high percentage of lay court users, the chapter (1) expands on the conceptualisation of the principle of orality and its tenets, (2) argues that orality is a crucial component of court users' access to procedural justice and procedural fairness and (3) identifies court procedures that enable or impede on the full implementation of the principle of orality.

In the English common law tradition, the principle of orality sits alongside the principle of publicity across most types of proceedings (in family courts, publicity is restricted due to the sensitive nature of substantive issues covered,

Funding statement: The chapter draws on research conducted as part of an AHRC funded project, reference number AH/S004882/1.

only the press have recently gained the right to observe family proceedings and report on them while keeping case details anonymous). The principle of publicity, as one of the components of orality, enhances the transparency of the justice system by securing the public's right to observe court cases, and the litigants' right to demand for their proceedings to be accessible to the public (Zuckerman 2003). In its fullest version, orality thus ensures that the public can hear all the evidence in a coherent and continuous manner (Zuckermann 2003: 86), which means that the witnesses give their evidence orally, other documentary evidence is introduced orally or read out, and the parties' narratives are introduced and consolidated through opening and closing speeches (Gibbons 2003).

In practice, across civil proceedings in England and Wales and in many other common law countries, the principle of orality has been deteriorating in the last decades (Roberts 2022). To cut cost and court time and increase efficiency, court procedures have shifted closer to different versions of trial by paper: litigants (or their representatives) are required to serve the court their submissions and any supporting documents in advance of each hearing, witnesses and parties submit their written statements instead of presenting their evidence orally and judges are expected to read the documentation in advance. The oral presentation of evidence is subsequently reduced to a potential cross-examination of witnesses, and opening speeches are limited to individual points which require clarification or an update (Zuckermann 2003: 87). Despite these considerable transformations, the principle of orality is often considered as a key part of court litigation, which essentially creates disparity between the theoretical model and legal practice (Lazer 2021).

The chapter offers a critical reflection on the theory and practice around the principle of orality: as developing legal systems across the world (e.g., Latin America, Eastern Europe) reform their justice systems to enhance democratisation and transparency, they often look towards such key common law principles as the principle of orality and publicity, and sometimes also lay participation in the justice system as an additional aspect of publicity (e.g., introducing juries). It is thus crucial to be aware of the advantages but also risks related to the implementation of orality and affiliated principles across different legal areas (cf. Ainsworth 2015). As a core design principle, orality functions as a starting point or even a safeguard for different access to justice measures. Firstly, orality is an expectation for the principle of publicity and is thus connected to elements of open justice. Secondly, orality is considered as a guarantee of a fair trial and procedural fairness (Zuckermann 2003), which envisions a provision of an opportunity for the party to present their story and respond to the other party's arguments and evidence. Thirdly, orality is an inherent part of procedural justice and contributes to court users' perceptions of procedural justice: orality creates the space for the parties (or their lawyers as proxies) to develop their narratives and, given that judges are impartial adjudicators whose judgement is based only on the evidence presented, the adversarial model creates optimal conditions for the parties' narratives to be heard (Ainsworth 2015, Zuckermann 2022). The list does not end here, as effective legal participation, access to information and access to courts are also linked to the extent court users are given opportunities to relate their narratives (cf. McKeever et al. 2022, Grieshofer 2024).

What is important to highlight from the analytical perspective is that linguistics offers a unique framework for analysing and conceptualising orality. The originality of the chapter thus lies in its methodological approach, which enables a detailed exploration of the principle of orality as a theoretical systemic concept of adversarialism while also facilitating a contextualised investigation of how orality is implemented across different lower court settings. Another distinctive feature of the study is that it explores three types of high-volume civil and family proceedings: post-separation child arrangements proceedings, post-separation financial remedy proceedings and small claims cases. Drawing on orality as an entry point for exploring court users' potential to be heard across three distinct settings, the chapter argues that the full implementation of orality (and what it stands for) can be fulfilled by combining the advantages that written and interactive modes of narrativisation offer, but this combined approach requires procedural adaptations to benefit courts, legal professionals and court users. The following section lays the groundwork by reflecting on how orality is viewed in research and practice, first in criminal contexts and then in civil contexts.

2.2 Principle of Orality in Research and Practice

In scholarly literature, the principle of orality has predominantly been discussed in the context of adversarial criminal proceedings (cf. Roberts 2022, Fairclough 2024). The focus on criminal proceedings is not surprising given that witness examination is a pinnacle of the oral adversarial tradition and (lay and expert) witness testimony is commonplace in criminal trials. By comparison, civil proceedings do not tend to involve many lay witnesses, and when expert witnesses are called, court procedures mainly require their written reports without the need for them to appear in court (see Civil Procedure Rules 2025). Viewed in the context of criminal proceedings, orality becomes somewhat conflated with witness examination, leading to inherently misleading preconceptions, such as that orality comprises of oral narratives, that oral narratives are narrations that come solely from witnesses and that witnesses are capable of presenting their stories in court and standing the test of cross-examination (Tkacukova 2016, cf. Lazer 2021: 10).

Linguistics research has challenged these assumptions, though often without explicitly referring to the principle of orality and instead focusing on narrativisation practices in criminal legal settings (Cotterill 2003, Gibbons 2003, Heffer 2005). For instance, what has been clearly established is that before defendants and witnesses appear in court for oral testimony, their narratives emerge through multiple retellings, including police interviews, which result in official written versions (see Haworth, this volume). As the criminal trial process does not allow for much deviation from those versions, such characteristics of orality as immediacy and publicity cannot be fully implemented. The other set of circumstances which restrict the scope of orality is linked to the goal-oriented, persuasive and confrontational discourse of adversarialism (Cotterill 2003). Witness examination is not an opportunity for a free narrative (Ainsworth 2015) and it is the examiners who have more control over the witness narrative: having the institutional power to ask questions enables them to determine topics and their sequence, phrasing of events or facts, and even the extent, length and suitability of responses (Tkacukova 2016). The principle of orality, as currently implemented in criminal settings, thus turns into a discursive tool which is used for the benefit of corroborating parties' narratives rather than providing an opportunity for witnesses to freely relate their stories in public.

Similarly, legal scholarship highlights that the centrality of parties' narratives in adversarialism enables court users to prioritise evidencing their stories as opposed to simply evidencing facts or seeking the truth (Roberts 2022). Furthermore, the coerciveness of cross-examination interactions is not conducive to eliciting reliable evidence or aiding accurate memory recall, and thus does not fully align with the truth-testing function embedded in the principle of orality (Block & Parker 2004, Firestone & Weinstein 2004, McIntosh et al. 2008, Ainsworth 2015). As a result, fact-finding mechanisms based on the assumption that witness performance during cross-examination can be reliably assessed as a measure of their credibility or truthfulness have been repeatedly challenged (Roberts 2022: chapter 7), and many witnesses and victims leave the court feeling they could not share their stories or, even worse, feeling distressed or even re-victimised and re-traumatised by the court experience (Ehrlich 2010, Hunter et al. 2020). In sum, contrary to the positive image of orality and its association with the principle of publicity and open justice (Roberts 2022), the adversarial oral tradition of witness examination in criminal proceedings has proven to be rife with challenges when it comes to ensuring the reliability of evidence, balancing the fact-finding practices and securing the citizen's trust in the justice system.

In civil settings, by contrast, the gradual decline of orality across many adversarial jurisdictions (e.g., England and Wales, USA, Australia) has resulted in oral testimony being largely substituted by written submissions filed to court and served on the other party in advance of the hearings. On the one hand, this contributes to pre-court stages being procedurally complex and filled with a multitude of distinct written genres (forms, witness statements, chronologies of historical events, skeleton arguments), which can be difficult to navigate (Grieshofer 2024). On the other hand, however, the undeniable advantage of submitting written statements is that parties have time to prepare and consider what they wish to include and how they wish to frame their narratives. Given the concerns around cross-examination practices, in family courts, for instance, it is generally believed that it is better for vulnerable parties to submit their witness statements and answer only complementary questions in court than to attempt to relate the entirety of their story from the witness box (Practice Direction 3aa of Family Procedure Rules). This practice, nonetheless, does not consider what happens to their written narratives during court hearings or the degree to which the written genres required by court procedures enable court participants to be heard and, as a result, these factors remain largely unexplored outside of linguistics (Grieshofer 2023). Balancing the advantages and disadvantages of oral and written narrativisation strategies presents a challenge.

The socio-legal research agenda pertinent to issues linked to orality in civil proceedings tends to focus on the wider themes of accessing justice. Given the high numbers of self-represented parties, it is unrealistic to expect that lay court users can engage with court processes and procedures on an expert level; the focus thus turns to assessing whether court processes enable the parties to be heard, which ties the principle of orality to effective legal participation embedded in the right to a fair and public hearing (under Article 6 of ECHR) and the overriding objective of the Civil Procedure Rules to deal with cases fairly and justly (McKeever et al. 2022). Grieshofer (2024) argues that existing court procedures reduce procedural fairness by limiting litigants' opportunities to relate their stories in court. As a result of diminishing orality, oral narratives are substituted with a plethora of distinct written genres, each fulfilling a different procedural aim and creating procedural burdens: for instance, court forms and other genres regularly come under criticism as overly complex and inefficient elicitation tools (Grieshofer 2023).

The complex nexus of legal procedures can only lead to muting parties' voices (Hunter et al. 2020, Grieshofer 2024). It is thus not surprising that in civil legal practice, there are widespread concerns that court users' voices are not heard. As the decline in orality has been accompanied by drastic austerity measures and, more recently, the introduction of digitisation services, it is crucial to redefine what the principle of orality stands for and assess how its implementation can be strengthened. Many citizens are likely to experience civil or family proceedings, and their experiences with the justice system will create wider public perceptions about the fairness of that system. Exploring access to justice and procedural justice by assessing the implementation of the principle of orality enables the chapter to integrate communicative practices with systemic legal principles.

2.3 Methodological Reflections

The chapter tests the principle of orality and what it stands for (orality, publicity, open justice) through empirical explorations based on mixed methods research, which included court observations of forty court hearings, complemented by textual ethnography, a survey of court users, interviews with court users and legal professionals (see Grieshofer 2024 for a detailed discussion of the data and methodology). Thanks to the diverse data sets collected, Grieshofer (2024) laid the groundwork for establishing the role of communication in procedural justice and detailed the impact of court procedures on legal-lay discourse and court users' perceptions of fair and due process. This chapter brings in a related but different perspective: investigating the principle of orality from the perspective of discursive practices enables the chapter to contribute a unique perspective on the core design principle of adversarial legal traditions.

One particularly useful linguistic concept to consider is voice projection. The concept is strongly embedded in the socio-political, socio-cultural and socio-legal epistemology of institutions, originating from Hymes' (1996) understanding of voice projection as a two-component act, which requires someone to use their voice and them being given an opportunity to do so. The concept of voice presumes relevant content framed in a context-appropriate style, and the notion of opportunity, as a separate criterion for voice projection, recognises that in institutional contexts, access to voice depends on institutional processes. The principle of orality in adversarial proceedings was designed, in part, to give a voice projection opportunity to court users (see the discussion in Section 2.2). Another way of exploring voice projection in court settings is through identifying elicitation and narrativisation practices (Grieshofer 2022), as it is mainly the legal-lay interaction which can increase the effectiveness of legal participation for lay court users in family and civil proceedings (Trinder et al. 2014, McKeever et al. 2022, Grieshofer 2024). Exploring the timing, scope and discursive practices around court users' voice projection opportunities is thus important when evaluating the implementation of the principle of orality in court proceedings.

The advantage of the linguistic insight into the principle of orality lies in the fact that it provides a methodological toolkit to break down orality as a communicative process (voice projection, narrativisation, elicitation) which aims to achieve a legal purpose (case presentation, publicity, transparency). The components of orality and its implementation are explored through discursive practices across three types of proceedings: child arrangements proceedings, financial remedy proceedings and small claims cases. The contrast between these 'high-volume' types of proceedings enables the chapter to reflect on the efficiency of different court procedures linked to the implementation of orality and consider how the benefits of the principle of orality can be retained across different legal contexts.

2.4 Principle of Orality in Child Arrangements Proceedings

Child-related private family proceedings resolve disputes between separating parents (or guardians) who cannot agree on living or contact arrangements for their children. Since family matters are emotionally charged, the cases where parties with parental rights cannot agree tend to be strongly disputed, and many include an element of alleged domestic abuse. Since in family matters parties' court experiences relate directly to their personal lives and their children, it becomes important for them to have an opportunity to project their voices and share their narratives. The principle of orality and what it stands for is thus crucial for the parties' sense of procedural justice, including their perceptions of whether they had a real chance to engage with the process effectively and their understanding of how and why the outcome was procedurally reached, even if they may not be happy with it (Tyler 2000). Reducing any component of orality can often be perceived by the parties as a systemic attempt to mute their voices, leading to them lose trust in the justice system, which is one of the persistent issues in family courts (Hunter et al. 2020, Grieshofer 2024).

Current standard proceedings present a multi-stage process, starting with safeguarding checks by child services even before the parties enter the courtroom for the first time. There are then at least two hearings (or more in cases where safeguarding concerns are identified) with a heavily procedural focus before the parties reach the final hearing. On average, it takes around a year to reach the stage of the final hearing (i.e., the main opportunity for the parties to present their stories before the judge in court). What happens before is a complex nexus of pre-court written narrative genres and procedural hearings focusing on the pre-court submissions and interim arrangements. As a result, for approximately a year, parents are limited to written narratives, which are partitioned across court forms, argument statements, witness statements, and child services reports. Each genre and each procedural step imposes further narrativisation restrictions, for example, only short responses are possible in court forms, and witness statements presuppose antagonistic accounts.

Child services reports are especially tricky from the discursive perspective, as child services collect information about the family situation through interviews with parents, and potentially children, and other education and health-related agencies. However, interviews are not recorded and note-taking practices differ, resulting in parties' narratives being presented from the third-person perspective, in a fragmentary manner, taken out of the conversational context and reinterpreted and recontextualised for the purposes of the reports. Grieshofer (2024) reports that the frequency of inaccurate child services' reports is alarmingly high, illustrating the inadequate processes used for capturing oral evidence, which breach discursive processes crucial for retaining the accuracy of accounts and transparency of the investigative and evidential process. These reports then become the most crucial piece of evidence, with child services occupying a quasi-judicial role (Holt et al. 2013), almost of similar significance as the judiciary (although the 'quasi-judicial' coinage is often contested). Admittedly, it is crucial for family courts to be guided by safeguarding checks and children services are experts in this, but without transparency it is very difficult to assess their influence over the case narratives.

The parties' pre-court narratives shared with child services are not recorded or stored as part of evidence and thus not shared with the judge in court (except through the filter of the reports), thus undermining the publicity factor and diminishing the transparency of the pre-court process. And so as the judiciary make procedural and case management decisions (i.e., the decisions that impact the scope and direction of the parties' main voice projection opportunities during the final hearing – Grieshofer 2024) in preparation for the final hearing, they mainly have access to the reports recontextualising the parties' narratives. The authentic parties' narratives do not feature in the process until the proceedings reach the pre-court preparations for the final hearing. Most attempts from the parties to project their voices in initial hearings are stopped with the justification that it is not the aim of those hearings (Grieshofer 2024). It is no surprise that the majority of litigants surveyed or interviewed across different studies feel that their voices are muted (Trinder et al. 2014, Lee & Tkacukova 2017, Hunter et al. 2020, Grieshofer 2024), as exemplified in this quote from an interview with a court user: 'You know what I would like to see? To have the opportunity to express yourself (…) Straightaway, you are shut up in the sense of, "No time, not now"' (LIP22).

One case involved a self-represented Parent 1 who was attempting to regain unsupervised contact and living arrangements for a teen with special needs, who started living with Parent 2 after an incident which involved the teen assaulting Parent 1 (case LIP16). As there was no space for a voice projection opportunity, Parent 1 attempted through frequent interruptions to raise several points fundamental to the well-being of the child (e.g., the teen child was not enrolled in school at the new address, special needs made it challenging to cope with supervised contact under certain circumstances). Nevertheless, the parent was stopped and asked to write a witness statement for the next court hearing, at which point Parent 1 expressed their distress about writing a witness statement (e.g., 'I don't understand how…', 'I need to say this…'). Had their narrative been elicited in an interactive format in court, it is likely they would have been better enabled to make their arguments count. One of the procedural changes previously considered for trialling across family courts in England and Wales envisaged the optionality of evidence presented in written form or orally in court at a preliminary hearing, if the court considers it appropriate (see amendments under 'Consideration of Information Gathering and Assessment Stage', section 5.2 para. (iii), sub-para. (e), *New Practice Direction* 36Z). But for now, such procedural flexibility is not implemented in the standard child arrangements hearings. Nevertheless, the fact that it was proposed reflects awareness of the challenges the binary system (oral vs. written) presents.

At the time of writing, a trial is under way of a new 'Pathfinder' model, which aims to settle disputes between parents through a multi-agency approach, incorporating children's voices from the very beginning of the proceedings and reducing court appearances to just one final hearing, with the potential for the arrangements to be reviewed at another hearing at a later stage (Private Law Pathfinder 2025). The pre-court stage thus gains in significance, as the family interacts with a Family Court Adviser who undertakes the information-gathering and assessments to compile a Child Impact Report, reflecting on the children's wishes, parents' opinions and family situation. The initial assessments of the model praise the early involvement of children, the focus on child impact, early interventions to support the family, and reduced court time (Barlow et al. 2025). Nevertheless, what remains unexplored is how the information from children and their parents is elicited and processed for the purposes of the Child Impact Report, especially since these conversations are not recorded. Given that these reports combine investigative, procedural and evidentiary functions, it becomes crucial to examine how the families' opinions and narratives are elicited, the extent to which they are heard, and how the information gathered is (re)framed for the final court hearing. Furthermore, as there are even fewer opportunities for judicial oversight, it also becomes important to explore how procedural fairness, specifically the principle of orality and publicity, can be achieved in the new model.

In sum, there are three barriers to the principle of orality in standard child arrangements proceedings. Firstly, parents' direct input in case narrativisation is limited to written genres, which are problematic for lay court users (Grieshofer 2024). Secondly, the main evidentiary narratives are expert-framed (children services reports), the discursive production of which obscures authentic narratives. Thirdly, direct access to the judiciary (and thus publicity before the judge) is denied, delayed and obstructed through communicative filters (child services reports). The principle of orality is thus side-tracked to written genres, other institutional actors and procedural priorities.

From the institutional perspective, it is crucial to recognise that orality is restricted and important to identify which components of orality put parties' voices at risk during pre-court and court stages. Once court proceedings end, parents still need to co-parent, and parents' control over their narratives is part of their legal participation, and an important part of the family (dynamics) history. Alternative approaches to child-related proceedings, such as the problem-solving investigative approach or Pathfinder model (Firestone & Weinstein 2004, McIntosh et al. 2008, Hunter et al. 2020, Barlow et al. 2025) do tend to highlight the need for more open and transparent communication between courts and child services as well as flexibility for parents to directly relate their wishes in different ways throughout the proceedings, but the provision of effective voice projection opportunities remains problematic to implement fully.

2.5 Principle of Orality in Financial Remedy Proceedings

The financial remedy proceedings deal with post-separation financial disputes as part of private family proceedings. Similar to the child-related proceedings, the pre-court stages involve multiple distinct genres, specifically two lengthy court forms, questionnaires, chronologies, witness statements and evidence about financial circumstances and financial needs (including the needs of shared children). In addition to the genre-complexity, the proceedings also involve distinct challenges related to the discourse of legal financial concepts and framing the parties' narratives as 'needs narratives' (Grieshofer 2024). It is important to note that the pre-court paperwork creates substantial challenges for all litigants, even those who have a legal representative, as they still need to compile the evidence about their finances. Nevertheless, despite the complex genre requirements with their distinct communicative aims, the parties have more control over the pre-court stages and the proceedings overall, especially in comparison to child-related proceedings, as there are no expert-framed genres involved (e.g., child services reports). The main difference is that the judiciary has access to all parties' narratives and evidence filed in court. Although these narratives are written, they are presented and related from the first-person perspective, in principle thus fulfilling the key requirements for the principle of orality, publicity and open justice.

The other strength of financial remedy proceedings is linked to their procedural design. The primary consideration is children's financial needs, which puts the procedural focus on children. As part of legal practice, this has historically evolved into adopting a more inquisitorial approach to the proceedings (The Family Court Practice: Part 9, section 9.15; Black et al. 2014), enabling judges to request the disclosure of additional evidence if needed. The case management and legal process are geared towards the judiciary playing an active role in defining the scope of the proceedings and parties' narratives. This is especially visible in the unique role of the penultimate hearing, which is a Financial Dispute Resolution Appointment (FDRA), before the proceedings reach the final hearing stage, that is, the stage with the witness examination and thus the main opportunity for parties' voice projection. The procedural purpose of FDRA hearings is for the judge to review all evidence, assess the strengths and weaknesses of each party's cases and consider possible outcomes, with the aim of encouraging out-of-court settlement. As a result, the judiciary step outside their neutral role and perform an advisory role (Holt & Thomson 2023, Grieshofer 2024). What is of significance is that with lay court users in my data, the judges helped frame their narratives through elicitation strategies, as illustrated in Example 2.1.

Example 2.1 (case 24, FDRA hearing with two self-represented parties):

Judge:	Who lives in the former matrimonial home?
[Parent 2]:	Me.
Judge:	Where does the child live?
[Parent 1]:	With me.
(…)	
Judge:	Are you arguing that anyone is entitled to more?
[Parent 1]:	Yes, I.
Judge:	Why?
[Parent 1]:	Because of the child.
(…)	
Judge:	(To Parent 2) You say, I should get more because [Parent 1] lives with a new partner. (To Parent 1) You say, I need to get more because I am looking after [child].

As this is not the final hearing, the judge is not asking questions to examine the parties; the communicative purpose of the questions is to summarise the evidence and clarify the parties' financial needs. As a result, the judge helps not only identify and frame parties' strongest arguments but also enables them to be heard in an efficient and legally relevant manner (cf. Reynolds, this volume). The parties' actual orality is reduced to minimal answers, but the purpose of the orality principle is fully met as the enhanced role of the judge enables the parties to effectively exercise their legal participation and project their voices. This procedural adjustment of the judiciary's role currently only applies to this type of proceedings in England and Wales, but has proven to be very successful: the predominant majority of financial remedy proceedings now settle at the FDRA stage, inspiring recommendations for a version of an FDRA hearing to be included in other types of family and civil proceedings (Holt & Thomson 2023).

In financial remedy proceedings, the implementation of the principle of orality heavily relies on full disclosure of evidence, that is, engagement with procedurally and discursively complex forms and written genres, which can be stressful for some litigants (e.g., in case 39, the litigant acknowledged that they have not complied with directions because 'I cannot deal with documents. I need help from [court support] and mental health'). Despite the complexity of written genres and pre-court steps, the procedural design of these proceedings is still considered exemplary with respect to the support parties obtain from the judiciary in the FDRA hearings and the fact that the evidentiary disclosure is fully overseen by the judiciary, who are often experienced in settling these cases. In sum, the proceedings meet all components of orality and publicity, despite the actual voice projection being often restricted to minimal responses to the judge's narrative framing questions, asked in the spirit of supporting parties to identify their strengths and be better informed in preparation for negotiations. This illustrates that voice projection does not need to be long and can be substituted by the open manner of elicitation that strengthens parties' legal participation.

2.6 Principle of Orality in Small Claims Cases

Small claims cases deal with financial disputes below the £10,000 threshold, with the common perception that as these are fairly straightforward cases of low value, they can be managed by lay court users. But the irony is that this is not reflected in the Civil Procedure Rules in any substantial manner: litigants in person still need to conduct cross-examination, instruct experts, prepare evidence and make submissions independently following the discursive practices expected from legal professionals; and the Civil Procedure Rules themselves are a technical professional text written by lawyers for lawyers and therefore do not provide any instructions for these processes.

When it comes to orality in the small claims court, on the one hand, these aspects prevent the extent to which court users' voices can be projected and heard in court due to frequent (and understandable) problems with their legal relevance. On the other hand, small claims cases are held in public, all evidence is presented directly before the judge, and proceedings offer many voice projection opportunities, as cases are mainly heard within the same court sitting, so the initial procedural stage is immediately followed by submissions and witness examination. Within the same hearing, parties can thus present their narratives through a variety of procedural and substantive stages: opening statements, submissions, witness examinations and costs narratives (Grieshofer 2024).

There are understandably limitations as to the degree to which lay court users can be expected to conform to the procedural and legal expectations and make their narratives legally relevant, and indeed lay narratives are often perceived as unfocused, unnecessarily chronological, inductive and overly emotional accounts (Conley & O'Barr 1988, 1998, Trinder et al. 2014).

Similar to Conley and O'Barr's (1988, 1998) findings, in this study lay court users were found to focus on their good intentions and character instead of presenting rule-oriented accounts, and without explicitly referring to actors' legal obligations and violations. The accounts, nevertheless, still included the necessary detail but needed a degree of probing and the right elicitation approach from the judiciary for their oral narratives to be relevant (Grieshofer 2024).

For instance, in case 36, the litigant did not manage to frame their narrative of dispute resolution (the steps they took to resolve the dispute out of court) appropriately, but did manage to bring up pre-court email communication. Although the judge was sceptical as to its relevance at first, when they agreed to read the email, this led to a favourable decision on costs, and the judge saying to the other party's solicitor: 'When I see an email like this, an offer, and you're saying you want the time in court. Court time is a valuable resource and shouldn't be used [like this]. It was reasonable to have some reservations about [the substantive matter in the case]'. It was only through the judge's interactive engagement with the litigant that this outcome – and procedural justice – was reached.

Similarly, in case 30, the cross-examination between two self-represented parties (a building company and client) was very chaotic and did not clarify anything with respect to any of the narrative threads in relation to the narrative of dispute onset, dispute resolution narratives or parties' case narratives. The lack of structure was further complicated by the use of contextually unsuitable interactive turns: what was supposed to be a cross-examination turned into an argument with claims instead of questions. It was only after the judge took over the questioning that the substantive matters could be established through relevant elicitation (e.g., 'Do you accept they offered to do extra work?', 'Why did you reject mediation?', 'Tell me why I should decide in your favour?'). The opportunity to project the voice only became useful to the parties once they were guided through the process by relevant questions from the judge. The framing of the questions ensured the legal relevance of the party's contribution, shortening the length of their voice projection but increasing its effectiveness. The principle of orality was thus essentially maintained through adapting the role of the judge towards a more inquisitorial role, despite it not being procedurally recognised as such. But in cases with two self-represented parties, it is the judicial style and individual adaptations the judges make that define the extent to which due process can be reached and parties' voices can be effectively projected. In sum, even in proceedings geared towards lay court users, court procedure rules do not envisage how the principle of orality can be most effectively met, and the judges thus have to resort to the usual procedures (e.g., lay parties cross-examining each other) before they can introduce adaptations (e.g., the judge asking questions).

2.7 Concluding Remarks

There are several conceptual frameworks which can be used for exploring access to justice, and the choice of orality is not accidental in this chapter. As opposed to exploring access to justice through the lenses of procedural justice (cf. Grieshofer 2024), legal participation (cf. McKeever) or other frameworks, which prioritise the focus on court users' challenges and needs, focusing on orality offers a novel perspective on the core design principle of adversarial legal systems. Investigating the core systemic principle enables this chapter to prioritise the exploration of court procedures and the context which court users have to navigate. At a time when orality is becoming diminished and potentially even further reconfigured by court reforms and digitisation of court services, exploring the concept gains in significance as it becomes instrumental to identify which components of orality can be reduced and which ones need to be retained to ensure the core premise of fair and due process is guaranteed.

The exploration of three different procedural settings across family and county courts has led to three interrelated findings and lessons to be learnt with respect to legal practice. Firstly, the publicity component of orality cannot be achieved if the main evidentiary investigations happen outside of court without transparent evidence preservation practices, resulting in the parties not being able to present their cases fully even before the judiciary (as is currently the case with standard child-related proceedings and the new Pathfinder model). Secondly, to be efficient and litigant-friendly, orality does not need to rely on lengthy narratives, but can effectively be accomplished with the help of guided elicitation firmly embedded in court processes and procedures (as is currently the case with financial remedy proceedings). Thirdly, orality enforced through legal discursive practices does not per se enable effective legal participation of lay court users, and without clear procedural precedent, any modifications of the process have to rely on individual judicial styles (as is currently the case with small claims cases). More broadly, what is perceived as reduced orality and increased written procedural burden can be reimagined as oral textuality and textual orality (transformations between digital, written and spoken formats), an osmosis the main function of which is to carry the voices of the parties in a way that honours their authenticity; enables judicial oversight, guided elicitation and input; and provides scope for procedural flexibility to address court users' challenges in a consistent way.

The final point to make is that the chapter illustrates that language- and communication-centred research can make a significant contribution to understanding the systemic principles of the justice system, facilitating their implementation across different legal settings and contexts, and identifying structural injustices through exploring communicative processes and discursive practices.

References

Ainsworth, J. (2015). 'Legal discourse and legal narratives: Adversarial versus inquisitorial models'. *Language and Law/Linguagem e Direito*, 2(1), 1–11.

Barlow, C., Richardson Foster, H., Scollay, C., Barter, C., Stanley, N. with Miskowiec., A. & Carruthers, W. (2025). Private law pathfinder pilot: Process evaluation and exploratory financial analysis. Ministry of Justice Analytical Series. Accessed 6 May 2025. www.gov.uk/government/publications/private-law-pathfinder-pilot-process-evaluation-and-financial-analysis

Black, Rt., Cleary, A. & Culworth, W. (2014). *The Family Court Practice*. Family Law. Lexis Nexis.

Block, M. K. & Parker, J. S. (2004). 'Decision making in the absence of successful fact finding: Theory and experimental evidence on adversarial versus inquisitorial systems of adjudication'. *International Review of Law and Economics*, 24(1), 89–105.

Civil Procedure Rules, Part 35. Experts and Assessors. Civil Procedure Rules. Accessed 30 March 2025. www.justice.gov.uk/courts/procedure-rules/civil/rules/part35

Conley, J. M. & O'Barr, W. M. (1988). 'Fundamentals of jurisprudence: An ethnography of judicial decision making in informal courts'. *North Carolina Law Review*, 66(3), 467–508.

Conley, J. M. & O'Barr, W. M. (1998). *Just Words: Law, Language, and Power*. Chicago: University of Chicago.

Cotterill, J. (2003). *Language and Power in Court: A Linguistic Analysis of the OJ Simpson Trial*. London: Palgrave.

Ehrlich, S. (2010). 'The discourse of rape trials'. In Coulthard, M. and Johnson, A. (eds.), *The Routledge Handbook of Forensic Linguistics*. London and New York: Routledge, 265–281.

Fairclough, S. (2024). 'Resilience building in adversarial trials: Witnesses, special measures and the principle of orality'. *Social & Legal Studies*, 33(4), 642–667.

Family Court Statistics Quarterly: October–December (2024). Accessed 30 March 2025. www.gov.uk/government/statistics/announcements/family-court-statistics-quarterly-october-to-december-2024

Firestone, G. & Weinstein, J. (2004). 'In the best interests of children: A proposal to transform the adversarial system'. *Family Court Review*, 42(2), 203–215.

Gibbons, J. (2003). *Forensic Linguistics: An Introduction to Language in the Legal System*. London: Blackwell.

Grieshofer, T. (2022). 'The importance of being heard: Stories of unrepresented litigants in small claims cases and private family proceedings'. *Language and Law – Linguagem e Direito*, 9(1), 1–19.

Grieshofer, T. (2023). 'Court forms as part of online courts: Elicitation and communication in the early stages of legal proceedings'. *International Journal for the Semiotics of Law*. https://doi.org/10.1017/9781009378031.

Grieshofer, T. (2024). *Legal-Lay Discourse and Procedural Justice in Family and County Courts*. Cambridge: Cambridge University Press.

Heffer, C. (2005). *The Language of Jury Trial: A Corpus-Aided Analysis of Legal-lay Discourse*. Basingstoke: Palgrave.

Holt, K. & Thomson, C. (2023). 'Autoethnography: A personal reflection on the work of the family bar in the North of England'. *Journal of Social Welfare and Family Law*, 45(1), 62–80.

Holt, K., Broadhurst, K., Doherty, P. & Kelly, N. (2013). 'Access to justice for families? Legal advocacy for parents where children are on the "edge of care": An English case study'. *Journal of Social Welfare and Family Law*, 35(2), 163–177.

Hunter, R., Burton, M. & Trinder, L. (2020). *Assessing Risk of Harm to Children and Parents in Private Law Children Cases.* Ministry of Justice. Accessed on 30 March 2023. https://assets.publishing.service.gov.uk/government/uploads/system/uploads/attachment_data/file/895173/assessing-risk-harm-children-parents-pl-childrens-cases-report.pdf

Hymes, D. (1996). *Ethnography, Linguistics, Narrative Inequality: Toward an Understanding of Voice.* London: Taylor & Francis.

Lazer, S. (2021). The Principle of Orality. Unpublished PhD thesis, University of Huddersfield.

Lee, R. & Tkacukova, T. (2017). 'A study of litigants in person in Birmingham Civil Justice Centre'. 2 *CEPLER Working Paper Series.* http://epapers.bham.ac.uk/3014/1/cepler_working_paper_2_2017.pdf

McIntosh, J. E., Bryant, H. D. & Murray, K. (2008). 'Evidence of a different nature: The child-responsive and less adversarial initiatives of the Family Court of Australia'. *Family Court Review*, 46(1), 125–136.

McKeever, G., Royal-Dawson, L., Kirk, E. & McCord, J. (2022). 'The snakes and ladders of legal participation'. *Journal of Law and Society*, 49(1), 71–92.

Private Law Pathfinder (2025). Ministry of Justice. Accessed on 30 March 2025. https://gov.uk/government/publications/private-law-pathfinder-pilot-process-evaluation-and-financial-analysis

Roberts, P. (2022). *Roberts & Zuckerman's Criminal Evidence.* 3rd ed. Oxford: Oxford University Press.

Tkacukova, T. (2016). 'Communication in family court: Financial order proceedings from the perspective of litigants in person'. *Journal of Social Welfare and Family Law*, 38(4), 430–449.

Trinder, L., Hunter, R., Hitchings, E., Miles, J., Moorhead, R., Smith, L., Sefton, M., Hinchly, V., Bader, K. & Pearce, J. (2014). *Litigants in Person in Private Family Law Cases.* Ministry of Justice Analytical Series. www.justice.gov.uk/publications/research-and-analysis/moj

Tyler, T. (2000). 'Social justice: Outcome and procedure'. *International Journal of Psychology*, 35(2), 117–125.

Zuckerman, A. (2003). *Civil Procedure.* Trowbridge: LexisNexis.

Zuckerman, A. (2022). 'Truth finding and the miracle of inquisitorial process'. In Ferrer Beltrán, J. and Vázquez, C. (eds.), *Evidential Legal Reasoning: Crossing Civil Law and Common Law Traditions.* Cambridge: Cambridge University Press, 71–83.

3 Linguistic Rituals in Faretta Waivers

Mel Greenlee

3.1 Introduction

This chapter examines linguistic rituals surrounding waivers of legal rights in the context of U.S. criminal prosecutions. The most familiar warning and waiver is the Miranda advisement to suspects at the time of arrest (*Miranda* v. *Arizona*, 384 U.S. 436 (1966)). Here, a second waiver of legal rights by laypersons in the criminal context is compared and discussed, which could be thought of as Miranda's close cousin: Faretta. A Faretta waiver is the renunciation of a defendant's constitutional right to defense counsel; lay defendants make these formal waivers when they elect to represent themselves (*Faretta* v. *California* (1975) 422 U.S. 806 (1975)). Courts may refer to self-representation as 'pro-se' or 'pro-per' representation, or a defendant's litigating 'in propria persona'. Regardless of labels, the form and content of Faretta waivers have received far less attention than Miranda. Yet these warnings and waivers are linguistically complex, with similarly weighty legal consequences, deserving close analysis.

In both contexts, courts have strongly emphasized the importance of informed autonomy, the notion that a person facing legal sanctions is not merely passive but has decisional rights – a suspect may choose to speak to police, for example. Informed autonomy implies that crucial decisions are made only after the affected person is fully advised and cognizant of potential legal consequences. Thus, the Miranda Court viewed its warning to suspects as a crucial safeguard against coerced decision-making. A similar notion of autonomous and informed decisions underlies the Court's jurisprudence on Faretta waivers. In reviewing the validity of laypersons' waivers, US constitutional law requires that judges 'thoroughly' investigate, as courts must indulge a 'strong presumption' against giving up a fundamental right (*Von Moltke* v. *Gillies*, 332 U.S. 708, 724 (1948)).

This chapter focuses on the language of Faretta waivers via readability and syntactic analysis, contextualizing these further via the analysis of courtroom discourse practices. A small sample of Faretta waivers is examined, aiming to compare the procedure and language of these legal admonitions to findings of research on Miranda warnings and waivers. The Faretta analysis draws on trial transcripts and appellate pleadings in the most serious cases – capital trials – where defendants opted to represent themselves. The discussion contrasts the legal language of written forms and the capabilities of the defendants, building on the analysis of defendant – judge interactions and exploration of discursive practices in Faretta hearings.

Although limited in scope, the linguistic analysis serves as an initial rationale for doubting the true thoroughness of judicial review, even in a high-stakes circumstance where the most exacting scrutiny might be expected. As will be seen, Faretta waivers share many communicative features and complications with Miranda. Just as linguists have recommended concrete improvements in Miranda language and procedure, linguistic expertise has much to contribute, through interdisciplinary collaboration and research, to ensuring that Faretta admonitions are sufficiently comprehended to serve as a basis for legal decisions.

3.2 Research on Communicating Miranda Rights

In Miranda, the Court determined that to protect suspects from undue coercion, police had to inform them upon arrest of their right to silence and against self-incrimination, as well as their right to counsel, prior to any interrogation. Any waiver must be made 'knowingly, intelligently and voluntarily' under the totality of the circumstances (*Miranda* at 444; *U.S.* v. *Garibay*, 143 F.3d 534 (9th Cir. 1998)). A suspect's waiver must be made with 'full awareness' of the right and 'the consequences' of giving it up (*Moran* v. *Burbine*, 575 U.S. 412, 421 (1986)). Yet the language of Miranda warnings gives no assurance that suspects will understand their rights. The Supreme Court provided no standard wording, and formulations vary greatly (Rogers et al. 2007; Rogers 2008).

Rogers and Drogin (2015: 152) found Miranda warnings were often syntactically convoluted with sophisticated vocabulary beyond the educational level of the average detainee (6th or 7th grade of US schools). Domanico et al. (2012) analyzed tape recordings of Miranda warnings as administered by police in Milwaukee, Wisconsin, using a standard readability metric, the Flesch-Kincaid test; the study confirmed that the reading level of the recorded Miranda warnings was on average 10th grade US, therefore exceeding suspects' education level. Some sections were so complex that 'even college-educated suspects' would not fully understand them (13–14).

Rogers (2008: 781) estimated that around 300,000 arrestees in the US waive their Miranda rights every year without understanding even half of them. In particular, suspects fail to comprehend the right to free counsel prior to interrogation (Rogers & Drogin 2015: 152). Most people overestimate their Miranda understanding, with many assuming that a failure to speak would be considered incriminatory (Rogers et al. 2010). Further, vulnerable lay populations, such as persons with limited English proficiency (Pavlenko et al. 2019) or persons with limited cognitive ability, mental illness or disability, are especially prone to misunderstandings (Erickson et al. 2020; Rogers et al. 2007; Tazi & Rogers 2023).

Further, Ainsworth (2008, 2021) has shown that courts' evaluation of suspects' responses to the Miranda warnings are based on 'flawed assumptions about language and human communication' (2021: 112). She examined recent cases where courts considered that suspects had waived their Miranda rights, as well as 'several hundred' cases in which judges evaluated suspects' attempts to invoke them (2008: 8). The study revealed a serious pragmatic imbalance: only the baldest and most direct suspect responses were considered an adequate invocation of constitutional rights, while minimal responses (or even lengthy silence) were considered a waiver. Ainsworth (2008: 19) concluded that the rights allegedly protected by Miranda are 'perilously easy to waive and almost impossible' to assert.

Given doubts about Miranda comprehension based on research, applied linguists and psychologists have recommended that suspects' true understanding of the warnings be evaluated with an 'own-words' paraphrase or a dialogue technique, rather than a simple yes/no (Pavlenko 2024; CORG 2016; Domanico et al. 2012; Ferguson 2012).

Parallel misunderstandings and difficulties in assessing laypersons' comprehension of legal warnings remain to be explored in the Faretta realm. Faretta waivers raise similar concerns with respect to the degree to which they are understood and the quality of the judiciary's assessment of laypersons' comprehension. By exploring both perspectives, this chapter thus fills an important gap in research and practice.

3.3 Case Law and Procedure of Faretta Waivers

Like Miranda, waivers of the right to counsel are evaluated under the 'knowing intelligent' and voluntary standard (*Faretta* v. *California*, 422 U.S. 806 (1975)). A lay defendant must make a decision to forgo counsel only after being fully informed of the disadvantages of self-representation (*Faretta*, 422 U.S. at 807; *Iowa* v. *Tovar*, 541 U.S. 77 (2004)). But unlike Miranda waivers, which are elicited in the interrogation room, Faretta waivers are recorded in court, by a judge, in the presence of counsel. Defendants fill out a written waiver form, which is later reviewed in court. Nevertheless, as will be detailed further, these apparent procedural safeguards do not necessarily make for greater guidance or comprehension by defendants.

Legal decisions concerning self-representation involve the interplay between two constitutional rights of US criminal defendants: the right to counsel and the right to self-represent. Most criminal defendants cannot afford to hire private counsel (Tafoya and Nguyen 2015). Thus, prior to trial, indigent defendants are appointed defense counsel by the courts (*Gideon* v. *Wainwright*, 372 U.S. 335 (1963)). Sociological studies of this attorney–client relationship have shown it can be a rocky one (Natapoff 2005; Clair 2021). The most common situation in which self-representation arises is where the defendant distrusts appointed counsel (Goldschmidt 2022: 348), feels that their voice cannot be heard or that counsel is not effective. In those circumstances, the defendant can ask the trial court to replace counsel (a motion which is usually denied) and/or move for self-representation.

In some instances, courts may deny self-representation. In *Indiana* v. *Edwards*, 554 US 164 (2008), the U.S. Supreme Court recognized that trial courts have discretion to deny self-representation where the defendant's severe mental illness may render a litigant incapable of trial advocacy. Nevertheless, courts and mental health experts have struggled to refine the definition of necessary self-representation skills and to accurately assess them (Im & Witherell 2023; Patton et al. 2019; White & Gutheil 2016; LeCluyse 2015). Studies of relevant appellate decisions since *Indiana* v. *Edwards* have generally found that despite the Supreme Court's provision for judicial discretion, even where defendants seeking self-representation manifest serious symptoms, trial courts tend to grant their motions, and these decisions are upheld (Yacoub & Briggs 2022; Blume & Clark 2011; Knoll et al. 2010).

Where a defendant moves for self-representation, the court will provide a form to fill out and will schedule a formal hearing at which answers to the form's questions are then discussed. Pro-se defendants thus engage directly with judges concerning their wishes, submit a document they personally have completed, and at the hearing, confirm their comprehension of legal rights, explicitly giving them up. Yet despite these extra measures compared to *Miranda*, the challenges common to lay-legal communication prevail, as the analysis presented later will show.

3.4 Data and Methodology

To explore communication of Faretta warnings, verbatim transcripts of court hearings in capital cases were examined, as part of a larger study of trial discourse in proceedings where defendants represented themselves. Self-represented cases were located by screening the California Appellate Project's large database of California capital transcripts and postconviction pleadings. Results indicated that approximately 60 of the 701 capitally sentenced prisoners in the state had represented themselves at some point in their proceedings. Some did so only briefly and most eventually accepted representation by counsel. A minority continued to represent themselves for their entire trial; for this latter pro-se group, 18 transcripts were available for analysis (Greenlee 2017, 2022).

Review of their trial records showed that all of them had originally been assigned defense attorneys by the court, as they could not afford to hire counsel. Case records showed the usual procedure and documentation in response to defendants' self-representation requests. Prior to allowing self-representation, judges relied on written waiver forms. These forms were available as part of the trial record for 11/18 cases, which spanned a period of over 25 years (1992–2019) and trials in eight different California counties. For these cases, the written Faretta waivers were reviewed, as well as trial transcripts, and depending on the stage of the appeal, postconviction pleadings ($N = 6$). Extracts from their trials are presented later via (anonymized) case letter and page of the Clerk's Transcript (CT) or Reporter's Transcript (RT) of trial proceedings.

The pro-se group was diverse: of the 11, 4 identified as white, 3 African American, and 4 Latinx. Under the Penal Code (Section 190.3), if convicted of the charged crime(s), their only possible sentences were either life in prison without possibility of parole or a death sentence. In capital cases, a convicted defendant undergoes a second penalty trial where the sentence is decided by a jury. Each of these defendants was self-represented throughout, and each received a death sentence.

Review of the defendants' records established their general level of education as high school (11–12 years) or a high school equivalency exam. One had only six years of education. Three defendants had taken some college courses. According to their records, half manifested serious mental health symptoms and had been subject to competency proceedings. Their disabilities and diagnoses included possible intellectual disability, as well as paranoia, paranoid schizophrenia, psychosis and other mental health symptoms. All defended themselves while incarcerated.

For some defendants, trial records included handwritten samples of writing at a low literacy level, which is typical of prisoners in the US (Pavlenko 2024; Sterngold 2006). One dyslexic defendant, in a note to the judge, wrote that the case charged two counts of '*murdur*' and remarked, '*Your decsition to grant me my case has stoped a lot of problems*' [sic] (Case K, CT 436). Other litigants misspelt the name of the high school they attended (Case E, CT 73) or of prior prisons (Case C, CT 688).

Self-representation usually began with an informal oral request by the defendant (e.g., 'I'd … like to go pro-per on this case' (Case K, RT 101). Judges' responses were uniformly discouraging. One commented, '[o]bviously, we're not dealing with a petty theft or a drunk driving …' (Case E, RT 14). Another warned, 'I've told you a bunch of times now I think it's crazy …' (Case F, RT 241). A third emphasized, '[T]he state does not allow me to let you represent yourself without going through a rather lengthy litany or rather lengthy advisement telling you what I am required to tell you of all of the dangers involved in self-representation …' (Case G, RT 11). When dissuasion failed, judges instructed defendants to fill out the Faretta form for the following court session, where they would check if the forms had been filled out by defendants and discuss their answers.

3.5 Written Faretta Forms

The language of the written waiver forms, similar to Miranda warnings, was complex. Neither length nor wording of the forms was identical, but admonitions were framed in a similar fashion across the 11 cases, as long statements followed by a check box or a blank in which the defendants were to put their initials to indicate understanding (see the Reference list for the current Advisement and Waiver of Right to Counsel (Faretta waiver) form used in a county not part of the sample).

Among the 11 cases, five Faretta forms requested basic biographical information, such as years of schooling or prior self-representation. One question on two of the forms asked defendants to 'please explain briefly why you wish to represent yourself'. To this query, one defendant responded with a single profane complaint about appointed counsel's performance (Case B, RT 249). In the other case, the judge pointedly remarked that he would not explore the defendant's written answer, which expressed a desire for 'the truth' (Case F, RT 230).

There were three problematic characteristics across the 11 forms: the language was generally too complex, the comprehension check was reduced to a tick box exercise and some forms contained irrelevant or inapplicable provisions. With respect to the first two points, see Example 3.1, which is drawn from a warning containing over 1,300 words. (In the interest of length, the following examples have been edited using ellipsis (…)). Unless otherwise indicated, text of the examples (including errors and capitalization) is as printed on the forms or in the case transcripts.

Example 3.1 Excerpt from Long Faretta Form (Case E)

DANGERS AND DISADVANTAGES TO SELF-REPRESENTATION
3. I understand there are many dangers and disadvantages in representing myself. Among those disadvantages of not having an attorney are the following: …

The form then sets out several admonitions to which the defendant should confirm understanding, for example, '… I will not be entitled to special consideration or assistance by the Court …'. [check box]

C. I understand that if I am permitted to represent myself, it will be necessary for me, WITHOUT THE ASSISTANCE OF A LAWYER, to conduct my own trial consisting of, but not limited to: Making pretrial motions; selecting a jury; making an opening statement; cross-examining the witnesses for the prosecution; subpoenaing and presenting my own witnesses; making appropriate objections and motions during the course of the trial; preparing and presenting proposed jury instructions to the Court; making the final argument; making appropriate motions after trial; representing myself at the time of the probation and sentencing hearing in the event of conviction.

At the end of Paragraph C, the form provides a single check box on the right for the defendant to put their initials, confirming comprehension. The sentence's length and complex wording are readily obvious, as is the inadequacy of a single check box for confirmation of understanding. For example, if a defendant did not know the meaning of 'appropriate objections', but understood other parts of the paragraph, there would have been no way to indicate partial comprehension. In addition, the task list is composed of multiple noun phrases (the object of 'consisting of') begun with a gerund (verb+ing). Such nominalization is common in academic and scientific texts, but is known to bedevil understanding (Fang et al. 2006). Further difficulty in processing is added by gratuitous capitals ('WITHOUT…') and unfamiliar legal terms of art (e.g., *subpoena, cross-examine*).

The reading level of the Faretta forms was initially evaluated using the Flesch-Kincaid test, as in Domanico's study of Miranda (Domanico et al. 2012). But this test is only one of several available readability metrics (Grieshofer 2023). The 11 Faretta forms were therefore also examined with three web-based readability tests: the Coleman-Liau test, the SMOG test and another which represents a 'consensus' of 7 readability tests. (These metrics, and their measurement formulae, are available at www.ReadabilityFormulas.com.) Like Flesch-Kincaid, SMOG and Coleman-Liau are based on length, either measuring syllables or characters (for words) as well as words per sentence.

Average readability levels for individual Faretta forms ranged from about US grade 7 to grade 13 (first year of university or college). The four readability metrics' scores were not in perfect agreement but still clustered in the range of 9th grade US (mean of four: 9.28). This reading level is only slightly below the overall measurement of Miranda (grade 10) in the Milwaukee study (Domanico et al. 2012). And, as in that prior research, some paragraphs required much more reading skill.

While readability tests work well as a rough indicator of complexity in comparing the warnings to studies of Miranda, they have obvious limitations (Grieshofer 2023; Grieshofer et al. 2021; Tiersma 1999: 227). As noted earlier, syntactic complexity also greatly influences comprehensibility (Martinez et al. 2022, 2024; Berk-Seligson 2016: 245–246; Stygall, 2002, 2021). In addition to the problems shown in Example 3.1, the sample documents shared other grammatical features identified by research as difficult and 'imped[ing] comprehension' (Tiersma 1999: 203).

Among these were frequent passive voice (e.g., 'all documents … will be handed to witnesses'; 'this petition will be forwarded') and vagueness of reference (e.g., 'such requests … will most likely be denied'). The forms also contained many layers of subordinate clauses (Martinez et al. 2022, 2024; Grieshofer et al. 2021; Shuy 1998a). Some used awkward conditionals and concessive clauses, which are known to complicate language processing (Stygall 2002). The conditional expression 'in the event' appeared in a paragraph common to seven of the cases, in one of which it was spelled incorrectly: 'I understand that the Court may terminate my right to self-representation *in the event* that I engage in serious misconduct and obstruct the conduct and progress of the trial. I understand that *in the even* [sic] that happens, I will have to be represented by a lawyer …' [italics added]

Review of the forms' content and organization also revealed some irrelevant provisions not applicable to proceedings for capital defendants. Irrelevant portions included: 'I understand that I have the right to be admitted to liberty on reasonable bail pending the trial' (6 cases). However, under the defendants' circumstances, there was in fact no possibility of bail, even if the defendant had understood the archaic phrase, 'admitted to liberty'. (See California Penal Code 1270.5: 'A defendant charged with an offense punishable with death cannot be admitted to bail, when the proof of his or her guilt is evident or the presumption thereof great'.) Other forms noted the possibility of probation in the event of conviction ('I am aware that … if after trial I am found guilty, I have a right to make an application for probation, but that I am not entitled to probation as a matter of right' (Case A), which is also inapplicable in a capitally charged case. But this irrelevant text occurred in the same paragraph as information concerning the minimum and maximum penalty for the offense(s) currently charged, a highly relevant matter. On the other hand, most forms failed to mention the specifics of capital proceedings. The California Supreme Court has held that such detailed warnings are not required even in capital cases (*People* v. *Riggs*, 44 Cal. 4th 248 (2008)). Only one (Case I) mentioned mitigation evidence at the second, penalty phase.

Given prior research on complex language, and in light of the relatively low educational level of these litigants, their mental symptoms, and their stressful legal circumstances, it seems most unlikely they fully understood the warnings despite their general affirmation when asked, 'Do you understand …?'. Nevertheless, the legal presumption is that defendants 'understand what they are told' regarding self-representation (*Arredondo* v. *Neven*, 763 F.3d 1122 (9th Cir. 2014)).

3.6 Judges' Questions at Hearing

When defendants came to court with their completed forms, the sessions generally consisted of lengthy remarks by the judge, closely shadowing the written forms.

Most judges did not ask open-ended or hypothetical questions, which might have revealed defendants' true naïveté concerning trial procedure. Instead, transcripts showed that judges' questions tended to require yes/no answers. Excerpts from the trial transcripts are shown later. While the examples have been shortened using ellipsis (…), or for longer abbreviations (***), the transcripts otherwise are as in the original.

An excerpt from the hearing of Defendant B shows the judge's initial question (Case B, RT 242–244).

Example 3.2 Judge addresses Defendant B

J: And did you sign and initial that form?
B: Yes.
J: All right. Let me go over that with you. ¶ Okay. B, you understand that it is generally unwise for a person, even a person who is a licensed attorney, to represent themselves in the case because, in the case of a person who is not a licensed attorney, they lack knowledge of and experience in the law and even for one who is a licensed attorney they lack the objectivity about their own case that a licensed – a separate lawyer would normally have. So do you understand, … that it is generally unwise and probably unwise, almost certainly unwise, in a case of this seriousness with a potential capital punishment or death penalty on the table for you to represent yourself? ¶ Do you understand that?
B: Yes.

I have used the paragraph symbol (¶) in Example 3.2 to graphically shorten the text, where the reporter had indicated a paragraph break in the judge's talk.

As seen in this Example, judges tended to dominate speech at the hearing, using closed questions. In general, like the admonition formulae of Miranda, Faretta procedures may leave little opportunity for display of misunderstanding, questions or doubt on the part of the affected layperson.

The continued hearing transcript of Defendant B, and Defendant M's hearing (Case M, RT 139–142), serve to further illustrate the ritualistic talk at these sessions. Defendant B had gone to school for only six years and was receiving medication for mental illness. At the Faretta hearing, B began to answer before the judge, who was clearly following a script, finished reading aloud. Rather than confirm that B understood the warnings, the judge expressed concern for the record. An excerpt is shown in Example 3.3. (The court reporter represented B's interruption of the judge with dashes (--).)

Example 3.3 Case B Faretta hearing (continued)

J: If you are convicted, you may not legally complain of not having had an attorney to represent you in the matter. Do you --
B: Yeah.
J: -- understand that? I'm going to go through it and do my job in the form in which I'm going to do it, and that means doing everything right, B, so I do not

appreciate it when you brush off the question and interrupt me as I'm asking you the question with the answer … Do you understand that, B?
B: Yes, sir.

In Example 3.4, Defendant M, who was previously assessed as intellectually disabled, was questioned about the Faretta form.

Example 3.4 Case M, Faretta hearing

J: I am going to go over some … things with you, M. You understand that the offenses with which you're charge with are serious. [sic] The Court is advising you it would be contrary to your best interest to refuse to accept the services of appointed counsel. The appointed lawyers that are selected by the Court can handle any type of criminal case, they have a great knowledge of criminal law, criminal procedure and an intricate workings of this court. [sic] It is your intention to not allow me to appoint a lawyer for you, is that correct?
M: Yes.
***
J: You … have the right to speedy and public trial, in this case it is within 60 days of the date the Court found you competent to complete the criminal proceedings unless you agree to a date beyond that time, do you understand this right?
M: Yes, sir.
***

While both defendants B and M continued to respond to the court's closed questions, their true understanding of their import, like many who waive Miranda, appears highly questionable. Checking a box at the end of a long, barely comprehensible sentence, or requiring forced-choice responses to convoluted, closed questions, seems guaranteed to allow misunderstandings to go undetected until the pro-se defendant is required to perform as an advocate.

A great deal of research has shown the ineffectiveness of closed questions, such as those in the Faretta form, for assessing comprehension or for information gathering (for review, see CORG 2016; Oxburgh et al. 2010). The legal presumption of Faretta understanding, as in Miranda, may again be based on a flawed legal conception of 'language and human communication' (Ainsworth 2008, 2021). Application of research-based linguistic expertise in document design and wording would be extremely valuable for delivering more understandable legal information to these lay litigants and in checking on their comprehension (Grieshofer 2023; Shuy 1998b; Tiersma 2021; Stygall 2002). A joint statement by psychologists and attorneys has suggested that in evaluating fitness to represent oneself at trial, defendants should be asked open-ended questions about their understanding of self-representation (Patton et al. 2019). Further, where judges assess defendants' responses to admonitions, the 'paraphrase' or 'own-words' techniques recommended for Miranda could be quite revealing as an initial step (see Pavlenko et al. 2019; CORG 2016; Ferguson 2012; Domanico et al. 2012).

For Faretta defendants suffering from mental health symptoms, detailed feedback on comprehension would be even more crucial. As the U.S. Supreme Court stated in *Indiana* v. *Edwards*, where it is not clear that a defendant has the mental ability to coherently represent him or herself, self-representation is likely to prove as 'humiliating as ennobling' (554 U.S. 164 at 176). Overall, more accurate and in-depth methods of probing understanding must be developed if self-representation is truly to be with 'eyes open' (Im & Witherell 2023).

3.7 Conclusions and Reflections on 'Informed Autonomy'

Although limited in scope, the linguistic analysis of Faretta cases above may serve as an initial rationale for doubting the true thoroughness of judicial assessment of informed autonomy, even in a high-stakes circumstance where the most exacting scrutiny might be expected. In these cases, while accepting defendants' written waivers, judges appeared to engage in largely ritualized questioning, with insufficient attention to factors which negatively affect the lay litigants' practical appreciation of the rights they formally renounced. Like the jurists whose language ideology was analyzed by Philips (1998: 77), judges' interactions at times appeared to prioritize the formal record at the expense of detailed probing.

In allowing laypersons to give up their fundamental constitutional protections in both Miranda and Faretta contexts, everyday US legal practice may thus show a considerable divide between theory and practice (Miller 2021). In theory, courts exalt the notion of defendant autonomy, but obstacles in practice, including linguistic ones, render that goal unattainable. The Faretta case study reported here has shown these problems deserve focused linguistic research and dedicated revision to promote fairness. The present analysis encompassed a small data sample with descriptive and qualitative tools, but to examine Faretta language and communication in depth, detailed linguistic research should be applied to a larger group of waivers, along with experimental methods of assessing comprehension. Ethnographic study of courtroom practices related to Faretta waivers would also contribute valuable nuanced information. The results could further inform communication improvements where defendants seek self-representation, as they have in other 'Plain Language' endeavours (e.g., Shuy 1998b; Tiersma 2021). Whether opting to speak in an interrogation or to represent oneself at trial, informed choices can only be made when the options are understood in the affected person's own circumstances – necessarily a task of concrete language comprehension where research-based forensic linguistic expertise has much to offer.

References

Advisement and Waiver of Right to Counsel (Faretta Waiver). Online: www.alameda.courts.ca.gov/system/files/ala-cr-060-faretta-waiver-form-eff-1-1-20201.pdf

Ainsworth, J. (2008). 'You have the right to remain silent… but only if you ask for it just so: The role of linguistic ideology in American police interrogation law'. *The International Journal of Speech, Language and the Law*, 15(2), 1–21.

Ainsworth, J. (2021). 'Curtailing coercion in police interrogation: The failed promise of *Miranda v. Arizona*', in Coulthard, M., May, A., and Sousa-Silva, R. (eds.), *The Routledge Handbook of Forensic Linguistics*, 2nd ed. London: Routledge, 95–111.

Berk-Seligson, S. (2016). 'Totality of circumstances and translating the Miranda warnings', in Erlich, S., Eades, D., and Ainsworth, J. (eds.), *Discursive Construction of Consent in the Legal Process*. Oxford: Oxford University Press, 241–263.

Blume, J. H. and Clark, M. J. (2011). 'Unwell: *Indiana v. Edwards* and the fate of mentally ill pro se defendants'. *Cornell Journal of Law & Public Policy*, 21, 151–174.

Clair, M. (2021). 'Being a disadvantaged criminal defendant: Mistrust and resistance in attorney-client Interactions'. *Social Forces*, 100(1), 194–217.

Communication of Rights Group (CORG). (2016). 'Guidelines for communication of rights to non-native English speakers in Australia, Wales & England, and the USA.' Online: www.aaal.org/guidelines-for-communication-rights

Domanico, A. J., Cicchini, M. D., and White, L. T. (2012). 'Overcoming Miranda: A content analysis of the Miranda portion of police interrogations'. *Idaho Law Review*, 49(1), 1–22.

Erickson, S. L., Salekin, K. L., Johnson, L. N., and Doran, S. C. (2020). 'The predictive power of intelligence: Miranda abilities of individuals with intellectual disability'. *Law and Human Behavior*, 44(1), 60–70.

Fang, Z., Schleppegrell, M. J., and Cox, B. E. (2006). 'Understanding the language demands of schooling: Nouns in academic registers'. *Journal of Literacy Research*, 38(3), 247–273.

Ferguson, A. G. (2012). 'The dialogue approach to Miranda warnings and waiver'. *American Criminal Law Review*, 49, 1437–1491.

Goldschmidt, J. (2022). *Self-Representation: Law, Ethics and Policy*. New York: Lexington Books.

Greenlee, M. (2017). 'Disorder in the court: Language use by "gray area" pro per defendants'. *Language & Law/Linguagem e Direito*, 21(1), 12–31.

Greenlee, M. (2022). 'It's not because I didn't warn you'. *Paper presented to the Global Meeting on Law and Society*, Law and Society Association, Lisbon, July 15th.

Grieshofer, T. (2023). 'Court forms as part of online courts: Elicitation and communication in the early stages of legal proceedings'. *International Journal for the Semiotics of Law-Revue internationale de Sémiotique Juridique*, 36(4), 1–39.

Grieshofer née Tkacukova, T., Gee, M., and Morton, R. (2021). 'The journey to comprehensibility: Court forms as the first barrier to accessing justice'. *International Journal for the Semiotics of Law-Revue internationale de Sémiotique juridique*, 35(5), 1–27.

Im, D. S. and Witherell, J. S. (2023). 'How experts advise evaluating pro se competence 15 years post-Edwards'. *The Journal of the American Academy of Psychiatry and the Law*, 51(4), 1–13.

Knoll, J. L., Leonard, C., Kaufman, A. R., and Way, B. B. (2010). 'A pilot survey of trial court judges' opinions on pro se competence after *Indiana v. Edwards*'. *Journal of the American Academy of Psychiatry and the Law*, 38(4), 536–539.

LeCluyse, E. (2015). 'The spectrum of competency: Determining a standard of competence for pro se representation'. *Case Western Reserve Law Review*, 65(4), 1239–1267.

Martinez, E., Mollica, F., and Gibson, E. (2022). 'Poor writing, not specialized concepts, drives processing difficulty in legal language'. *Cognition*, 224, 105070.

Martinez, E., Mollica, F., and Gibson, E. (2024). 'So much for plain language: An analysis of the accessibility of United States federal laws over time'. *Journal of Experimental Psychology: General*, 153(5), 1153–1164.

Miller, K. E. (2021). 'The myth of autonomy rights'. *Cardozo Law Review*, 43(2), 275–441.

Natapoff, A. (2005). 'Speechless: The silencing of criminal defendants'. *New York University Law Review*, 80, 1449–1504.

Oxburgh, G. E., Myklebust, T., and Grant, T. (2010). 'The question of question types in police interviews: A review of the literature from a psychological and linguistic perspective'. *International Journal of Speech, Language, and the Law*, 17(1) 45–66.

Patton, C. L., Johnston, E. L., Lillard, C. M., and Vitacco, M. J. (2019). 'Legal and clinical issues regarding the pro se defendant: Guidance for practitioners and policy makers'. *Psychology, Public Policy, & Law*, 25(3), 196–211.

Pavlenko, A. E. (2024). 'Language proficiency as a matter of law: Judicial reasoning on Miranda waivers by speakers with limited English proficiency (LEP)'. *International Journal for the Semiotics of Law-Revue Internationale de Sémiotique Juridique*, 37(2), 329–357.1

Pavlenko, A., Hepford, E., and Jarvis, S. (2019). 'An illusion of understanding: How native and non-native speakers of English understand (and misunderstand) their Miranda rights'. *International Journal of Speech, Language & the Law*, 26(2), 181–207.

Philips, S. (1998). *Ideology in the Language of Judges: How Judges Practice Law, Politics and Courtroom Control*. New York: Oxford University Press.

Rogers, R. (2008). 'A little knowledge is a dangerous thing. Emerging Miranda research and professional roles for psychologists'. *American Psychologist*, 63, 776–787.

Rogers, R. and Drogin, E. Y. (2015). 'Miranda rights and wrongs: Matters of justice'. *Court Review*, 51, 150–156.

Rogers, R., Harrison, K. S., Hazelwood, L., and Sewell, K. W. (2007). 'Knowing and intelligent: A study of Miranda warnings in mentally disordered defendants'. *Law and Human Behavior*, 31, 401–418.

Rogers, R., Harrison, K. S., Shuman, D. W., Sewell, K. W., and Hazelwood, L. L. (2007). 'An analysis of Miranda warnings and waivers: Comprehension and coverage'. *Law and Human Behavior*, 31, 177–192.

Rogers, R., Hazelwood, L., Sewell, K. W., Harrison, K. S., and Shuman, D. W. (2008). 'The language of Miranda warnings in American jurisdictions: A replication and vocabulary analysis'. *Law and Human Behavior*, 32, 124–136.

Rogers, R., Rogstad, J. E., Gillard, N. D, Blackwood, H. L., and Shuman, D. W. (2010). 'Everyone knows their Miranda rights: Implicit assumptions and countervailing evidence'. *Psychology, Public Policy, & Law*, 16, 300–318.

Shuy, R. W. (1998a). *The Language of Confession, Interrogation and Deception.* Thousand Oaks, CA: Sage.
Shuy, R. W. (1998b). *Bureaucratic Language in Government and Business.* Washington, DC: Georgetown University Press.
Sterngold, J. (2006). 'Illiteracy reinforces prisoners' captivity.' *San Francisco Chronicle*, 27 December 2006.
Stygall, G. (2002). 'Textual barriers to United States immigration', in Cotterill, J. (ed.), *Language in the Legal Process.* Houndmills: Palgrave, 35–53.
Stygall, G. (2021). 'Complex documents/Average and not-so-average readers', in Coulthard, M., May, A., and Sousa-Silva, R. (eds.), *The Routledge Handbook of Forensic Linguistics*, 2nd ed. London: Routledge, 32–47.
Tafoya, S. and Nguyen, V. (2015). '*California criminal courts: Fact sheet*'. Public Policy Institute of California. www.ppic.org/publication/californias-criminal-courts/
Tazi, K. Y. and Rogers, R. (2023). 'Falling through the cracks: Failing to identify compromised Miranda abilities for defendants with limited cognitive capacities'. *Behavioral Sciences & the Law*, 41(5), 326–342.
Tiersma, P. M. (1999). *Legal Language.* Oxford: Oxford University Press.
Tiersma, P. M. (2021).'Instructions to jurors: Redrafting California's jury instructions', in Coulthard, M., May, A., and Sousa-Silva, R. (eds.), *The Routledge Handbook of Forensic Linguistics*, 2nd ed. London: Routledge, 267–280.
White, M. M. and Gutheil, T. G. (2016). 'A proposed model for assessing defendant competence to self-represent'. *Journal of the American Academy of Psychiatry and Law*, 44, 425–436.
Yacoub, A. R. and Briggs, B. (2022). 'Suicide by court? The role of advisory counsel in assisting courts to determine a defendant's competence to proceed pro se'. *Southern California Interdisciplinary Law Journal*, 31, 245–275.

Cases Cited

Arredondo *v*. Neven, 763 F.3d 1122 (9th Cir. 2014)
Faretta *v*. California, 422 U.S. 806 (1975)
Gideon *v*. Wainwright, 372 U.S. 335 (1963)
Indiana *v*. Edwards, 554 U.S. 164 (2008)
Iowa *v*. Tovar, 541 U.S. 77 (2004)
Miranda *v*. Arizona, 384 U.S. 436 (1966)
Moran *v*. Burbine, 575 U.S. 412 (1986)
People *v*. Riggs, 44 Cal. 4th 248 (2008)
U.S. *v*. Garibay, 143 F.3d 534 (9th Cir. 1998)
Von Moltke *v*. Gillies, 332 U.S. 708, 724 (1948)

Statutes Cited

California Statutes (Westlaw, 2024)
Penal Code 190.3: Determination of Death Penalty or Life Imprisonment.
Penal Code 1270.5: Capital Offenses; Nonbailable Where Proof of Guilt Evident or Presumption Thereof Great.

4 Navigating the Challenges of Legal Practice in Lawful Surveillance of Multilingual Communication

Nadja Capus, Cornelia Griebel and Franziska Hohl Zürcher

4.1 Introduction and Background

In covert surveillance operations, the police monitor the activities of suspected individuals to gather information for their investigations. This information is then used by public prosecutors and judges in subsequent legal proceedings. Surveillance is conducted around the clock and includes monitoring conversations on wiretapped telephones or in bugged premises and vehicles. Often, surveillance extends over several weeks or months, resulting in an overwhelming volume of communications. This constitutes a significant intrusion into privacy and requires judicial authorisation. Consequently, it is primarily used in cases of serious offenses such as human trafficking, drug trafficking, economic crimes, and terrorism. However, its effectiveness is compromised by two primary challenges: the comprehensibility of the intercepted communications and the transmission of these contents within the scope of investigations and court proceedings. These challenges are exacerbated when the suspects do not communicate in the language of the law enforcement agencies.

In this intricate field, interpreters and translators, hereafter referred to as intercept interpreters/translators (IITs), play an indispensable role. Their main responsibility involves attentively listening to recorded conversations in the source language to identify any relevant information connected to ongoing investigations and then conveying these conversations in the target language, mainly in writing but also orally. Consequently, the IIT's work exemplifies a unique hybrid translational activity requiring the use of strategies relevant to both (oral) interpreting and (written) translation, as highlighted by Capus and Havelka (2022).

Communication surveillance differs from triadic interpreting activities, such as in police or court interpreting, where the interpreter takes part in the

Funding statement: This contribution results from a research project funded by the Swiss National Science Foundation (project no. 10001_184896).

communication between the interviewed person and the interviewer, in that the interlingual transfer does not serve the purpose of ensuring understanding between the interacting parties at the time of the communicative act itself. Instead, the transfer by the IIT is unidirectional, guided by the investigative context, and serves the scope of information gathering and evidence collection. Furthermore, for oral source information, the transmission is intersemiotic when intercepted oral communication is converted into a written *translatum* (Reiss & Vermeer 1984/2014). To fulfil their specific translational task, IITs need to combine their translational competences with forensic and criminalistic competencies (Griebel & Havelka 2024). However, they are not explicitly required to perform forensic and criminalistic tasks such as voice recognition, deciphering coded language, or information analysis. In fact, in Switzerland, as in most jurisdictions, engaging in these activities would exceed their legal authority (Capus & Griebel 2021). Nevertheless, in practice, the police often rely on IITs having these criminalistic and forensic skills. As a result, these tasks are informally undertaken by many IITs (Griebel & Hohl Zürcher 2023).

The product of the translational process, the *translatum*, can manifest in various forms, such as a brief note indicating the conversation's relevance or lack thereof to the criminal inquiry, a summary of the conversation's content, an informal oral report of key details to police investigators, or a written interlingual translation of the entire conversation or parts of it, hereafter referred to as translated intercept record (TIR). The TIR can be used as evidence in subsequent criminal proceedings. In most countries, including Switzerland, the oral conversation in the source language is directly transferred into a written *translatum* in the target language without prior intralingual transcription (Capus & Griebel 2021; Capus & Havelka 2022; Gradinčevič-Savič 2020; Salaets et al. 2015). However, in some countries like the US and Australia, an intralingual transcript must be created before interlingual translation. In these cases, the interlingual translation of the transcript can occur later and be performed by translators not involved in the actual communication surveillance (Capus and Gilbert 2024; Gilbert & Heydon 2021; Lai 2023; NAJIT 2019).

The work of IITs is crucial yet opaque but has been increasingly explored in recent years (see, e.g., Lai 2023, for a recent overview). Their role and activity in the context of criminal proceedings are of interest from legal, sociological, and translation studies' perspectives. This chapter triangulates major findings across diverse research threads and various theoretical frameworks such as taxonomy of the translational activity and products of intercept interpreting and translation according to the functionalist approach (Reiss & Vermeer 1984/2014), the processes of decontextualisation and recontextualisation (Bauman & Briggs, 1990), indexicality (Garfinkel 1967/1984), and street-level bureaucracy (Lipsky 1980/2010). The study originates from interdisciplinary research (see Capus et al. 2024) aimed to fill a significant knowledge gap, particularly regarding the activities, responsibilities, and competences of IITs (Capus & Havelka 2022; Drugan 2020; Salaets et al. 2015). It was conducted in Switzerland, where a comprehensive data set was collected, consisting of case files, participant observation during ongoing communication surveillance at a police station, semi-structured interviews with IITs and police investigators, and audio recordings of monitored conversations. The data primarily covered drug trafficking cases. The main analysis method applied was qualitative content analysis (Kuckartz 2018; Mayring 2022), which categorises and interprets manifest and latent content to describe specific topics and patterns. Quantitative content analysis was also employed for systematic text counting, and multimodal (inter)actional analysis (Norris 2004) was used to understand the multiple modes of communication (see Capus & Grisot 2022; Havelka 2024).

In this contribution, we start from the original communication between the secretly monitored suspects that represents phase 1 (Section 4.2). The second phase corresponds to the situation in police premises, where the IITs listen to these conversations and are, in collaboration with the police, responsible for the interlingual transfer and the production of *translata* (Section 4.3). Hence, in phase 2, the IITs and police officers are the active participants in the communication and the monitored individuals change to being the object of communication. The third phase involves further processing of the *translata* (Section 4.4): on the one hand, excerpts from the *translata* are used for questioning the suspects; on the other hand, they are incorporated into written documents such as police reports, indictments, and court judgments. In addition to the police, prosecutors and judges are key actors in this phase of communication. While the IITs no longer actively participate, the monitored individuals may intermittently become subjects in the communication, at least if they are being questioned. In the last section, we discuss the overall roles and responsibilities of IITs within the communication surveillance and criminal proceedings (Section 4.5).

4.2 Phase 1: Original Communication – Fragmented, Ambiguous, and Encoded

The first communication phase consists of the original communication between the monitored individuals. As secret surveillance of communications takes place during the 'everyday life' of the persons being monitored, it is characterised by the authenticity and immediacy of naturally occurring communication, along with potential ambiguities and contextual specifics. From a sociological perspective, such conversations have an 'indexical' character (Garfinkel 1967/1984). Participants, especially those familiar with each other, often use pronominal, temporal, or spatial references such as 'they', 'this', 'later', 'here', or 'there' rather than explicit designations for people, places, or times. These conversations are understandable to them due to their shared background knowledge (Bergmann & Meyer 2021: 45). According to Garfinkel (2022), indexical expressions unfold their meaning only *in situ*, that is, in a specific situation at a particular time and place, and with respect to the occasion and the 'biography of interaction in which they have been spoken' (129). This is illustrated by the following telephone conversation shown in Example 4.1 between person A and person B, who are involved in drug dealing (Case file 3; see Hohl Zürcher & Capus 2024). All data examples used in this chapter were translated from French or German into English by the authors and fully anonymised. Square brackets in data examples denote changes made by the authors, such as fictitious information for anonymisation purposes (e.g., [MARC] in Example 4.1), explanations (e.g., [one of the IITs] in Example 4.4), or omissions (e.g., […] in Example 4.1). The annotations in parentheses or round brackets were added by the IIT (e.g., '([MARC] asks an unintelligible question, he seems to be eating)').

Example 4.1

A: (incomprehensible)
B: Yeah, hey [MARC], how are you doing?
A: Hello.
B: Hello, hello. How are you?
A: Good, and you?
B: Doing alright.
A: Not better?
B: A little tired but alright.
A: Mm. You're sorting things out over there?
B: Yeah, yeah, slowly.
A: Mm… ([MARC] asks an incomprehensible question, he seems to be eating).
B: Nothing special.
A: Mm. You're not here?
B: No. I might… maybe tonight if I have a moment, I'll still swing by for a bit.
A: Ok, ok.
[…]

The indexicality of the conversation between person A and person B can be seen, for example, in A's question 'Not better?', which indicates shared background knowledge. Obviously, B wasn't feeling well before, and A refers to this by asking if B is feeling better now. Another evidence for shared background knowledge is the use of deictic expressions, 'there' and 'here'. Additionally, both persons are speaking in ellipses and allusions, for example, when speaker A says, 'You're sorting things out over there?' and speaker B replies with 'Yeah, yeah, slowly'. This exchange implies that there are shared experiences or context between the speakers, which is alluded to without being directly stated. While the meaning of the conversation seems to be clear to its active participants, the conversation is vague and ambiguous for uninvolved third parties such as the police and IITs.

The example pertains to a telephone conversation that is characterised by a specific purpose and a clearly defined scope of time, content, and participants, much like written and oral communication via messaging services. In contrast, bugged vehicles or apartments involve varying combinations of participants, adding complexity to communication as multiple separate conversations can occur simultaneously, participants may switch between discussions or engage in phone calls with absent third parties, and overlapping speech often results from several individuals speaking or interrupting each other at the same time. For intercept interpreters, this creates significant challenges, as they must not only discern and differentiate between overlapping voices but also maintain clarity and accuracy when interpreting fragmented or disrupted exchanges.

The communication in phase 1 is further characterised by linguistic aspects such as sociolects or milieu and group languages. What is much more important, however, is the above-mentioned 'biography of interaction' (Garfinkel 2022: 129). In the context of communication surveillance, this biography includes the fact that, within organised crime, it is widely known that law enforcement agencies may monitor communication. This means that even spontaneous communication is adapted to a certain extent to the risk that there may be external listeners, namely the monitoring police. Especially on the phone, experienced criminals try to talk as little as possible, as illustrated in the following quote from an IIT saying:

Example 4.2

You can tell he's small fry. [Name of another suspect] would never talk like that, you always have to listen to him twice or three times, there are always hidden messages. (Observation day 1)

In addition, some monitored individuals obscure their talk and pronunciation either by eating something or putting something in their mouth (e.g., a plum), as reported by an IIT during the participant observation at the police station:

Example 4.3

An IIT recounts a story about a dealer from [mentions country of origin] who worked as a taxi driver and always had something in his mouth during relevant conversations. The IIT suggests it might have been a plum, and laughs. Thus, both his voice and what he said were difficult to understand. (Observation day 4)

Another way of making communication less comprehensible is the use of code words: according to our interviews with police officers and IITs, criminally relevant information is often encoded or encrypted by the monitored individuals. Our quantitative content analysis of TIRs shows that this applies to most telephone conversations (Hohl Zürcher & Capus 2024): only in 12 out of 538 translated phone calls referring to drug transfers, the monitored individuals explicitly talk about 'drug', 'cocaine', or 'hashish'. The suspects much more frequently use circumlocutions such as ‘stuff’ or the pronoun ‘it’, or codes like the names of clothing or vegetables, while individuals are mentioned by using vague descriptions or nicknames. The deliberate obfuscation of conversation content reinforces the inherent indexical character of communication and increases the ambiguity and incomprehensibility of the conversations for uninvolved individuals.

4.3 Phase 2: From Audio Recording to IIT to Police Investigator

In communication phase 2, the IITs come into play. As soon as they put on their headphones and start to listen to the communication recorded on audio tapes, they are confronted with the naturally occurring communication between the monitored individuals, including the occurring obstructions as described in phase 1. They listen to the conversations and start producing different *translata* (cf. Section 4.1). This process involves interlingual transfer as well as triaging the conversations based on their relevance to the actual criminal investigations. It represents an initial step of entextualisation (Bucholtz 2009; Park & Bucholtz 2009), specifically decontexualisation, where communication is extracted from its original context (Bauman & Briggs 1990). The original communication is thus reconstructed by the IITs, often in co-operation with the police and with a focus on the needs of law enforcement agencies (Griebel & Hohl Zürcher 2023; Griebel & Havelka 2024). The initial communicators are no longer active participants but become subjects of communication between third parties.

IITs, as uninvolved third parties, require ‘professional hearing’ (Bucholtz 2009) to understand and transfer investigative information. This involves interpreting the inherent vagueness and indexicality of conversations. Although not formally tasked with investigative responsibilities, in practice, IITs are guided by questions such as: Who is speaking? About what? With what intent? Where and with whom? While their primary role is interlingual transfer, they understand that investigators rely on these insights to guide further investigation steps (Griebel & Havelka 2024). Therefore, the IITs endeavour to use as many modal resources as feasible for capturing communication. Havelka (2024) describes five levels of multimodal speech perception during the listening process: the acoustic, linguistic, communicative, situative and forensic level. When listening, the IITs must perceive the modal cues on all these levels and document them in the *translatum*. The key difference to transcription, however, is that an interlingual transfer is simultaneously taking place. So, the true meaning of the source language statement can only be understood on both the linguistic and communicative – that is, (socio-)cultural – levels if the IITs provide interpretive aids in the form of explanations or clarifications.

The following court case (judgment 501 2018 106 of the Cantonal Court of Fribourg, dated March 18, 2019, consideration 2.4.2) demonstrates the importance of IITs providing interpretive aids to ensure that both linguistic and communicative (socio-cultural) nuances are understood by the investigating authorities. In an investigation of drug trafficking offenses, the alleged offenders were street-level cocaine dealers connected to a Senegalese woman residing in Fribourg. When translating the intercepted communication of the Senegalese woman from Wolof into French, the IIT added the following comment: *'en parlant des chaussures, c'est de la drogue qu'elle est en train de parler'* (translation by the authors: 'by talking about shoes, she is actually talking about drugs'). It then turned out that this comment added by the IIT was very helpful. In a police interrogation at a later stage, an accomplice of the accused Senegalese woman was confronted with the audiotape of the intercepted conversation and the accomplice confirmed that they were indeed talking about drugs not shoes. This illustrates how, in some cases, codes and the true meaning of a conversation can only be understood on a deeper level with interpretive aids. In such cases, cultural and communicative contexts need to be considered, but such interpretation must be carefully managed within the legal framework to avoid overstepping the boundaries of the interpreter's role. Therefore, unlike the widespread legal fiction that a strictly literal interlingual transfer suffices for comprehending intercepted communication (Capus & Griebel 2021), it is essential to recognise that paralinguistic, situational, and contextual elements are vital for understanding (see, e.g., Chakhachiro 2016; Havelka 2024).

The primary modal resources perceived and conveyed by the IIT are what individuals say. However, the language transfer is not always simple and unambiguous due to the indexicality. If we return to the previously cited excerpt of the recorded conversation, we can, for example, see that expressions such as 'sorting things out' (as in person A's question 'You're sorting things out over there?') are clearly open to various interpretations. Given that both individuals are engaged in drug trafficking, it is conceivable that 'sorting things out' could pertain to activities related to drug transportations or financial transactions. However, it cannot be ruled out that 'sorting things out' has a completely different meaning that is not relevant from an investigative point of view. Through the decontextualisation (Bauman & Briggs 1990) of the communication from the preceding conversations as the larger context, the statement gains a vagueness that it did not possess in the original communication situation. In this example, the IIT leaves the interpretation of all indexical expressions to the reader. In another example, the IIT interprets and explains such expressions with bracketed comments: '[...] to those people over there (SPAIN)' (Hohl Zürcher & Capus 2024: 706) or 'I'm fine, I want to go to the car so I don't know when we're going to get the rest of this stuff from the guy (the rest of the drugs from ANDERSON)' (Hohl Zürcher & Capus 2024: 703).

To resolve indexicality, IITs rely on the background knowledge they have acquired during the course of communication surveillance in the respective case. If their own knowledge is insufficient, they often consult the police for additional information that may have been obtained from other investigative measures (e.g., police observation). The extent to which IITs engage in such forensic interpretations and explanations is contingent upon their perceived role (Hohl Zürcher & Griebel, 2024): IITs who primarily regard themselves as external service providers tend to reproduce indexical expressions verbatim without engaging in their own interpretative analysis. Conversely, seasoned IITs, who closely identify with investigative work and often have substantial case knowledge, occasionally assert themselves over police interpretations in some cases. This range of interpretative involvement highlights the need for clearer guidelines on the scope of IITs' responsibilities, particularly when their interpretations might significantly impact the investigative process (Capus & Gilbert 2024).

In communications surveillance, it is not just the content of speech that matters, but also how it is delivered. The IIT must assess various modal cues, such as speech patterns, stuttering, lisping, speech rate, dialect, and paralinguistic elements like prosody shifts. These non-verbal, audible cues help the IIT infer the context or mood, such as a high-pitched voice indicating fear or anger, or laughter hinting at hierarchy (Havelka 2024). Additionally, these non-verbal resources aid in identifying individuals, as IITs often recognise voices during surveillance. In fact, although IITs are not professionally trained experts in voice recognition, the police do attribute expertise to them, repeatedly emphasising how IITs successfully recognise voices even after several years (Griebel & Havelka 2024). Examples 4.4 and 4.5 are extracts from transcriptions of interviews that we have conducted with police officers:

Example 4.4

They [knew] about other proceedings that we had conducted much earlier, three or four years earlier, and they were already IITs, then he [one of the IITs] came and said: 'The voice, it had already appeared in the previous action. But we told him differently'. And then, when we checked everything and also with/perhaps with the telephone connections, we had to say: 'He's right'. He only heard it because of the voice: 'I recognise that voice'. […] Then I said: 'That's fantastic'. (Police officer 4)

Example 4.5

[…] our IITs can say, 'Hey, we've heard that one before. We've heard him there, there and ten years ago'. They know these voices so well. (Police Officer 3)

While this can be valuable, it carries risks of error, as their identifications are not based on formal expertise. This practice should be explicitly acknowledged to prevent overreliance on informal judgments, ensuring it supports investigations without undue influence.

Background noise is another key modal resource in surveillance. In phone calls, it could be traffic or train sounds; in vehicle surveillance, the radio; and in apartments, the noise of a television or coffee machine. Background noise can provide clues to a suspect's location. It can also clarify deictic references like 'here' that are not evident through other means. Furthermore, background noise from the speaker, such as a knife hitting a board or packaging sounds, becomes part of multimodal communication. Mondada (2019) calls this 'multiactivity', where various modal resources overlap. Accurately documenting these resources is crucial for investigations.

An IIT describes in an interview their perception, interpretation, and documentation of potentially criminally relevant background noise as follows ('-' describes a word or sentence break):

Example 4.6

IIT 5: That- that's so. Or- I say- we must not interpret, two- for example two young men meet and they wrap up the drugs. But how do I write now 'they wrap up the drugs' if they say NOTHING? It rustles all the time, it could be paper, it could be plastic wrap, it could be a plastic bag. It could be that they are consuming themselves. And suddenly one of them says very quietly: 'Damn foil! It keeps tearing'. And THEN I know they are packaging. Or how do I know that one is preparing drugs and the other is packaging weed? You only hear 'tuck, tuck, tuck, tuck, tuck, tuck, tuck'. That's someone with the knife. It's like [cutting] a [gingerbread?] and the co- the cutting board is made of wood, I suppose, or someone else is in the kitchen and then it goes 'tuck, tuck, tuck, tuck, tuck'. And with the weed, they're snipping the weed, it goes 'zz-K, zz-K, zz-K' ((imitates cutting noise)) and THOSE are the sounds, but that's really experience.

Interviewer: But also- also that wouldn't appear in the TIR?

IIT 5: No. I must not write 'they wrap it', I may only write 'chopping-like sounds' or 'snipping-like sounds'. That I may write.

Against this backdrop, it becomes apparent that IITs play a key role in the process of decontextualisation (Havelka 2024). Additionally, they have a crucial influence on the comprehensibility of the original communication between the suspects, both by omitting certain elements of communication (e.g., intonation) or making note of such elements (e.g., comments on unclear pronunciation), and by rendering opaque statements word for word without indicating their vagueness ('sorting things out'). This is especially true for written interlingual products – the written *translata*. In the subsequent criminal proceedings, these *translata* become independent communication objects with their own distinct function and between, again, new communication participants (see Section 4.4).

Finally, real-time, oral communication between IITs and the police plays a crucial role during the second communication phase. This exchange involves both the IITs providing critical, often urgent information and the police offering broader contextual details from other investigative efforts. This collaborative 'metacommunication' between IITs and police transcends the primary communication of the suspects and becomes a space where the two parties jointly decipher coded language, ambiguity, and paralanguage to make the communication understandable to external authorities, such as prosecutors and judges (Griebel & Hohl Zürcher 2023). In many cases, IITs and police prefer oral rather than written communication. Oral communication serves as the primary 'coping mechanism' (Lipsky 1980/2010) for ensuring mutual exchange of information, particularly if it includes criminalistic interpretations of IITs, notwithstanding the fact that the legal regulations do not provide for it (Griebel & Hohl Zürcher 2023). This informal and invisible exchange is crucial for investigations, filling in gaps and providing an initial recontextualisation by integrating quotes or summaries of earlier communication (Bauman & Briggs 1990).

This collaboration raises questions about role boundaries. While IITs are not formally tasked with forensic or investigative duties, their active participation in deciphering and interpreting communications suggests a blending of roles. This expanded involvement may influence the outcome by potentially shaping how evidence is understood and used, but it also blurs the lines between translation and investigation, impacting both the IITs' objectivity and the police's reliance on their input. Thus, there is a need to clearly define and manage these roles to ensure that IITs' contributions do not overextend into areas beyond their legal scope.

The outcome of the second communication phase is written translations or, potentially, intralingual transcripts, which may serve as evidence or be archived if deemed irrelevant. Those that are deemed pertinent advance into the case files, involving new participants in the communication process.

4.4 Phase 3: Translated Conversations as Evidence in Transition from Investigation to Court

The communication from the second phase plays a pivotal role throughout the criminal proceedings, particularly in how police investigators utilise the TIRs. Early in the investigation, this communication often provides crucial information about the suspects, such as their involvement, roles, and planned activities. These insights enable law enforcement to make strategic operational decisions, such as expanding surveillance to additional individuals, initiating targeted police monitoring, or planning the timing of raids. The information is also incorporated into police reports and investigative interviews, where officers may directly quote translations provided by the IITs. Example 4.7 illustrates how police investigators put the TIRs to practical use in shaping their actions and case strategy:

Example 4.7

I read every- we have to, anyway, every record [TIR] that is written down, comes into a different system for us, where we then have a better search function. And then it is read [...] I also always note it down if it's an important sequence. If I now see that- this record will definitely be needed at some point in the further course of the investigation, during investigative interviews and whatever else, then I mark it accordingly (Police investigator 2)

Besides yielding investigative insights, the first two communication phases also generate evidence that the prosecution may use when bringing the case before the court. So, TIRs are included in the criminal court file as part of the evidence considered by the court. These TIRs generally present conversations in a verbatim format, faithfully reflecting the original wording of the intercepted communication. The court then evaluates whether to rely on this evidence, among other factors, in reaching its judgment. In Swiss criminal proceedings, judgments are formal written decisions issued by the court at the conclusion of a case. They provide an official summary of the evidence considered, including extracts from communication surveillance, but lacking direct references to original TIRs or audio recordings. This underscores the extent of decontextualisation. The omission raises concerns about the representativeness of the summaries, as the selective inclusion of only brief extracts, sometimes reduced to single words, risks distorting the content and intent of the original communication. Example 4.8 (also discussed in Capus & Grisot 2022: 7) illustrates how selected verbatim accounts are integrated into the judgment:

Example 4.8

In a subsequent telephone conversation, S explains to M that the mule is a train worker and that he is coming to L. He asks him if he can't find a car to pick him up. When the latter is reluctant, S points out that they are cowards, and that the transporter working on the trains makes deliveries every week, to which M replies that he will try to find someone to take him to L. S then asked him why he was 'stuck like that'. [Judgment, A5]

The extent of the selectivity becomes clear when considering that a single TIR might represent an interaction lasting several minutes or comprising dozens of conversational lines in the original TIR, and the specific case file included 240 TIRs covering over 150 weeks of communications surveillance.

Moreover, as Capus and Grisot (2022) also demonstrated, very little of the original content remains when surveillance evidence is summarised and incorporated into judgments. In fact, instead of citing the verbatim text from the TIRs, police officers in their police reports, prosecutors in their indictment, and judges in their judgments often provide their own summaries of the content. This process significantly reduces the level of detail and nuance. Original quotes from TIRs, when included at all, are usually limited to very brief extracts, such as short passages, single sentences, fragments of sentences, or even isolated words. As Example 4.9 illustrates, expressions like 'stuck like that' or similarly short phrases reflecting a discussion about money may appear verbatim (Capus & Grisot 2022: 7):

Example 4.9

-at 11:37, P contacts C to ask him 'you can have how much money I want to know'; the other one answers 'I will give you everything' [Judgment, A5]

However, as stated, these are exceptions rather than the norm. Most references to monitored communication in judgments consist of summaries, often stripped of the original conversational context. This selective use raises questions about the representativeness and interpretative accuracy of evidence derived from communication surveillance in judicial decisions.

Another concern is decontextualisation. In criminal practice, communication within case files is often fragmented and recontextualised. Monitored conversations are presented in isolated parts, detached from their original context, affecting interpretation and understanding (Haworth 2018; see Komter 2019 for similar findings related to statements of police investigative interviews). This decontextualisation is further exacerbated by the absence of direct links to the TIR or audio recordings in legal documents, enabling selective use of information and obscuring implicit intertextual references. Crucially, this practice frequently omits mention of IIT involvement, and so-called quotes from TIR are presented to the judges without clarification that they are translations (Capus & Grisot 2022). This lack of transparency raises serious concerns about fairness and accuracy in the interpretation of multilingual communications, highlighting the need for greater accountability and precision in how evidence is presented and contextualised in criminal proceedings.

This style of recontextualisation ensures that communication is both precise and legally substantiated, as mandated in lawful proceedings. However, it also presents significant problems. The invisibility of the translation process not only applies to the recontextualisation of information gathered from communication surveillance in earlier stages of proceedings but also extends to more fundamental dimensions. Capus and Griebel (2021) demonstrated how the criminal justice system tends to render IITs and the process of interlingual transfer completely invisible. This invisibility can lead to misunderstandings and misinterpretations, as the courts and involved parties may not fully recognise how the *translata* were produced, what decisions and assumptions were made in the transfer process, and what potential inaccuracies and distortions this could entail.

4.5 Discussion and Conclusions

While communication occurs over three temporally staggered phases involving different participants, our contribution demonstrates that these participants share a common perspective: the criminal proceedings. The original participants from phase 1 rarely play an active role in phases 2 and 3; once the *translata* are available, audio recordings are typically no longer played back. The suspected and accused individuals primarily engage in communication through police questionings or courtroom proceedings. Similarly, IITs typically disengage from communication in phase 3, their involvement becoming indirect through the written *translata*.

Communication in these phases not only changes in terms of who is involved but also undergoes significant shifts in content. It is reconstructed, with certain elements discarded, reinterpreted, or placed into new contexts. What ultimately remains is the core information deemed crucial for judgment. In cases like drug trafficking, this core may be the details surrounding the transfer of drugs and money, distilled from the broader, more complex exchanges that took place earlier.

Our findings unveil the pivotal role recontextualised communication assumes in criminal proceedings. Fragmentation and recontextualisation of original conversations in legal files result in targeted yet potentially distorted use of information. This process is particularly evident in the third phase, where intercepted communication enters court proceedings. Here, significant recontextualisation occurs, often obscuring the original communication context and subsequent IIT activities. We contend that the pervasive invisibility of IITs throughout the process poses critical concerns. Although they provide investigative support to the police, this often has to remain invisible so that they formally do not exceed their competences (Capus & Griebel 2021). This also prevents an open discussion about their qualifications, which in communication surveillance go beyond linguistic competence (Griebel & Havelka 2024), and, finally, conceals the fact that IITs and the police often work closely together (Griebel & Hohl Zürcher 2023). Invisibility, therefore, jeopardises the reliability and equity of the process, as there is no guarantee that the transformed content is an accurate and unadulterated reproduction of the original communication.

In conclusion, we assert the imperative for a clearly defined delineation of roles and responsibilities for IITs within the criminal justice system, or at the very least, the acknowledgement of the absence of such delineation in legal procedures. This is indispensable to mitigate misunderstandings and misinterpretations and uphold the integrity of judicial proceedings. Consequently, there is a pressing need for enhanced transparency concerning the utilisation and functions of IITs in the realm of criminal law. This entails unambiguous identification of translated content in legal files pertaining to criminal proceedings, along with the acknowledgement that translation processes do not take place in isolation but are intricately interwoven with and linked to criminal proceedings.

To sum up, the practice of criminal law stands to benefit from a critical re-evaluation and adaptation of the existing protocols. Ensuring the active involvement of IITs throughout the communications surveillance and evidence-gathering process is essential to uphold the rule of law and ensure fair criminal proceedings. Particular attention must be paid to safeguarding the right to be heard of those whose communications have been intercepted, especially if they later become suspects. Interdisciplinary contributions such as this one are invaluable in shedding light on these challenges and providing fundamental steps towards improving day-to-day legal practice in the surveillance of multilingual communications.

References

Bauman, R. and Briggs, C. L. (1990). 'Poetics and performance as critical perspectives on language and social life'. *Annual Review of Anthropology*, 19, 59–88.

Bergmann, J. R. and Meyer, C. (2021). 'Reflexivity, indexicality, accountability', in Bergmann, J. R. and Meyer, C. (eds.), *Ethnomethodologie Reloaded: Neue Werkinterpretationen und Theoriebeiträge zu Harold Garfinkels Programm*. Bielefeld: Transcript, 37–54.

Bucholtz, M. (2009). 'Captured on tape: Professional hearing and competing entextualizations in the criminal justice system'. *Text & Talk*, 29(5), 503–523.

Capus, N. and Griebel, C. (2021). 'The (in-)visibility of interpreters in legal wiretapping. A case study: How the Swiss Federal Court clears or thickens the fog'. *International Journal of Language & Law*, 10, 37–98.

Capus, N. and Grisot, C. (2022). 'Ghostwriters of crime narratives: Constructing the story by referring to intercept interpreters contributions in criminal case files'. *Crime, Media, Culture*, 19(3), 1–20.

Capus, N. and Havelka, I. (2022). 'Interpreting intercepted communication: A sui generis translational activity'. *International Journal for the Semiotics of Law*, 35, 1817–1836.

Capus, N., Griebel, C. and Havelka, I. (2024). *Multilingual Communications Surveillance in Criminal Law*. Cheltenham: Edward Elgar Publishing.

Chakhachiro, R. (2016). 'Contribution of prosodic and paralinguistic cues to the translation of evidentiary audio recordings'. *The International Journal of Translation and Interpreting Research*, 8(2), 46–63.

Drugan, J. (2020). 'Complex collaborations. Interpreting and translating for the UK police'. *Target*, 32(2), 307–326.

Garfinkel, H. (1967/1984). *Studies in Ethnomethodology*. Englewood Cliffs, NJ: Prentice Hall.

Garfinkel, H. (2022). *Harold Garfinkel: Studies of Work in the Sciences*. London: Routledge.

Gilbert, D. and Heydon, G. (2021). 'Translated transcripts from covert recordings used for evidence in court: Issues of reliability'. *Frontiers in Communication*, 6, 1–13.

Gradinčevič-Savič, D. (2020). Anforderungsprofil für Polizei, Staatsanwaltschaft, Rechtspflege und Gericht zum Erkennen und Umsetzen des Dolmetsch- und Übersetzungsbedarfs. *Babel. International Journal of Translation*, 66(2), 172–187.

Griebel, C. and Havelka, I. (2024). 'Interpreter, translator or investigator? Framing the competences of a hybrid translational field – intercept interpreting'. *Perspectives*, 33(3), 615–633.

Griebel, C. and Hohl Zürcher, F. (2023). 'The work of intercept interpreters in lawful communication surveillance: A daily trade-off between formal requirements and informal needs'. *International Journal of Law, Crime and Justice*, 74, 1–13.

Haworth, K. (2018). 'Tapes, transcripts and trials: The routine contamination of police interview evidence'. *The International Journal of Evidence & Proof*, 22(4), 428–450.

Havelka, I. (2024). 'Interpreting intercepted communication: From talk to evidence'. *Translation & Interpreting*, 16(1), 17–37.

Hohl Zürcher, F. and Capus, N. (2024). 'Redefining interpreters' and translators' roles: Unveiling forensic expertise in lawful interception of communication'. *Journal of Institutional Studies*, 10(2), 689–712.

Hohl Zürcher, F. and Griebel, C. (2024). 'Role making in translational contexts: A qualitative study on the different roles of intercept interpreters/translators in covert communication surveillance'. *Translation in Society*, 3(2), 177–201.

Komter, M. (2019). *The Suspect's Statement: Talk and Text in the Criminal Process*. Cambridge: Cambridge University Press.

Kuckartz, U. (2018). *Qualitative Inhaltsanalyse: Methoden, Praxis, Computerunterstützung*, 4th ed. Weinheim: Beltz.

Lai, M. (2023). 'Transcribing and translating forensic speech evidence containing foreign languages: An Australian perspective'. *Frontiers in Communication*, 8, 1–18.

Lipsky, M. (1980/2010). *Street-Level Bureaucracy: Dilemmas of the Individual in Public Services*. New York: Russell Sage Foundation.

Mayring, P. (2022). *Qualitative Content Analysis: A Step-by-Step Guide*. London: Sage.

Mondada, L. (2019). 'Contemporary issues in conversation analysis: Embodiment and materiality, multimodality and multisensoriality in social interaction'. *Journal of Pragmatics*, 145, 47–62.

NAJIT. (2019). General guidelines and requirements for position paper. *Transcription Translations in a Legal Setting for User and Practitioners*. https://najit.org/wp-content/uploads/2016/09/Guidelines-and-Requirements-for-Transcription-Translation.pdf.

Norris, S. (2004). *Analyzing Multimodal Interaction: A Methodological Framework*. London: Routledge.

Park, J. S.-Y. and Bucholtz, M. (2009). 'Introduction. Public transcripts: entextualization and linguistic representation in institutional contexts'. *Text & Talk*, 29(5), 485–502.

Reiss, K. and Vermeer, H. J. (1984/2014). *Towards a General Theory of Translational Action: Skopos Theory Explained* (Christiane Nord, Trans.). London: Taylor and Francis.

Salaets, H., Alsulaiman, A. and Biesbrouck, S. (2015). 'Tap interpreting: From practice to norm: A Belgian case study'. *Turjuman*, 24(2), 11–49.

5 Process, Procedure and Professional Practice in the Creation of Police Interview Evidence

Kate Haworth

5.1 Introduction

Police–suspect interviews in England & Wales (E&W) are a key tension point between legal treatment of communication as evidence and linguistic understanding of the dynamics of spoken interaction. Studies have addressed how police–suspect interview interaction is co-constructed between interviewer and interviewee (e.g., Johnson 2008; Haworth 2017; cf. Reynolds, this volume); this chapter goes a stage further in showing how subsequent institutional practitioners also become active participants in the data through the construction of the official written record. It will demonstrate how legal process and procedure have a discernible presence in the ultimate interview 'product' alongside the original participants; yet this same legal system institutionally reinforces the fiction that these verbal accounts are not subject to change and holds the suspect criminally liable when inconsistencies emerge (s.34 Criminal Justice and Public Order Act 1994).

The specific focus of this chapter is to demonstrate the importance of the administrative processes undergone by an interviewee's words post-interview, revealing how they shape – indeed, create – the resulting evidential product. Importantly, this can substantially undermine the significant efforts which have gone into improving and professionalising police interviewing in E&W over several decades. The journey from 'live' interaction in an interview room, to an official evidential record, is largely taken for granted within the legal system, with little-to-no internal or external scrutiny; yet this is a much more significant, and underestimated, aspect of policing than is currently understood (Fraser 2022). The argument of this chapter is that it should instead be recognised as a substantial contribution to – and transformation of – the resulting evidence, with all the dangers that potentially entails, especially when it goes so unnoticed.

Funding statement: This research was supported by Research England's Expanding Excellence in England (E3) fund.

I gratefully acknowledge the contributions of Drs Emma Richardson and Zoë Adams in the collection, redaction and anonymisation of some of the data presented in this chapter.

5.2 E&W Police–Suspect Interview Records

Legal requirements around police interviews with suspects, and the consequent institutional procedures and processes for making records of those interviews, vary considerably from one jurisdiction to the next. It is therefore important to identify the particular applicable legislative and administrative framework, if we are to have a fuller understanding both of the interview interaction itself, and of any subsequent version of it we might be examining (either for legal or academic reasons). In E&W, the jurisdiction which this chapter covers, the interview recording process is governed by Codes of Practice attached to the Police and Criminal Evidence Act 1984 (widely known as PACE). Code C, s. 11(B) requires that all police–suspect interviews must be recorded (with only rare exceptions); Codes E and F make detailed provision for audio- and video-recording, respectively.

There is no express requirement in PACE or its Codes for a transcript to be made of these recordings. However, for cases which are likely to proceed, and are serious enough for Crown Court rather than Magistrates' Court disposal, a written version of the recording is produced, known as a ROTI/ROVI (Record Of Taped/Video Interview). This is created on an official form known as an MG15, a 'national file standard' agreed by the Home Office, Crown Prosecution Service and the police (Home Office 2020: 4). It is this version which is presented as evidence of the interview in court, as a routine part of the prosecution case file. It is also the version which is most heavily relied upon in the criminal justice system, rather than the audio/video recordings (Haworth 2018).

Each E&W police force has a pool of administrative staff employed specifically to produce these written versions of the video and audio recordings of suspect interviews (and occasionally other similar data, such as emergency calls). This reflects the fact that this is seen as simply a basic typing task, requiring no case knowledge or particular skill other than reasonable typing speed. (Compare with, e.g., the Netherlands or Norway, where formal written records of interview are produced by the actual interviewing officers – see van Charldorp 2013; Komter 2019; and Diepeveen 2024, respectively.)

Police interviews with suspects have a fascinating dual function, being simultaneously both investigative and evidential (Haworth 2010/2021), in that their primary function is as a key part of the police's initial investigation of a potential crime, while the words spoken in that interview also become a piece of evidence, exhibited through the physical artefact of the official record. This evidential role becomes particularly significant in E&W due to s.34 Criminal Justice and Public Order Act 1994, which provides that inferences can be drawn at court about any failure on the part of a defendant to mention something at an earlier stage, including their police interview, which they then seek to rely on as part of their defence. In other words, if what a defendant says at court appears to be different from what they said at interview, this can be taken as a sign of guilt. This, of course, assumes that the version of what was said at interview which is being used as the point of comparison is accurate and fair. Yet this assumption is currently made uncritically, despite the potential enormity of the consequences and despite the fact that almost no attention is being paid to the actual process of production (see Fraser 2022; also Walker, this volume). It is precisely this gap which this chapter seeks to address.

5.3 Data and Method

This chapter draws on a broader project on police interview evidence, 'For The Record' (FTR), which analyses police interview records through multiple stages of the criminal justice process, from interview room to courtroom. A significant and novel part of the FTR project involves capturing and integrating the practitioner perspective; we are thus able to gain their insight and reflection on a process which has hitherto been almost entirely invisible to those outside the police. The project incorporates several data types, including official police audio/video recordings, their corresponding MG15s, and focus groups and questionnaires with police practitioners. For the first phase, data were collected and analysed from one police force (Force A), as reported in Haworth et al. 2023 and Richardson et al. 2025; further data were subsequently collected from three other forces (Forces B, C and D).

The full interview dataset, which will be drawn upon in this chapter, comprises 41 pairs of police audio/video recordings and MG15s, featuring crimes such as online child sexual offences and supplying drugs. Since MG15s are generally only produced for cases which are likely to go to Crown Court, these are all of a relatively more serious nature. The focus groups were conducted by the author on police premises between August 2021 and July 2024. A total of 41 interviewers participated in 6 focus groups; a total of 9 transcribers participated in 5 focus groups, and 11 transcribers (including the entire cohort of one force) also completed an online questionnaire, which used Likert scales and closed questions to obtain more basic factual information. The focus groups ranged from 1¼ to 2¼ hours in length, and were semi-structured to ensure consistency across groups while allowing free discussion and topic introduction. Although these were arranged through a known contact within each force, participation was entirely voluntary, and fully informed consent was obtained.

Note that not all data types could be accessed for all participating forces; for example, transcriber focus groups could only be conducted at Forces A and C, and we were not able to obtain interview data from Force B. Nevertheless, overall the FTR dataset is a substantial and unique resource for qualitative research, particularly given the immense challenges of gaining access to both interview data and police personnel. All data were redacted, anonymised and transcribed; any personal details which appear in the data extracts below are pseudonyms. Given that transcription is our focus, it is worth adding that the data extracts in this chapter are not transcribed in full linguistic detail, since this is not required for our specific research purpose here (following, e.g., Cook 1990; Lapadat 2000).

5.4 How the Process Shapes the Product

We will now turn to an examination of where the institutional processing described earlier has a discernible presence in the official interview record. These records are treated legally as mere 'copies' of the original interview interaction (s.133 and 134(1) Criminal Justice Act 2003; *R* v. *Rampling*); a neutral and accurate representation of the interviewee's own words. What soon becomes apparent, however, is that they are nothing of the sort, in ways which go beyond the immediately obvious. For reasons of space, this chapter will focus on three main aspects of transcriber practice: summarising, opening preliminaries and representation of emotion.

Perhaps the most substantial transformation of interview evidence occurs due to the practice of transcribers summarising some parts of an interview in the MG15, rather than rendering the interaction 'verbatim' (a term which in this context is used to mean writing down every word spoken). While this third-person summarising of some parts of the interview is overt and highly visible in the record, the argument presented here is that it is a far more challenging, and less neutral, task than appears to be currently recognised. This has parallels with the related phenomenon of interviewer 'formulations' of interview talk, which are effectively real-time summaries of the interaction during the interview itself; studies have shown these to be a complex and challenging institutional task for interviewers (e.g., Ferraz de Almeida & Drew 2020, Stokoe & Edwards 2008; see also Diepeveen 2024), so it seems likely that without the benefit of their professional knowledge, transcribers will not fare any better. We will consider this practice in Section 5.4.1. In Section 5.4.2 we will focus on an element which is routinely summarised in MG15s across all our participant forces: the opening section of the interview where basic procedural information is relayed and rights administered. Finally, in Section 5.4.3 we will shift attention to a different type of omission from the MG15, evaluating how transcriber avoidance of conveying emotion has a potentially serious detrimental effect on the evidential value of the interview record.

5.4.1 Summarising

Regarding the summarising of interview interaction in the MG15, a striking finding is that despite the MG15 being intended as a means of standardisation, there is in fact no standardisation in how it is actually used in practice. Transcribers at Force C reported always transcribing ‘verbatim’, which was largely borne out in our interview data, although with minor exceptions; in Forces A and D there was much more prevalent use of summarising, with stretches of talk frequently presented only in summary (e.g., ‘PC 1234 continued to go through items seized from the property’, D-IV04). Given that the dataset includes both interview data and transcriber focus groups for Force A, this section will focus specifically on practice in that force.

First, it emerged that Force A transcribers receive no training or guidance to assist them in this task. In fact, they are given a seemingly large amount of individual discretion as to whether, and how much, to summarise a given interview. In other words, in this force there does not seem to be any specific procedural requirement behind the extent to which an interview record entails summarised talk; it is simply up to the transcriber to decide. When asked about this process in the questionnaire, all respondents referred to including anything ‘relevant’ or ‘pertinent’ to the interview, or ‘salient points’. Many specific factors were listed, such as in Example 5.1:

Example 5.1 Transcriber questionnaire response: Deciding what to include in full

Q: How do you decide what to include and what to omit? Please list as many factors as you like.
A: Include:
Salient points: when/where/what happenend [sic].
Admissions: intent, dishonesty, consent.
Defence/mitigation: duress, self-defence, drink/drugs, accident, provocation, permission.

It is notable how many of these are complex legal concepts, such as consent, mitigation or duress, yet these transcribers have no legal background or training to assist them in understanding or applying such concepts. Similarly, they have little to draw on in determining what might be ‘relevant’ or ‘salient’ to a particular interview or investigation. Yet this is what transcribers are attempting to apply when determining whether part of an interview is fully recorded in the MG15, summarised, or perhaps not worthy of inclusion at all. This is an aspect which is recognised by the Force A interviewers as being problematic. As one interviewer put it, ‘… you need to be massively well trained if you’re going to summarise those documents around the court process, around the points to prove, defence, mitigation, the- all the legal elements of it’ (FG4). It seems rather a tall order to provide transcribers with suitable training to cover all such aspects, however.

A further aspect which arose in one of the transcriber focus groups is that some subject matter presents more difficulties than others, and hence may be treated differently. The transcribers raised the example of fraud cases, which they find difficult to understand. As a consequence, they are more likely to put more 'in full' because, as one put it, 'it's really hard … to summarise something that you don't understand' (FG3). An important factor to consider here is that the transcribers likely understand less than they realise in other cases.

As well as content not being understood, a similar issue arises regarding lack of understanding of the underlying purpose and function of particular lines of questioning. A great deal of effort is put into training interviewers in effective interviewing techniques, including application of the PEACE model (e.g., Clarke, Milne & Bull 2011), and it is now well recognised, in E&W interviewing at least, that the structure and sequencing of specific questions can have a direct impact on the quality of evidence produced by the interviewee (e.g., Griffiths & Milne 2006). It can also be highly significant tactically for the interviewer, especially for ensuring that an interviewee has been given every opportunity to mention something while being questioned, for the later purposes of s.34 CJPOA 1994. The fact that the questioning sequence is often not preserved in the transcript is therefore a source of frustration for interviewers, as seen in Example 5.2:

Example 5.2 Interviewer perspective on summarising questioning sequences

> … my biggest bugbear with the transcript is when you get like four or five questions just put into one answer … I don't think it gives you the bigger picture of, you know, why you're going down a certain line of questioning sometimes. … to get to one point, you might ask five questions to get to that one point because you're giving them an opportunity to answer snippets of the question before you go to the blockbuster question if you like, whereas by paraphrasing you miss, you know, this is why I'm going down this line of questioning and the fact that you haven't been given a truthful answer at question one and it's not until you get to question five perhaps where the suspect gives that answer. (FG4, Force A Interviewers)

Unsurprisingly, the evidential significance of such subtleties may not be obvious to a transcriber. This knowledge gap between interviewers and transcribers is illustrated by the anecdote shared by a transcriber in Example 5.3:

Example 5.3 Transcriber perspective on summarising questioning sequences

> I think I had one years ago where an officer had asked, it was something to do with a mobile phone, and they'd asked this lad if he had a mobile phone, and he denied having the phone, … and he asked about four or five times through the interview if he got a mobile phone, 'no', so I only put it say twice, I thought well he's asked him already and he's asked him again, I'll leave it at that and then the officer came back to me later and said 'I wanted them five times in' to show that he was actually, he'd been asked time and time again and he denied having it, and I thought two was probably enough. (FG1, Force A Transcribers)

Despite this, Force A transcribers did not consider the task of choosing what to summarise to be particularly challenging, as evidenced from the questionnaire. When asked 'how easy do you find it to select what goes into the official record?', all categorised it as either 'easy' (4/9) or 'neither easy or hard' (5/9). This is perhaps surprising, since it is extremely challenging to perform this task to an appropriately high and consistent standard, given the stakes involved and the fact that they are effectively performing an assessment of the evidential value and relevance of what is said during the interview. Any move away from 'verbatim' transcribing, and into decision-making as to what goes in the record, is therefore always likely to present difficulties.

When we look at examples of summarising in the Force A interview dataset, it is often unclear why one part of an interview has been summarised, while others have not. Figure 5.1 shows a substantial amount of summary, including

3:40		Lee BRAITHWAITE'S statement was then put to DAVIDSON. DAVIDSON denied calling him them fucking idiots as described and said he called him (DAVIDSON) a fucking idiot. He denied the comment of making mincemeat out of him. DAVIDSON made comments when the statement was put to him but due to the distorted sound quality, they were inaudible. The Officer continued with the statement and when asked if he punched him, DAVIDSON said no and he didn't touch him. DAVIDSON explained again about asking the police if he had any marks and the police telling him about the blood 15 minutes later.
		PC FELIX continued putting the statement to DAVIDSON, who said the son came out with a shovel and said he didn't walk towards him as described. DAVIDSON said it was him against all of them because they were all together with the next door neighbours.
		When it was described how he had a go at Kieran who lived next door, DAVIDSON admitted he did that. He disputed the police took him away and said they went to him in the kitchen.
8:15	Q	... so that's what he says
	R	Yeah, yeah, that's fine
	Q	It's fair to say that you don't agree with that
8:19	R	Not at all, not one bit

Figure 5.1 Summarised section of interview record (A-IV14)

what would appear to have been significant sections of the interview. Numbers in the left column are transcriber time stamps.

In Figure 5.1 we see numerous contributions by the interviewee *described as* being denials or admissions ('he denied…'; 'DAVIDSON admitted…'), rather than presenting us with what the interviewee actually said, despite the potential significance of this. We also have a section at the end of this extract which *is* transcribed verbatim, despite being seemingly of far less significance or relevance. We have also lost the referent of 'that': given that an entire statement has just been put to the interviewee, what exactly does he not agree with? Overall, this shows how decisions about what to write verbatim and what to summarise can have a substantial effect on how much detail can be lost or distorted, and hence on the evidential value of the interview record.

It is possible that the reason for the summarising, and then the switch to verbatim here, is due to the fact that a witness statement is being relayed to the interviewee for their response, a practice which transcribers reported finding difficult to know how to deal with. This is understandable from their perspective, since that witness statement will be fully available elsewhere; it can therefore seem not to be a good use of the transcriber's time simply to type it out again. However, this overlooks the legal and evidential significance of recording the interviewee's responses to the specific points raised in those statements. This is, of course, why interviewers present witness statements to suspects during interviews. This is therefore a good illustration of how the practice of leaving this editorial process to staff with no legal training can lead to valuable evidence being lost (through no fault of their own, it must be emphasised).

5.4.2 *Procedural Preliminaries*

An element which was routinely summarised across the data from all our partner forces is the opening formalities, which as a minimum includes introductions, delivery of the caution and conveying rights around legal representation. This is often largely formulaic and dictated by relevant legal and procedural requirements, so it is perhaps understandable that this is seen as of less importance by transcribers and hence not worthy of 'verbatim' treatment. Indeed, its significance is also often underplayed by interviewers to interviewees (e.g., 'Before we get to asking questions Mr Gerrard I need to go through some admin with you', C-IV07). However, this belies the very important legal and interactional function of these sequences, as evidenced in several linguistic studies (Heydon 2005: 49–57; Rock 2007, 2021: 115–119; Diepeveen et al. 2022; see also Greenlee, this volume).

This part of the interview is treated in a similarly understated and formulaic way by transcribers, although with variation across forces. In the Force A and D interview data there are multiple different summarised versions of the opening section, with transcribers developing their own personal practices. The Force C interview dataset, however, has a notable level of uniformity. Out

Tape Counter Times	Person Speaking	Text
		THE INTERVIEW PROCEDURE WAS EXPLAINED. PERSONS PRESENT INTRODUCED THEMSELVES. ADVISED OF ENTITLEMENT TO FREE AND INDEPENDENT LEGAL ADVICE. CAUTIONED. CAUTION WAS EXPLAINED AND UNDERSTOOD.
00:04:43	AB123	So you're here today, you've been arrested on suspicion of a common assault,

Figure 5.2 Force C standard summary of interview opening sequence (C-IV04)

of nine Force C MG15s, seven display identical text in the opening text box, an example of which is given in Figure 5.2. (Of the remaining two, one contains this same wording but in a slightly different order and with some extra detail added; the other can be seen in Figure 5.3 discussed later.)

Focus group discussion with Force C transcribers confirmed the suspicion that this uniformity is due to the use of a standard template.

Example 5.4 Force C introduction standardisation

KH: Is there a standard wording for those introductions, or do you do it your own way?
C-T1: No, there's standard, it would- so when, when you pick up a template, the MG15 interview template, it, it's on there.
KH: Oh okay.
C-T1: It's already on there.
C-T2: Yeah.
C-T1: And you can just add what you want.
(FG12, Force C Transcribers)

While this pre-filled template is undoubtedly an administrative efficiency, and therefore understandably procedurally appealing, analysis of the actual interactions these purport to represent reveals that it can give rise to potentially important errors and omissions. As a preliminary observation, despite the consistency of these MG15 openings, an analysis of the corresponding audio recordings reveals that in reality there was considerable interactional deviation, with the sequence represented by this same text ranging from 1 minute 31 seconds (C-IV02) to 6 minutes 5 seconds (C-IV09). The adequacy of the information and explanations being given is beyond the scope of this chapter, since we are focusing on the record and not the interaction itself, so for present purposes we will limit our observations simply to whether or not the stated elements actually occurred. While the majority of these opening summaries can be described as accurate in this sense, in some cases there are potentially significant misrepresentations.

To take one of these cases, although the MG15 for interview C-IV06 contains the template assertion 'ADVISED OF ENTITLEMENT TO FREE

AND INDEPENDENT LEGAL ADVICE', this turns out not to be true. The only actual interaction regarding this legal right is as shown in Example 5.5.

Example 5.5 Not advised of entitlement to free and independent legal advice

SOL: Also present is duty solicitor Simon Scarlett.
IR1: Thank you. Have you had sufficient opportunity to talk privately with your legal representative, Frank?
IE: I have, yeah.
IR1: Yeah, thank you. If you wish to stop the interview to speak with your legal rep again, you can do so at any point, just let me know and we can pause the recording for you to do that, all right?
IE: Mmm hmm.
(C-IV06, our transcript)

The right in question is specified in PACE Code C, para 11.2: 'Immediately prior to the commencement or re-commencement of any interview at a police station or other authorised place of detention, *the interviewer should remind the suspect of their entitlement to free legal advice and that the interview can be delayed for legal advice to be obtained …*' (my italics). While the interviewer covered the second part of this right, which is not reflected in the record, he failed to give the first part, which *is* given in the record. It is perhaps not surprising that a transcriber might be unaware of the intricacies of the PACE Codes and hence not appreciate this distinction; it is worth noting, however, that para 11.2 goes on to state that 'It is the *interviewer's* responsibility to make sure all reminders are recorded in the interview record' (my emphasis). Since this interviewee clearly does have a free legal representative present, I do not wish to argue that any injustice was done here; however, it is an indication of the dangers of standard text being used unquestioningly.

Finally, the C-IV08 MG15 is the only instance where part of this standard text is apparently removed by a transcriber, since it does not include 'Caution was explained and understood'. This is shown in Figure 5.3.

		THE INTERVIEW PROCEDURE WAS EXPLAINED. PERSONS PRESENT INTRODUCED THEMSELVES. ADVISED OF ENTITLEMENT TO FREE AND INDEPENDENT LEGAL ADVICE.
01.50 01.54	D5D5D	A breach of non-molestation order is what you were initially arrested for, I'm also arresting you for harassment, okay.
		PC GREEN states time of arrest as 14.04 hours.
02.08		**CAUTIONED.**
		PC GREEN starts to explain the caution ...
03.01	DP	Actually I don't agree with the harassment part, because like I said, I've been

Figure 5.3 C-IV08 MG15 opening

The amendment of the template wording we see in Figure 5.3 is in some respects an example of good practice by the transcriber, since (unlike Example 5.5) it correctly reflects that the comprehension check for the caution in fact never takes place. However, it also implies that the explanation of the caution was incomplete, which is not entirely borne out by the audio recording: although a very small 'continuing' rise in intonation indicates that the interviewer was potentially about to continue their turn, they had in fact already given an explanation of all elements of the caution. It also gives the impression that the interviewee interrupts the interviewer, which again is not a fair reflection: on listening to the audio, there is a potential 'transition relevance place' (TRP) in Conversation Analysis terms (Sacks, Schegloff & Jefferson 1974) at this point, with a completed unit of meaning and (micro) pause in the interviewer's turn, so this switch in speaker is far more benign than the MG15 suggests. Further, 'actually' is a mistranscription: although the audio is somewhat unclear, my hearing (shared with a second independent listener) is that the interviewee begins their turn with the far less confrontational '*like I say*, I don't agree…'. The transcriber's input therefore generates a somewhat misleading and unfair impression of this interviewee.

Overall, then, this indicates that using pre-set 'template' MG15 content is not necessarily wise, especially if it leads transcribers into an assumption of procedural conformity rather than paying full and close attention to what actually occurs in each interview. It also highlights the dangers for all those who later rely on these records of taking them at face value, even for seemingly routine and mundane content.

5.4.3 Emotion

Finally, a key aspect which is routinely omitted from our MG15 dataset is non-verbal expressions of emotion, such as crying or laughter. As documented in Richardson et al. 2025 (157–161), the Force A MG15s contained no markers of emotion of any kind, despite there being a wealth of such features available in the audio recordings from which the transcribers were working. This finding has largely been replicated in the Force C and D interview data, with only the following exceptions: in the Force C data, which is largely rendered 'verbatim', there are two instances of added commentary – '(laughs)' (C-IV01) and 'DP BECOMES UPSET' (C-IV02); and in one Force D MG15, the transcriber notes in a descriptive summary that the interviewee 'became upset and apologised' (D-IV04). These three instances amount to the only indications of emotion across our dataset of 41 official records, despite the fact that frequent instances of highly charged emotion such as anger, distress and frustration are readily observable in the corresponding audio/video source material. The interactional significance of such communicative features is obvious from a linguistic perspective, especially in terms of our perception of the speaker. This routine absence from our MG15 dataset is therefore striking.

Focus group discussion with transcribers reveals that the decision to omit markers of interviewees' (or indeed interviewers') emotions during the process of producing the official record is a deliberate and conscious one on their part, due to a concern not to go beyond what they are 'entitled or should be conveying' (Force C, FG13). While recognising the often powerful impact of the emotion they hear on their own perception, they regard this as 'only our own viewpoint' (Force A, FG1) and therefore too subjective, when they are aiming to make the record as objective as possible. However, the removal of such features is a subjective decision in itself, which has a substantial transformative effect on how interviewees are represented in the official record, and can therefore be described as anything but neutral. (Interview participants may be treated the same, but it is rare that a police interviewer would be displaying emotion, nor is it their behaviour or character which is under scrutiny.) It also appears to contradict one of the intended purposes of introducing mandatory audio/video recording, with PACE Code E stating that 'the provisions of this Code … and the provisions of Code F … provide safeguards for suspects against inaccurate recording of the words used in questioning them *and of their demeanour during the interview*' (Code E, 1.5A, my emphasis). It is another highly significant way in which the institutional process manifests itself in the evidential record, to the potential detriment of the very fairness and balance the transcribers are seeking.

In terms of consequences for criminal practice, FTR experimental work has demonstrated that choosing whether or not to represent such features in a police interview transcript, and how to represent them, can directly affect people's perceptions of the interviewee (Deamer et al. 2022; Tompkinson et al. 2023; Tompkinson & Haworth 2024). However, this research indicates that it is a highly complex and difficult matter to resolve satisfactorily. We cannot yet state with confidence whether omitting or including such features in the record is better practice; however, we can certainly state that this is a decision with direct consequences for criminal justice, and which therefore needs to be based on evidence, not an unscrutinised administrative decision.

5.5 Implications for Practice

From a purely linguistic perspective, it would be easy to reach the conclusion that these written evidential records ought to be abandoned completely and to recommend that those in the legal process who need to access an interview for any reason should always use the version closest to the original, that is, the audio or video recording. However, while theoretically sound, that does not take into account the practical reality of this particular professional context. Time constraints, caseloads and general workload pressure mean that this is usually an unaffordable luxury for those conducting the investigation, so a written record serves a useful time-saving purpose, as highlighted by several interviewers.

Example 5.6

…in terms of being able to just go back through and work your way through it and jump to the point that's relevant to what you're dealing with at that moment. The paper record is much quicker and easier than the audio, in terms of- in terms of referencing back and forth quickly. (FG11, Force C Interviewers)

Example 5.7

And then when you're constantly dipping in and out of multiple files, it is really helpful when we've got big workloads, to just be able to, right, for me, look back at my highlighted thing, I need to do <u>that</u> now. (FG5, Force A Interviewers)

However, if the written version is inaccurate, partial or unreliable, such a short-cut is very much a false economy for the investigation. But as well as potentially negatively affecting an investigation, current written records are also falling short evidentially. For example, several participant interviewers specialise in rape and serious sexual offences and reported actually experiencing attempts at controlling behaviour from interviewees during interview. Yet they felt that this was not reflected in the written version, despite the fact that this very behaviour often corroborated the victims' accounts in such cases.

Example 5.8

I think, coming back to Anthony's point it's really important, we deal with loads of offences which are about power and control … it's quite evidential and we're not- that isn't captured. That's not translated into the transcript. (FG9, Force B Interviewers)

This omission of potentially evidentially relevant detail from the record, especially regarding the interviewee's emotional state, was mentioned across numerous focus groups.

Example 5.9

You don't picture- you don't get someone's nervousness on a transcript or anger, and actually from victim suspect point of view, if you have an angry suspect interview and a very nervous victim, that is very good evidence. But if they don't say anything, if what they say isn't- doesn't highlight that then CPS [Crown Prosecution Service] aren't gonna know that, are they, without watching them. (FG4, Force A Interviewers)

It seems clear, then, that the current process for producing official interview records is detrimental both investigatively and evidentially, and that the consequences are potentially far more serious than currently realised – not least, simply in terms of wasted time and effort at multiple stages and across multiple personnel.

5.6 Discussion

The analysis presented in this chapter, and the FTR project more broadly (see Deamer et al. 2022; Haworth et al. 2023; Richardson et al. 2025; Tompkinson et al. 2023; Tompkinson & Haworth 2024) demonstrates that the institutional processes undergone by police–suspect interview data can cause substantial transformations to the evidence, yet they are largely invisible, unnoticed and unacknowledged. Creating an official written version of spoken interview interaction is treated as a mundane, unskilled administrative task, when in fact, to be done to what is arguably the appropriate standard, it demands a large degree of both legal and procedural knowledge and understanding of the nature of language and communication. It is important to emphasise that the intention here is very much not to lay blame at the feet of those given this task, but instead to highlight the collective institutional misunderstandings which lead to this predicament.

Linguistic studies have done a good job of uncovering the largely unacknowledged influence of interviewers over police interview interaction, and hence over an interviewee's account (e.g., Rock 2001; Johnson 2008; Haworth 2017). I wish to frame this as a parallel situation, where process and procedure are the invisible agents with substantial influence over what is still presented as the interviewee's own account in their own words. This conceptualisation provides new insight into the interrelation between legal procedure, language-in-action and professional practice. While scrutiny of the 'frontstage' activities of police interviewers is of course essential, this chapter shows that the 'backstage' institutional practices surrounding the interview are overlooked at our peril. It is hoped that this study demonstrates the importance for practitioners and researchers alike to pay closer attention to the format of the data they are examining and to actively reflect on and seek out the many voices and actors which have shaped it (cf. Reynolds, this volume). At the very least, it invites legal practitioners to perhaps reevaluate the level of trust they currently place in these official records – a point also amply demonstrated by Walker, this volume.

In summary, this chapter has shown just some of the ways in which background administrative processes have a significant, but largely unrecognised and unchecked influence over what is subsequently presented as criminal evidence against a suspect. It appears, at least in part, to stem from misunderstandings within the legal process of the nature of language and communication, especially around the conveyance of meaning. It is therefore also a prime example of an area where linguistics can make a vital contribution to increasing understanding of language as evidence, and – hopefully – to drive positive change.

References

Clarke, C., Milne, R., and Bull, R. (2011). 'Interviewing suspects of crime: The impact of PEACE training, supervision and the presence of a legal advisor'. *Journal of Investigative Psychology and Offender Profiling*, 8, 149–162.

Cook, G. (1990). 'Transcribing infinity: Problems of context presentation'. *Journal of Pragmatics*, 14(1), 1–24.

Deamer, F., Richardson, E., Basu, N., and Haworth, K. (2022). 'For the record: Exploring variability in interpretations of police investigative interviews'. *Language and Law / Linguagem e Direito*, 9(1), 25–46.

Diepeveen, A. (2024). 'The suspect's statement in interaction: Responding to "formulations" in the investigative interview'. *Journal of Pragmatics*, 220, 47–61.

Diepeveen, A., Svennevig, J., and Urbanik, P. (2022). 'Suspects' opportunities to claim their legal rights in police investigative interviews'. *International Journal of Speech, Language and the Law*, 28(2), 171–200.

Ferraz de Almeida, F. and Drew, P. (2020). 'The fabric of law-in-action: "Formulating" the suspect's account during police interviews in England'. *International Journal of Speech, Language and the Law*, 27(1), 35–58.

Fraser, H. (2022). 'A framework for deciding how to create and evaluate transcripts for forensic and other purposes'. *Frontiers in Communication*, 7. http://doi.org/10.3389/fcomm.2022.898410

Griffiths, A. and Milne, B. (2006). 'Will it all end in tiers? Police interviews with suspects in Britain', in Williamson, T. (ed.), *Investigative Interviewing: Rights, Research, Regulation*. Devon: Willan Publishing, 167–189.

Haworth, K. (2010/2021). 'Police interviews as evidence', in Coulthard, M., May, A., and Sousa Silva, R. (eds.), *Routledge Handbook of Forensic Linguistics, First/Second Edition*. London: Routledge, 144–158.

Haworth, K. (2017). 'The discursive construction of evidence in police interviews: Case study of a rape suspect'. *Applied Linguistics*, 38(2), 194–214.

Haworth, K. (2018). 'Tapes, transcripts and trials: The routine contamination of police interview evidence'. *International Journal of Evidence and Proof*, 22(4), 428–450.

Haworth, K., Tompkinson, J., Richardson, E., Deamer, F., and Hamann, M. (2023) '"For the Record": Applying linguistics to improve evidential consistency in police investigative interview records'. *Frontiers in Communication*, 8. http:// doi .org/10.3389/fcomm.2023.1178516

Heydon, G. (2005). *The Language of Police Interviewing: A Critical Analysis*. Basingstoke: Palgrave.

Home Office. (2020). *Manual of Guidance and MG Forms, Version 11*. London: Home Office.

Johnson, A. (2008). 'From where we're sat…: Negotiating narrative transformation through interaction in police interviews with suspects'. *Text & Talk*, 28(3), 327–349.

Komter, M. (2019). *The Suspect's Statement: Talk and Text in the Criminal Process*. Cambridge: Cambridge University Press.

Lapadat, J. C. (2000). 'Problematizing transcription: Purpose, paradigm and quality'. *International Journal of Social Research Methodology*, 3(3), 203–219

Richardson, E., Hamann, M., Tompkinson, J., Haworth, K., and Deamer, F. (2025). 'Understanding the role of transcription in evidential consistency of police interview records in England and Wales'. *Language in Society*, 54(1), 135–166. (First published online 15th August 2023.)

Rock, F. (2001). 'The genesis of a witness statement'. *Forensic Linguistics*, 8(2), 44–72.

Rock, F. (2007). *Communicating Rights: The Language of Arrest and Detention*. Basingstoke: Palgrave.

Rock, F. (2021). 'Collecting oral evidence: The police, the public and the written word', in Coulthard, M., May, A., and Sousa Silva, R. (eds.), *The Routledge Handbook of Forensic Linguistics (Second Edition)*. Abingdon: Routledge, 112–126.

Sacks, H., Schegloff, S., and Jefferson, G. (1974). 'A simplest systematics for the organisation of turn-taking for conversation'. *Language*, 50(4), 696–735.

Stokoe, E. and Edwards, D. (2008). '"Did you have permission to smash your neighbour's door?" Silly questions and their answers in police suspect interrogations'. *Discourse Studies*, 10(1), 89–111.

Tompkinson, J. and Haworth, K. (2024). 'The effect of linguistic detail in police interview transcripts on perceptions of an interviewee'. *Language and Law / Linguagem e Direito*, 11(2), 55–78.

Tompkinson, J., Haworth, K., Deamer, F., and Richardson, E. (2023). 'Perceptual instability in police interview records: Examining the effect of pauses and modality on people's perceptions of an interviewee'. *International Journal of Speech, Language and the Law*, 30(1), 22–51.

Van Charldorp, T. (2013). 'The intertwining of talk and technology: How talk and typing are combined in the various phases of the police interrogation'. *Discourse & Communication*, 7(2), 221–240.

Cases Cited

R *v*. Rampling [1987] *Criminal Law Review* 823

Statutes Cited

Criminal Justice Act 2003, ss. 133 and 134(1)
Criminal Justice and Public Order Act 1994, s. 34
Police and Criminal Evidence Act 1984, Codes C, E and F

6 Evidence and Assessing Verbatim Transcription Quality of Black English and Standard American English

L. Alexander Walker III

6.1 Introduction

Transcripts flood the United States' legal systems. For permanence and convenience, lawsuits and prosecutions build mountains of paper that reduce the spoken to the written. If those transcripts contain mistakes and a lawyer, judge, or jury relies upon such a transcript, they are more likely to make a legal error. Like a machine learning algorithm, a legal system's outputs are only as good as its inputs. What remains understudied is how transcription services currently used by US courts fare when producing transcripts of nonstandard varieties of English and dialects. This chapter reports a first-of-its-kind study which tests whether private transcription services are worse at transcribing Black English than Standard American English, assessing the number and kind of mistakes and whether those mistakes are significant, in both the statistical and legal senses.

Black English pervades modern life in the United States, and the legal system is no different. However, the consequences of Black English's linguistic differences with Standard American English remain to be fully recognized and explored. Due to a wide range of socioeconomic reasons, a disproportionate number of Black English speakers go through the legal system – and the criminal system in particular – yet few legal professionals, judges, and professional transcribers are native speakers of the language variety. Sociolinguistics has long identified the difficulties speakers of related language varieties can have when interpreting language varieties they do not

Funding statement: This research was funded by the Harvard Law School Center on Legal Profession.

I want to thank Isaiah Garlin, Justin McElderry, Nicholas Harvey, Jaden Owens, Malcolm Fields, Maxwell Rodney, Holger Spamann, Malia Gesaule, Joseph Knee, Alexander Stremitzer, Eric Martínez, Rosina Curren, Noah Feldman, Kate Haworth, Tatiana Grieshofer, Ed Cheng, and all the participants at the Evidence Summer Workshop 2024. I also thank Roop Patel and Danilo Linhares for excellent research assistance. Errors and opinions here are my own.

speak themselves (Hockett 1958: 321–330; Delsing & Lundin-Åkesson 2005). For many of the same sociocultural reasons that explain the overrepresentation of Black English in the criminal system, those who do not speak Black English tend to have lower levels of comprehension of the variety. To be sure, Black English and Standard English are very similar language varieties at the highest level of generality, but there are differences in lexicon, syntax, and pronunciation between them that might very well create problems for transcribers if they do not speak Black English themselves (Walker 2025). A just legal system cannot blind itself to meaning-bearing differences between varieties of English if they cause transcribers to introduce factual errors into the official record.

This chapter presents the results of a 'linguistic audit' of two private transcription companies, empirically testing the accuracy of their human and AI transcription in both Black and Standard American English. The chapter aims to improve legal professionals' awareness of three important aspects of Black English in a legal system primarily administered by speakers of Standard American English. First, because transcriptions of in- and out-of-court audio are regularly outsourced to private companies, this study investigates the role those companies play in Black English's relationship with the legal system. At present, it remains unclear if these private transcription companies will rise to the task of transcribing Black English accurately. Any comparative advantage or disadvantage private transcription companies have over public staff should inform both policymaking and what lawyers representing their clients should prefer.

Second, current research is insufficiently intersectional. Men who speak Black English are more likely to interact with the criminal system than women who do, and this carries import because men who speak Black English are much more likely to employ certain linguistic features of Black English than women. For example, <a nigga> can function as a first-person singular pronoun in Black English, but men are much more likely to use it that way than women, who are in turn more likely to use <a bitch> for that purpose. Additionally, both Black men and women are overrepresented in the criminal system, but Black men are much *more* overrepresented. If markedly male linguistic features are more likely to be misinterpreted, that might hold special moral weight as far as the legal system is concerned.

Third, both in the private and legal spheres, machine transcription and so-called 'generative artificial intelligence' are of increasing interest. The Black English legal-linguistic scholarship has not tested the actual effectiveness nor pondered the theoretical desirability of machine transcriptions of Black English in the legal system. Because private transcription services often have machine and human transcription options, they represent an opportunity to begin these conversations.

6.2 Black English and Legal Process

There is a small but growing literature documenting and critically examining how Black English interacts with the legal systems of the United States both from the legal and the sociolinguistic vantage point (Walker 2023: 1958 n.4). Institutional actors at various stages of the process from audio recording to legal ruling have misinterpreted Black English. Such mistakes underscore the importance of sociolinguistically informed inquiries into the legal system's relationship with Black English.

Judges making easily disprovable linguistic mistakes when faced with Black English is perhaps the most dramatic way the legal system might fail. Likely the most famous of these cases – and one intelligible even to those who do not speak Black English – is the case of the 'lawyer dog'. Courts enforce *Miranda* rights by excluding testimony obtained via violation of a suspect's right to counsel (see Greenlee, this volume). In *State* v. *Demesme*, 228 So.3d 1206 (La. 2017), the Louisiana Supreme Court was faced with the question of whether the following (as transcribed by the district attorney's office) was a request for counsel for the purposes of *Miranda* such that a confession obtained after not giving the suspect a lawyer must be excluded: 'if y'all, this is how I feel, if y'all think I did it, I know that I didn't do it so why don't you just give me a lawyer dog cause this is not what's up'. This case would be unremarkable if the court excluded the confession, but it did not. In concurrence, Justice Crichton argued that the 'ambiguous and equivocal reference to a 'lawyer dog' does not constitute an invocation of counsel that warrants termination of the interview'. Charitably, this is a misunderstanding of Black English, where <dog> or <dawg> can mean something close to 'sir'.

Some mistakes judges have made are more technical, however. There are three things of note in *United States* v. *Arnold*, 486 F.3d 177 (6th Cir. 2007), which involved whether the evidence was sufficient to find that the accused possessed a firearm. First, the majority and the dissent adopted different versions of what was said on an audio recording (in Black English) after listening to it themselves. Second, the dissenting judge, Judge Moore, made a gross misstatement as to Black English grammar with which the majority did not disagree if the dissent's reading of the audio was correct. The dissent believed the audio recorded Tamica Gordon as saying 'he finna shoot me'. And, because Judge Moore believed whether Gordon's statement was admissible turned on whether the sentence was in the present tense, she argued that the 'lack of an auxiliary verb renders determination of whether Gordon intended to imply the past or present tense an exercise in sheer guesswork'. This is false. In Black English, the auxiliary verb may be omitted in the present tense but not in the past tense (Walker 2023: 1963, 2025; Wolfram 2004: 111, 117–118, 128 tbl.3).

Third, and most worrying, is that Judge Moore relied on Urban Dictionary for her interpretations of the sentence's 'slang'. If Judge Moore had relied instead upon, say Lisa Green's *African American English*, which was published in 2002, she would not have made this mistake (Green 2002: 34–75). A combination of untrustworthy sources, a lack of competence, and a lack of awareness led to Black English being misinterpreted.

Judges are not alone in their misinterpretations. Jones et al. (2019) documented accuracy of publicly employed court reporters on Black English and found disheartening results:

> Despite certification at or above 95% accuracy ..., the court reporters performed well below this level .... 40.5% of the utterances were incorrectly transcribed in some way. The best performance on the task was 77% accuracy, and the worst was 18% accuracy. ... [T]he very best of these court reporters, all of whom are currently working in the Philadelphia courts, got one in every five sentences wrong on average, and the worst got more than four out of every five sentences wrong, under better-than-normal working conditions, with the sentence repeated (Jones et al. 2019: 230).

These results were necessarily preliminary and only focused on publicly employed court reporters. But these results, along with the knowledge that juries might be negatively influenced by the use of Black English (Kurinec & Weaver 2019), mean that legal scholarship in the United States should follow in the footsteps of legal-sociolinguistics research in other jurisdictions. For example, research in the United Kingdom and Australia has considered the factors that would affect the ability to use automatic speech recognition in police interviews and forensics, including audio quality and native language variety (Harrington 2023; Loakes 2022). Such research has also considered the effects of non-native English on the accuracy of transcriptions (Meyer et al., 2020; DiChristofano et al., 2022; Markl, 2022). Eades' influential research considers how Aboriginal English interacts with the Australian legal system. She has gone beyond just looking at how differences in formal grammar and lexicon might affect understanding and explains how the cultural clashes create misunderstanding. For example, she raises awareness of 'gratuitous concurrence', the 'common Aboriginal conversational pattern of freely agreeing to propositions put to them in Yes-No questions, regardless of their actual agreement, or even their understanding of the question' (Eades 2012: 478–479). A failure to consider this sociolinguistic distinction in reacting to questions might gravely impact the accuracy of judicial proceedings.

In the case of Black English, we are just beginning to appreciate the legal consequences of its differences. This chapter aims to supplement the literature by investigating a still unexamined actor: the human and machine transcription of private transcription companies.

6.3 Method

The study's metiendum is the difference in transcription quality when private companies process Black English versus Standard English. I wrote a monologue in informal Black English (417 words, 36 sentences) and translated it into informal Standard American English (423 words, 36 sentences). It consists of a one-sided fictional jail call. The speaker might be talking to his brother. It includes many features that are common to Black English, that make the variety unique, and that have given trouble to legal actors before (Walker 2025).

The participants selected to voice the monologue were six young Black men (under 35): five bidialectal speakers (Black English and Standard American English) and one monodialectal Standard American English speaker. The bidialectal speakers, like most bidialectal speakers, retain some features of Black English phonetics when speaking Standard American English. Additionally, all of the speakers had at least some college education. Socioeconomic differences also filter through into phonetics and broaden the difference between Standard American English and Black English (Labov 1972: 297–354). The bidialectal speakers read both scripts naturalistically, randomly assigned to which script was read first. And the monodialectal speaker read just the Standard English version. The men read the scripts on their own and delivered the audio files to me electronically, which I transcribed myself to create a 'key transcript' against which the private transcription companies would be measured.

The choice of comparison is necessarily difficult here. The most realistic scenario is to compare less highly educated White readers to less highly educated Black readers. And we might expect the greatest disparity between more highly educated White readers and less highly educated Black readers. This initial study chose a practicable but conservative scenario – highly educated Black readers compared to themselves. It eliminates the confounding factors associated with comparing one individual to a different one, is practical because many Black English speakers are bidialectal, and is conservative because we should expect highly educated Black readers to be more easily understood in Black English than less highly educated Black readers, decreasing mistakes in those transcripts. But we should also expect Black readers to be less likely to be understood than White readers when speaking Standard American English, increasing those mistakes. Therefore, any disparity is smaller than we might imagine otherwise. Part of the difficulty in choosing the comparators arises from the fact that there is a societal asymmetry. Many Black people speak standard American English, but few White people speak Black English. The monodialectal speaker was included because we might expect some difference in Standard American English comprehensibility between bidialectal and monodialectal Black readers.

For this initial study, two prominent private transcription companies were tested and anonymized: Company 1 and Company 2. Both companies' transcripts have been used in United States courts. They both hold themselves out as 99% accurate in human transcription and 90% accurate in machine transcription, which seems to be industry standard.

Each of the 11 audio files was transcribed four times, one machine and one human from each company. For both companies, options (which increased price) for 'full verbatim' transcripts as opposed to 'clean verbatim' transcripts were chosen, meaning that 'ums' and other speech disfluencies were to be included. The companies made various statements regarding 'accent' and 'dialect' with no clear distinction between the two. Company 1 claimed their AI was trained on different 'accents', and Company 2 made clear they were available to transcribe 'dialects', though it might take longer. They have a 'heavy accent' option, which I used for all transcripts at Company 2, increasing the price. I used the standard turnaround time for both companies, which was three days.

Also relevant are this study's differences from Jones et al. 2019. Jones et al. used a mix of men and women, tested court transcribers, and seemingly tested on single sentences with some sort of acute time pressure. This study used just men, tested private transcription companies, and tested a monologue with no study-imposed time restraint – the test was open book.

To measure the accuracy of individual transcriptions when compared with the key transcript, the analysis relied on the normalized Word Error Rate (Wang et al., 2003; Park et al. 2008; Kuhn et al. 2023). The Word Error Rate formula is: $\frac{S+D+I}{N}$. *S* is substitutions, (e.g., the word <bad> is changed to 'bat'); *D* is deletions (e.g., <what had happened> to 'what happened'); *I* is insertions (e.g., <matter fact> to 'matter of fact'); *N* is the total number of words in the script. (For notation, I will indicate my own transcription with <> and what was transcribed by the companies with quotation marks.) Normalization in this context means ignoring unimportant differences. Since the context is legal and not, say, standardization for a digital library for easy digital search, I was as lenient as possible with differences that did not change the meaning of the phrase. So, I did not count orthographic differences (e.g., <LaTanya> to 'Latonya' and <going> to 'goin'') or punctuation differences unless it changed the meaning of the phrase substantially. Normalization was chosen here for two reasons. First, Black English has no standard orthography. The purpose here is to capture *mis*transcriptions rather than just *different* transcriptions. Second, normalization makes any estimate more conservative because it only decreases the number of mistakes counted.

Without venturing too far into the forest of Word Error Rate debates, it is important to note that in this case, more important than the ratio of errors to total words or sentences is the *type* of errors made (Harrington 2023).

For example, the occasional deletion of an introductory <and> is much less serious than changing <in that bitch> to 'in a bit' or <eight police> to 'a police.' So, to analyze the results properly requires qualitatively assessing the mistakes.

In sum, to say there is a problem here worth remedying, three things need to be true: (1) there is a disparity in transcript quality conditioned on dialect; (2) the size of the disparity is meaningful; and (3) the types of mistakes made in at least the Black English transcripts are liable to misinterpretation in a legally meaningful way. The results section undertakes to show that (1) and (2) are met by presenting the quantitative data. The discussion section shows (3) is met by analyzing the qualitative aspects of the mistakes. Then the final part notes the limitations, implications, and conclusions from this study with respect to the companies, transcribers, AI programs, and extant evidence law.

6.4 Results

Figures 6.1 and 6.2 show the average number of mistakes (per transcript) and word error rates for both companies investigated. The bars are the 95% confidence intervals, assuming the underlying distribution is normal.

There are several things of note. First, regardless of who transcribed, AI or human, Company 1 or 2, the average number of mistakes and word error rates were significantly (to 95% confidence) higher for Black English. These

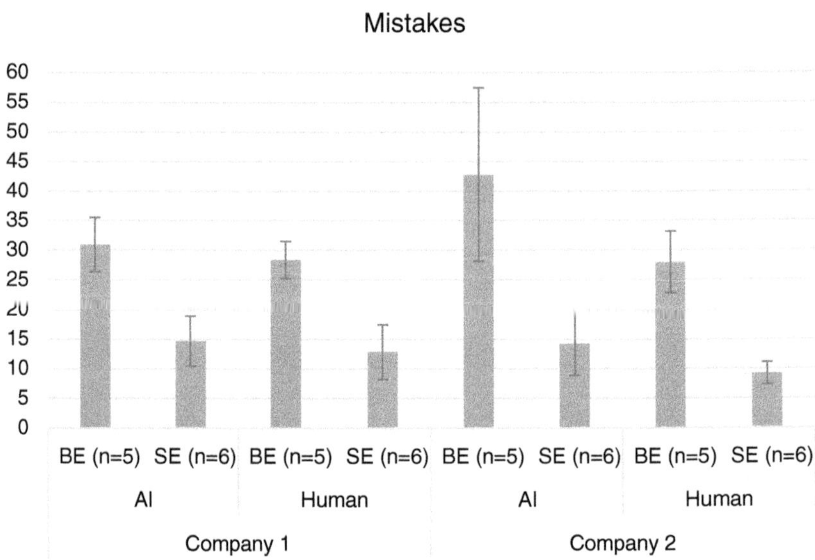

Figure 6.1 Private transcription companies' average mistakes per transcript

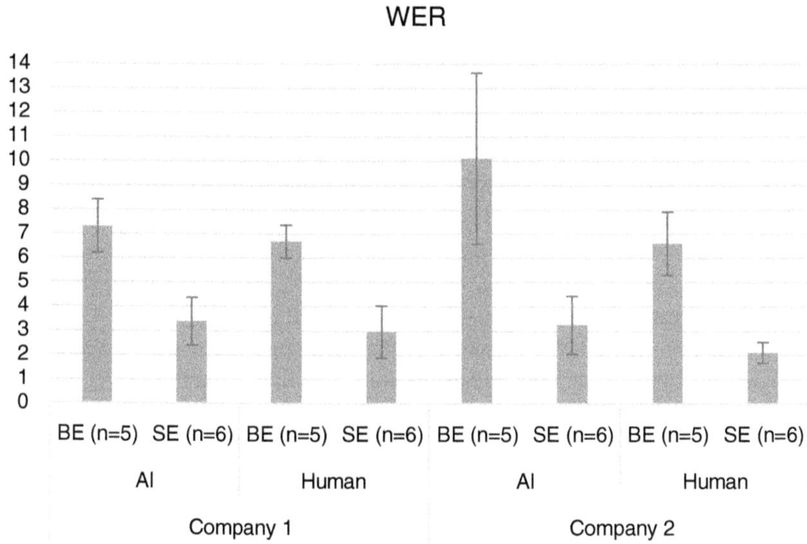

Figure 6.2 Private transcription companies' word error rates

results are also robust to removal of the monodialectal speaker, removal of the bidialectal speaker that precipitated the most mistakes in Black English, and removing both simultaneously. The bidialectal speaker that precipitated the most mistakes in Black English did so uniformly in Black English but did not always precipitate the most mistakes in Standard American English. Nothing concerning this speaker was qualitatively different than other speakers at first brush.

Second, and more important than the mere statistical difference, is the disparity's magnitude. Assuming (falsely) that the mistakes are uniformly distributed across sentences, the *best* performance was more likely to transcribe a sentence with a mistake than one without. In practice, we are likely to get a sentence that is either mostly fine or one with many mistakes. If the mistakes are not just aesthetic – and calling any mistake merely aesthetic is fraught (Tompkinson et al. 2023: 22) – these results cannot be dismissed as unimportant.

Third, while the companies themselves claim a higher level of accuracy for human over AI transcription, the results here do not bear that out. Although humans always averaged fewer mistakes, in no category were humans significantly better than the AI at transcribing the Black English *or* the Standard English.

Fourth, neither company performed better than the other. The humans of company 2 would be the Bayesian bet, but the fact that these two unrelated companies performed so similarly is notable.

6.5 Qualitative Analysis

What remains is to justify the idea that the mistakes are of a type that matter. It is useful to categorize the types of mistakes and why they seem to happen. I will not list all the mistakes but instead show some representative examples of different kinds. Dialectal and cultural differences might lead to three types of mistakes: (1) mistakes resulting from divergent phonetics and phonology of Black and Standard American English, (2) sociological factors causing transcribers to, consciously or subconsciously, view something as 'wrong' and correct it, and (3) mistakes resulting from divergent grammar between the varieties. I do not have data about the transcribers and so cannot know their backgrounds. Nor can I assert with confidence why a particular mistake occurred. That said, given the mistakes that occurred, all pathways seem plausible at different points because the mistakes run the gamut – wherever Black and Standard American English diverged, errors filled the cracks.

Furthermore, some mistakes seem particular to humans or particular to AI programs. For transcriptions, I will indicate in parentheses (translator type, company), so (AI, 1) means the AI transcribers from Company 1.

Starting with the phonetics, Black English has different sounds than Standard American English (Green 2002; Walker 2025). This seemed to precipitate substantive mistakes for both AI and human transcribers. For example, strings of consonant sounds can be reduced to fewer sounds in Black English. This essentially looks like the deletion of sounds. The word <trustin> has two such strings, the /tʃ/ + /r/ sequence at the beginning and the /st/ in the middle. Black English speakers might reduce the first to just a /tʃ/ and the second to just an /s/. This caused confusion. The word was transformed into various other words that yielded something different or nonsense, like in Example 6.1:

Example 6.1

<it's no good reason for trustin that nigga>
there's no good reason for trusting that guy

'it's no good reason for us in that nigga' (AI, 2)
'it's no good reason for touching that nigga' (Human, 2) & (AI, 1)

Sounds can also just be different. For example, the sounds represented by 'th' can be produced like /d/, /f/, or /v/, sounds at the end of words might be less strongly pronounced, if at all, and, as Example 6.2 demonstrates, vowel quality might also be different. A combination of these factors seems to be at play in the following examples.

Example 6.2

<into LaTanya's crib>
into LaTanya's residence

'and took LaTonya's crib' (Human, 2) & (AI, 2)

Example 6.3

<Even though they at LaTanya's place>
Even though they are at LaTanya's place

'Even though dead latanya place' (AI, 1)
'Even though a day at a Latonya place' (AI, 2)

Both Examples 6.2 and 6.3 show how different sounds might confuse. Example 6.2 has multiple potential causes. One is that 'into', when unstressed and before a consonant in Standard American English ends in a schwa /ə/. This speaker's final vowel possibly seemed (to the transcribers) to sound more like the vowel in 'push', leading to a transcription of 'and took' rather than <into>. Another possibility is that the semantic context of 'abode' was less available than 'manger', which had the effect of making 'took' more coherent than 'into' as the fuller context was <the cops done busted down into LaTanya's crib>. Cops do not usually 'burst into' baby beds. This along with an implicit understanding that consonant clusters (here /kl/) are readily reduced in many varieties of English could have led to a transcription of 'took'. It is unclear how much these understandings have seeped into machine transcription algorithms. Example 6.3 is simpler and shows how the pronunciation of <they> with an initial /d/ sound can trick AI into hearing 'day' and 'dead'.

With respect to differences that might have been subconscious or conscious 'corrections' of Black English, these types of mistakes were more common in humans than AI, but some AI mistakes seem fairly characterizable as such because the training data might bias the AI to expect Standard English in certain contexts. For example:

Example 6.4

<LaTanya's crib>
LaTanya's residence

'Latanya's house' (Human, 1)

Example 6.5

<I ain't>
I didn't/I'm not

'I didn't' (Human, 2), (AI, 2), (AI, 1), and (Human, 1)

Example 6.6

<we ain't even do nothing>
'we ain't even do anything' (Human, 1)

Some of these mistakes change meaning more than others. The change from <crib> to 'house' in Example 6.4 injects an implication (a freestanding building) absent from the original, and changing <ain't> to 'didn't' in Example 6.5 might create assuredness as to tense when there is none. That said, in

Example 6.6, the change from <nothing> to 'anything' does not change the substance in most circumstances. It is striking, however, that these mistakes happened when the task is to produce *verbatim* transcriptions of the audio.

Finally, there are the mistakes that might have resulted from unfamiliarity with certain Black English grammatical constructions. These mistakes were frequent and often devastating to correct transcription. In Black English, especially for men, <a nigga> can be a first-person pronoun (Walker 2025). Human transcribers from both companies changed the meaning to indicate someone other than the speaker being the subject of the sentence, like in Example 6.7.

Example 6.7

<A nigga been knew>
I have known for a long time

'that nigga been knew' (Human, 1)
'That nigga Ben knew' (AI, 2)
'A nigga Ben knew' (Human, 2)

This example also highlights the phenomenon we can call 'fictitious Ben'. The stressed <been> in Black English can indicate the remote past (Walker 2025), but it was often confused with the name 'Ben' (a name that does not appear in the transcript). <Been> to 'Ben' was also observed in Jones et al.'s investigation of court transcribers (2019). For human transcribers, there seemed to also be a priming effect. If 'Ben' was identified early in the transcript, they seemed to misidentify it more than once. Examples 6.8 and 6.9 show further appearances of fictitious Ben.

Example 6.8

<I been don't fight no more>
It has been the case for a long time that I don't fight

'I bend don't fight no more' (AI, 1)
'I been done fight no more' (Human, 1)
'I… Ben don't fight no more' (Human, 1)
'I Ben don't fight no more' (AI, 2)
'I've been to a fight no more' (Human, 2)

Example 6.9

<LaTanya sister friend Janiya *been* told you>
LaTanya's sister's friend Janiya told you a long time ago

'Latanya is just a friend, Jania, Ben told you' (Human, 2)
'Latanya's just a friend. Jania Ben told you' (AI, 2)
'Latanya's sister's friend Janaya, Ben told you' (Human, 1)
'The time your sister friends and I have' (AI, 2)
'Latanya's sister friend Janiah. Ben told you' (AI, 1)

Example 6.10 shows a similar phenomenon of how the combination of Black English's ability to use contact relative clauses and a zero copula can cause confusion.

Example 6.10

<the me'd fight people long gone>
the me that would fight people is long gone

'the media fight people long gone' (AI, 1)
'the media fight people, long gone' (AI, 2)
'the me fight people long gone' (AI, 1)
'the mead fight people long gone' (AI, 1) & (AI, 2)
'the me that fight people long gone' (Human, 1)
'To me, fightin' people long gone' (Human, 1)

To explain, in Black English one can delete relative conjunctions like 'that', 'which', or 'who' in places they would be required in Standard English (Walker 2025). And, in the present tense, the word 'is' is often not required (Walker 2025). Combining these can lead to ambiguity. <The man saw John shot him> can either mean, 'the man saw that John shot him' or 'the man, who saw John, shot him'. The shooter could either be 'the man' or John. The sentence in the audio <the me'd fight people long gone> is not ambiguous but does use both features in a way that seemed to confuse transcribers.

Example 6.11

<I'onno if they be listening to calls on this phone like it be in the movies>
I don't know if they usually listen to calls on this phone like it often is in the movies

'I don't know if they'd be listening to calls on his phone like it'd be in the movies' (AI, 1) & (AI, 2)

As shown in Example 6.11, when transcribers were faced with the Black English habitual (or invariant) <be>, they often inserted a '*d* before <be>. In Black English, an unconjugated <be> indicates something that is often, usually, or habitually the case (Walker 2025). So, for example, <she swimming> means 'she is swimming', but <she be swimming> approximates 'she often swims'. Both human and AI transcribers regularly inserted an apostrophe-d (and therefore the word 'would') where it does not exist in the original. The meaning of 'they often listen' changes to 'they would listen'.

Example 6.12

<He walk in – I ain't even doing nothing – come talkin' bout I'mma steal a TV right in front of LaTanya baby father Jaquan>
He walked in, I wasn't even doing anything, saying 'I will steal a TV', right in front of LaTanya's baby's father Jaquan.

'He walk in – I ain't even doing nothing – come talking about I'm going to steal the TV right in front of Latonya, baby, father, and Jaquan.' (Human, 2)

In Example 6.12, one person turned into four. Since the transcriber misunderstood the nature of possession in Black English, which makes apostrophe-s optional, the father of LaTanya's baby, turned into LaTanya, a baby, a father, and Jaquan. To make their interpretation make sense, they inserted an 'and' not present in the original.

Example 6.13

<Don't nobody never say nothing to nobody, but soon as he get invited, the cops done busted down into LaTanya's crib. Worst part, the time they had rolled up…>
Nobody ever says anything to anybody, but as soon as he got invited, the cops burst into LaTanya's place. Worst part, by the time they came…

'Don't nobody never say nothing to nobody, but as soon as he get invited, the cops done bust it down and took Latonya's crib. Worst part, Latonya had rolled up…' (Human, 2)

All the names I chose for the monologue are distinctly Black names, but they all have spent time in the top hundred most common baby names in the United States according to the Social Security Administration's baby name popularity searcher (www.ssa.gov/oact/babynames/) in one spelt form or another. The name <LaTanya> often gave trouble to transcribers. Besides the mistakes in tense in Example 6.13, 'Latonya' was inserted for 'the time they'. Confusing names and identities is possibly one of the gravest mistakes a transcript could make in the legal context.

Example 6.14

<Like stealing a TV hard or something. A nigga been know… a nigga been knew he messed up in the head>
As if stealing a TV is hardcore or something. I have known… I've known for a long time he is messed up in the head.

'Like stealin' a TV hard or sum'. Ay, nigga Ben though… That nigga Ben knew he messed up in the head' (Human, 1)

Finally, Example 6.14 shows how combinations of mistakes often cascaded into something unrecognizable from where we started. In this example, fictitious 'Ben' appears, and the first-person singular <a nigga> changes to 'that nigga' and 'Ay, nigga', which yields something extremely far from the meaning of the original.

Any of the mistakes that seem to result directly from differences in Black English from Standard American English should be worrying, and the breadth and severity of the mistakes indicate these transcripts would not give the reader an accurate portrayal of what was said. Even mistakes as simple as getting a name wrong can lead investigators in the wrong direction and implicate people with no involvement. Verbatim transcripts should, of course, be as close to verbatim as possible, with uncertainties notated as such. And while this chapter has not focused on orthography, transcription companies should consider developing internal, standardized orthography and notation for Black English. The purpose of such standardization would not be to 'standardize' Black English – legal transcription is unlikely to affect the orthographic creativity of the general population (Walker 2025: § 27) – but having clear rules for when to write 'nigga' vs. 'nigger' or 'been' vs. '*been*' vs. 'BIN' would alert transcribers to linguistic differences they should pay attention to.

6.6 Concluding Remarks

This study is small and preliminary, but its results are stark. Two unrelated private transcription companies that the United States courts rely upon are significantly worse at transcribing Black English than they are at transcribing Standard American English, and those mistakes are both of a magnitude and quality that the substance of what Black English speakers say has been changed in legally relevant ways.

Possibly the largest source of potential bias in this study is that the participants were not blinded to the study's aims. In theory, they might have made their Black English much less intelligible than their normal speaking patterns in the hope of exacerbating the results, but having transcribed the recordings myself, I do not believe the final recordings were out of step with run-of-the-mill Black English speech. In my personal estimation, the Black English recordings were much *clearer* and well-enunciated overall than casual speech, again maybe because the participants were not blinded to their being recorded. Regardless, however, the study should be replicated with blinded participants and a blinded transcriber competent in Black English against which to measure the mistakes. Other avenues of research might include using naturally recorded speech, but the comparator there will require more creativity.

If these results do in fact prove generalizable, considerations for policy emerge. First, whatever the two companies are doing to train on dialect is insufficient. It seemed whenever Black English had a particular difference from Standard American English, the transcribers erred. Second, the methodology here and in Jones et al. (2019) was quite different, but the results were the same. Third, the implications for machine transcription are unclear. Humans did not perform better than the AI to 95% confidence, and the machines are much cheaper and might be cheaper to improve if high-fidelity training data can be acquired (Briva-Iglesias 2021). That said, monologues with good audio quality are likely the optimal conditions for machine transcription. If the conditions were less favourable, humans might begin to significantly outperform machines (Harrington 2023; Loakes 2022).

There are also implications for evidence law in the United States. The proper analytic framework for transcripts remains unclear. Jurisdictions disagree about whether transcripts are mere aids to understand a recording or opinion evidence as to what the recording says (Fishman 2006: 487–491; Miller 2016: 373). And if they are opinion evidence, it is unclear whether they should count as lay opinion testimony or expert opinion testimony. Either way, it is unclear that a transcript prepared by someone incompetent in Black English should be admissible.

There is little comfort in the fact that the procedural rules in federal criminal cases allow for the objection to inaccurate transcripts prior to trial (Federal Rules of Criminal Procedure 12 & 16). If the Black English at issue was spoken by a witness or neither the defense lawyer nor judge is proficient in Black English, mistakes might well go unnoticed. The proper formality might be to say that authentication of a transcript should require proof that the transcriber is competent in Black English.

I have previously argued that due process requires safeguards against the mistranscription of language varieties characterizable as 'English' (Walker 2023). This chapter does not aim to delimit the boundaries of what law or justice requires here, but the results support two conclusions. First, for the purposes of the legal system, being a qualified transcriber in Standard American English does not make one qualified in Black English. And second, flowing from the first, a competent Black English speaker needs to be *somewhere* in the transcription process, whether as the transcriber or as a check.

The full relationship between Black English, linguistics, justice, and the legal system is not even close to being fully explored. This study is but a small window into a fruitful area of study where seemingly mundane assumptions in the courts – the transcript represents what was said – might be questioned. We still do not have a handle on the problem's scope, and further research is necessary on Black English and all the other common nonstandard varieties of English in the United States and across the anglosphere. For example, this chapter has focused on 'substantive' mistakes in transcription, but Kurinec and Weaver demonstrate that juror perceptions of witnesses are negatively influenced when that witness speaks Black English (2019: 819–823). It remains unclear how orthographic differences in a transcript might affect juror appraisals (Tompkinson et al. 2023). In the immediate future, however, when Black English is identified, qualified experts should be called, if not by counsel, then by the courts *sua sponte* to affirm accuracy and interpret Black English for factfinders. If not, injustice will result. Ignorance can no longer be a defense.

References

Briva-Iglesias, V. (2021). 'Traducción humana vs. traducción automática: Análisis contrastivo e implicaciones para la aplicación de la traducción automática en traducción jurídica', *Mutatis Mutandis*, 14(2), 571–600.

Delsing, L. and Lundin-Åkesson, K. (2005). *Håller språket ihop norden? En forskningsrapport om ungdomars förståelse av danska, svenska och norska.* København: Nordic Council of Ministers, Nordic Council of Ministers Secretariat.

DiChristofano, A., Shuster, H., Chandra, S., and Patwari, N. (2022). 'Global performance disparities between English-Language Accents in automatic speech recognition'. The Thirty-Seventh AAAI Conference on Artificial Intelligence (AAAI-23), 16200–16201. Available at: https://arxiv.org/abs/2208.01157

Eades, D. (2012). 'Communication with Aboriginal speakers of English in the legal process', *Australian Journal of Linguistics*, 32(4), 473–489.

Fishman, C. (2006). 'Recordings, transcripts, and translations as evidence', *Washington Law Review*, 81, 473–524.

Green, L. J. (2002). *African American English.* New York: Cambridge University Press.

Harrington, L. (2023). 'Incorporating automatic speech recognition methods into the transcription of police-suspect interviews: Factors affecting automatic performance', *Frontiers in Communication*, 8, 1–17.

Hockett, C. F. (1958). *A Course in Modern Linguistics.* New York: The Macmillan Company.

Jones, T., Kalbfeld, J. R., Hancock, R., and Clark, R. (2019). 'Testifying while Black: An experimental study of court reporter accuracy in transcription of African American English', *Language*, 95(2), e216–e252.

Kurinec, C. A. and Weaver III, C. A. (2019). 'Dialect on trial: Use of African American vernacular English influences juror appraisals', *Psychology, Crime and Law*, 25(8), 1–53.

Kuhn, K., Kersken, V., Reuter, B., Egger, N., and Zimmermann, G. (2023). 'Measuring the accuracy of automatic speech recognition solutions', *ACM Transactions on Accessible Computing*, 16(4), 25, 1–23. https://doi.org/10.1145/3636513.

Labov, W. (1972). *Language in the Inner City.* Philadelphia: University of Pennsylvania Press.

Loakes, D. (2022). 'Does automatic speech recognition (ASR) have a role in the transcription of indistinct covert recordings for forensic purposes?', *Frontiers in Communication*, 7, 1–13.

Markl, N. (2022). 'Language variation and algorithmic bias: Understanding algorithmic bias in British English automatic speech recognition', in *2022 ACM Conference on Fairness, Accountability, and Transparency*, 521–534.

Meyer, J., Rauchenstein, L., Eisenberg, J. D., and Howell, N. (2020). 'Artie bias corpus: An open dataset for detecting demographic bias in speech applications', in *Proceedings of the Twelfth Language Resources and Evaluation Conference* (Marseille: European Language Resources Association), 6462–6468.

Miller, A. E. (2016). 'Jury suggestibility: The misinformation effect and why courts should care about inaccuracies in transcripts that accompany recorded evidence', *Law & Psychology Review*, 40, 363–382.

Park, Y., Patwardhan, S., Visweswariah, K., and Gates, S. (2008). 'An empirical analysis of word error rate and keyword error rate', in *Proceedings of the International Conference on Spoken Language Processing* (Brisbane, Australia).

Tompkinson, J., Haworth, K., Deamer, F., and Richardson, E. (2023). 'Perceptual instability in police interview records: Examining the effect of pauses and modality on people's perceptions of an interviewee', *The International Journal of Speech, Language and the Law*, 30(1), 22–51.

Walker III, L. A. (2023). 'Dialectal due process', *Harvard Law Review*, 136(7), 1958–1979.

Walker III, L. A. (2025). 'Black English for lawyers: A primer', *California Law Review*, 113, 101–159.

Wang, Y. Y., Acero, A., and Chelba, C. (2003). 'Is word error rate a good indicator for spoken language understanding accuracy', *Automatic Speech Recognition and Understanding*, 577–582.

Wolfram, W. (2004). 'Urban African American vernacular English: Morphology and syntax', in Kortmann, B. and Schneider, E. W. (eds.), *A Handbook of Varieties of English*. Berlin: Mouton De Gruyter, 1511–1532.

7 Judicial Exceptionalism and the Potential for Misinterpretation

Michele Ruyters, Miranda Lai and Gregory Stratton

7.1 Introduction: Linguistic Presence and Access to Interpreters

In adversarial justice systems, legal presence is a major tenet of a fair trial (Mikkelson 2014). In addition to the right to physical presence, legal presence requires that defendants have the right to be linguistically present in their proceedings (*Ebatarinja* v. *Deland* (1998) 194 CLR 444, 454). 'Linguistic presence' is a term coined by US scholars González et al. (1991) quoting *Arizona* v. *Natividad* (1974) (JUSTIA US Law n.d.) and later used by De Jongh (2008). The concept recognises that criminal matters must be communicated to defendants in a language they understand through qualified interpreters so that they are 'meaningfully present' (De Jongh 2008; González et al. 1991). Linguistic presence is a critical procedural assumption fundamental to the principle of access to justice because it empowers individuals to have a voice and to understand and navigate the criminal justice system (De Jongh 2008; *Ebatarinja* v. *Deland* (1998) 194 CLR 444, 454 [26]; González et al. 1991).

Defendants must understand the court's language at all stages of the criminal justice system. Linguistic presence during police interviews is particularly important to ensure that suspects understand matters put to them, because confessions resulting from police questioning can have a powerful impact on decision-makers at trial (De Jongh 2008; Kassin et al. 2010; Shifton 2019). While, in Australia, the right to silence protects defendants from incriminating themselves during police interviews and at trial, linguistic presence is crucial to understanding these rights and any subsequent questioning by police. Judges play a vital gatekeeping role in determining the admissibility of police interviews and in assessing the language proficiency of defendants who participate in interviews without an interpreter.

This chapter examines Australian judges' perceptions of the English language proficiency of 21 criminal defendants when evaluating the admissibility of police interview evidence where English was not their first language. We posit that when judges form opinions about defendants' English language proficiency, they make assumptions about their own competence to decide matters that are typically in the province of experts and about their own imperviousness to bias (Edmond & Martire 2019: 633). Judges' beliefs in their superior competence and objectivity over laypeople have been described as a form of 'epistemic exceptionalism' (Edmond & Martire 2019: 633; Prescott, 2020: 116; Steiner-Dillon 2019: 208). We caution that judges' overestimation of their ability to evaluate English language proficiency can result in gatekeeping errors that can compound systemic errors stemming from the police interview and lead to miscarriages of justice.

7.1.1 Judicial Gatekeeping and the Right to an Interpreter

In Australia, the right to an Interpreter is embedded in most criminal justice processes to ensure linguistic presence is addressed. While there is no absolute common law right to an interpreter in criminal proceedings, access to interpreters is assured under the defendant's right to a fair trial (Barnett 2006; Grimes 2021; *Ebatarinja* v. *Deland* (1998) 194 CLR 444). Access to interpreters at trial is also safeguarded in each Australian jurisdiction through legislation. Section 30 of uniform legislation adopted by six Australian jurisdictions, collectively referred to as the *Uniform Evidence Acts* ('UEA'), provides that witnesses may give evidence through an interpreter, and there are similar provisions in non-uniform evidence jurisdictions. Proscriptions on courts hearing cases without appropriate interpretation typically depend on the court's assessment of a person's language proficiency. For instance, under section 335 of the *Criminal Procedure Act 2009* (Vic), the court must not proceed without a competent interpreter if it determines that a person's English skills are insufficient for understanding the proceedings.

Statutory rights to an interpreter are also provided for people in custody who lack adequate English to understand questioning. For example, section 464D(1) *Crimes Act 1958* (Vic) mandates that where the person in custody lacks sufficient knowledge of English to understand police questioning, police must arrange a competent interpreter and defer questioning until the interpreter is present. Under section 139 of the UEA, defendants' statements will be taken to have been obtained improperly if they were not cautioned about their right to silence in a language in which they were reasonably fluent before the interview commenced. Access to competent interpretation in police interviews, therefore, is critical in ensuring fairness for suspects and that suspects are not later disadvantaged by miscommunications should the interview later be admitted into evidence (Conway, Daly & McEvoy 2021: 606).

This requirement highlights the judicial responsibility to assess defendants' English language ability when determining the admissibility of police interviews alleged to have been conducted without appropriate interpretation. Judges have a crucial gatekeeping role in ensuring that inadmissible evidence is not placed before the jury for its consideration (Schweitzer & Saks 2009; Nir & Liu 2021). For this reason, decisions about evidence admissibility in Australia are made in the jury's absence during voir dire hearings (e.g., UEA s.189). Judicial gatekeeping is particularly critical when confessional evidence has been obtained through the police interview in the absence of an interpreter. Confessions can be excluded because of unfairness to the defendant, they were not made voluntarily, or because they were improperly obtained, such as police failure to communicate the caution in a language the person understands (Alceste & Kassin 2021; High 2021; *DPP* v. *Natale (Ruling)* [2018] VS 339). This judicial responsibility underscores the importance of assessing language proficiency accurately. Judges may face challenges in this area, however, as their assumptions about language competence can inadvertently introduce bias into the gatekeeping role.

7.2 Judicial Impartiality

When judges evaluate defendants' language proficiency in police interviews, they can overestimate the value of common sense and make risky assumptions about their own capabilities in areas that typically require expert input (Guthrie et al. 2000). This approach may lead them to underestimate their susceptibility to bias in their decision making. While judges are expected to apply common sense, experience, and legal knowledge (ALRC 2021c; Fallon & Snook 2020; Sheldon 2016), there is a danger that their cultural and social perspectives could unconsciously influence their decision-making, potentially undermining the fairness of their gatekeeping (ALRC 2020a; Guthrie et al. 2002; Rachlinski et al. 2007; Rechlinski et al. 2008).

Judicial impartiality is crucial for maintaining public trust in the justice system (ALRC 2021b, p. 3). The Australian Law Reform Commission noted that perceptions of bias can arise when judges fail to recognise the importance of interpreters for people who lack English fluency, as this implies that the court undervalues their involvement in the proceedings (ALRC 2021c: 547). Judicial training in Australia has increasingly included cultural awareness programs and training on recognising and addressing bias, whether actual or perceived (ALRC 2021a).

Despite these efforts, studies indicate that judges tend to overestimate their ability to resist bias in decision-making (Guthrie et al. 2009; Rachlinski et al. 2007; Rachlinski et al. 2008; Sagiv 2015). This phenomenon is consistent with egocentric bias observed in many individuals (Ross & Sicoly 1979). Judges' egocentric bias might prevent self-awareness of their own limitations, leading to critical decision-making errors (Guthrie et al. 2002). Drawing on research indicating a link between the 'bias blind spot' and error, the Australian Law Reform Commission cautioned in its review of judicial impartiality: '[b]ecause of their "bias blind spot", people believe they are less susceptible to, and better at identifying, bias than others. Intelligence does not limit a person's exposure to the blind spot effect' (ALRC 2021b: 16).

Judges' confidence in their ability to resist bias can foster risky beliefs in exceptionalism, which is characterised by the idea that judges' 'intelligence, legal training, and good faith grant them a competence and objectivity beyond that of which laypersons are capable' (Steiner-Dillon 2019: 208; see also Edmond & Martire 2019: 633; Prescott 2020: 116). Steiner-Dillon termed this belief 'epistemic' (Steiner-Dillon 2019: 208). Assumptions of immunity to bias, inherent in exceptionalism (Edmond & Martire 2019: 633), can create problematic blind spots and undermine the judicial gatekeeping role. There is a genuine risk that judges' lack of expertise in evaluating English language proficiency and language usage in context, combined with exceptionalist beliefs and egocentric bias, will result in mistaken assessments of defendants' language capabilities. This is a particular risk when judges gatekeep confessional evidence in the voir dire.

7.3 Educated Common Knowledge or Expertise?

The voir dire is a preliminary hearing where defendants who challenge the admissibility of their police interviews can present evidence, including expert opinion, and cross-examine witnesses (UEA s189). Expert opinion evidence is admissible when experts have specialised knowledge beyond that of laypersons (McClellan 2009; UEA, s79(1)). As Fraser has observed elsewhere in relation to admitting indistinct covert recordings as evidence provided by police, where judges simply rely on their own perceptions and 'educated common knowledge' (Fraser 2018: 587), at the voir dire judges also often do not see it necessary to employ expert language assessments to gauge defendants' English proficiency when deciding the admissibility of police interviews.

Understanding how second languages work in high-pressure situations like police interviews arguably exceeds the scope of 'educated common knowledge'. As English (2020) has contended, the 'linguistic demands associated with arrest, interview, and court interactions … are far more complex' (481) than the more instrumental understandings of language assumed within the judicial system. There is a risk, therefore, that judges' deference to their own education and experience may result in mistaken assessments of English language proficiency.

7.4 Assessing Language Proficiency

Despite the high stakes, there is no prerequisite for evidence of English language proficiency in criminal legal contexts from arrest to hearing (Dissake 2022; English 2020). Conversely, evidence of language proficiency is required for participation in many governmental and institutional contexts. For example, evidence of English proficiency must be provided for entry to university study or visa eligibility (e.g., Australian Department of Home Affairs 2024).

A person's language proficiency can be self-assessed. Self-assessment is commonly used in educational settings including second language acquisition through methods such as reflections, journalling, and rubrics. Research suggests, however, that individuals are unsuited to evaluate their own linguistic competence and may significantly misjudge their language abilities (Dissake 2022: 231; Ross 1998). Some language experts suggest that language proficiency in legal contexts such as litigation and immigration should be tested by linguistic experts using task-based approaches (Dissake 2022; English 2020; Shuy 2002). English's (2020) methodology, for instance, involved obtaining a linguistic profile of the defendant through activities which included reading comprehension, listening comprehension, explaining a sequence of events, and juxtaposing the linguistic profile against the defendant's performance in police interviews.

The emphasis on task-based assessment aligns with the framework established in Australia by the *Recommended National Standards for Working with Interpreters in Courts and Tribunals*. First developed by the Judicial Council on Cultural Diversity (JCCD; now Judicial Council on Diversity & Inclusion, or JCDI) in 2017, the standards recommend a four-part test for judicial officers and legal practitioners to assess whether a person needs the assistance of an interpreter in proceedings:

1 Directly asking the person if they need an interpreter.
2 Assessing the person's speaking ability by asking questions requiring a narrative response.
3 Assessing comprehension and speaking ability by asking the person to explain relevant information communicated to them in their own words.
4 Arranging an interpreter where two or more of the following apply to the person:
   - Difficulty articulating back what was said.
   - Very short sentences or mainly one-word answers.
   - Consistently agreed with questions or propositions put to them.
   - Frequent inappropriate answers, for example, answering 'yes' to 'what' or 'where' questions.
   - Unclear meaning even though the words and grammar used were fine.
   - Unaware of contradictions in what they said.
   - Have limited vocabulary and rely on using the words and phrases from what was just said to them.
   - Grammatical errors in what they said.
   - Need to frequently repeat or simplify questions for them. (Refer to Annexure 4 in JCDI 2022: 95.)

If doubt remains after the test has been completed, the guidelines recommend that an 'English proficiency assessment' should be obtained from a 'suitably qualified linguist' as to the person's level of English competence in a voir dire hearing (JCDI 2022: 51). The standards include training for judges on assessing the need for interpreters (JCDI 2022: 51).

The standards emphasise the importance of linguistic assessments and judicial training to ensure procedural fairness for individuals with limited English proficiency in legal proceedings. With this in mind, this chapter explores approaches Australian judges have taken to evaluate defendants' language proficiency during police interviews.

7.5 Methodology

Using a systematic review of published judgments, we investigated how judges perceived the English linguistic proficiency of criminal defendants where language was raised as a concern regarding the admissibility of police interview evidence.

To ensure a widespread of cases over time, we searched for the term 'no interpreter' at multiple instances from the year 2000 across Australia by AustLII and Westlaw AU legal database searches. This search resulted in an initial 2823 cases, as the search term drew all cases in which an interpreter was simply referred to in the judgments. From this set of 2823, we removed all civil cases and all cases where the court was silent on the defendant's English language capability. From the remaining 80 cases, we eliminated cases that did not involve the admission of police interviews and cases in which an interpreter was present at the police interview. This process resulted in 21 criminal cases where interpreters were not present at the police interview and language was subsequently raised as an issue at trial. These are presented in Table 7.1. For consistency, we use medium-neutral citations using pinpoint paragraph references when referring to these cases in the following discussion.

The outcome of the criminal proceedings, namely whether the defendant was convicted, is not included in the table. This information was not available for most cases, as reported judgments were primarily decisions on the admissibility of police interviews. Police interviews were admitted in 10 cases and excluded from evidence in 11 cases. Interviews in several cases were excluded on grounds that did not directly relate to language proficiency, such as being unlawfully detained in custody. These cases were retained in the dataset because our purpose was to examine how judges evaluate language proficiency.

Table 7.1 *Cases of police interviews without interpreters in which English language capacity was a threshold consideration in determining admissibility*

	Jurisdiction	Case	Interview admitted into evidence	Nature of offence
1	Northern Territory	*R* v. *Weston & Anor* [2005] NTSC 49 ('*Weston*')	×	Sexual intercourse without consent
2		*R* v. *BL* [2015] NTSC 85 ('*BL*')	×	Sexual intercourse without consent
3		*R* v. *Cotchilli* [2007] NTSC 52 ('*Cotchilli*')	×	Murder
4		*R* v. *Tupou* [2016] NTSC 56 ('*Tupou*')	✓	Driving dangerously causing death
5		*R* v. *Lawrence* [2016] NTSC 65 ('*Lawrence*')	×	Sexual intercourse without consent & unlawful assault
6		*R* v. *Durilla* [2014] NTMC 26 ('*Durilla*')	×	Assault & breach domestic violence order
7	New South Wales	*Regina* v. *Deng* [2001] NSWCCA 153 ('*Deng*')	✓	Supply prohibited drugs
8		*R* v. *HS* [2019] NSWDC 575 ('*HS*')	✓	Assault, indecent assault
9	Queensland	*R* v. *Karalasingham* [2014] QDC 247 ('*Karalasingham*')	×	Indecent assault
10		*R* v. *D Bastos De Frietas* [2012] QDC 354 ('*Bastos de Freitas*')	×	Rape and assault
11		*R* v. *Cho* [2001] QCA 196 ('*Cho*')	✓	Murder
12		*R* v. *Trinh* [2002] QSC 471 ('*Trinh*')	×	Possess prohibited drugs
13	South Australia	*R* v. *Lem* [2004] (No. 1) SASC 416 ('*Lem*')	✓	Murder
14	Tasmania	*State of Tasmania* v. *Stojakovic* [2008] TASSC 48 ('*Stojakovic*')	✓	Rape, indecent assault, attempted rape
15		*Tasmania* v. *Liu* [2021] TASSC 53 ('*Liu*')	✓	Trafficking in fish
16	Victoria	*R* v. *Mohammed (Ruling)* [2004] VSC 408 ('*Mohammed*')	×	Murder, attempted murder
17		*R* v. *Natale (Ruling)* [2018] VSC 339 ('*Natale*')	×	Incitement to murder, extortion, threat to kill
18	Western Australia	*The State of Western Australia* v. *Gibson* (2014) 243 A Crim R 68 ('*Gibson*')	×	Manslaughter
19		*Narrier* v. *The State of Western Australia* [2014] WASC 21 ('*Narrier*')	✓	Murder
20		*The State of Western Australia* v. *Talib* [2015] WADC 85 ('*Talib*')	✓	Unlawfully cause grievous bodily harm
21		*George* v. *The State of Western Australia* [2020] WASCA 139 ('*George*')	✓	Child sexual offences

7.6 Evaluating Defendants' English Language Capacity

When assessing defendants' English language capacity and understanding, courts in this study considered similar factors and terminology: defendants' understanding of police questioning; the need for questions to be repeated; responsiveness to questions including demeanour and other non-verbal responses; monosyllabic responses; 'broken English'; and defendants' use of 'understandable' English and reasonable English fluency.

Most judges were confident using their observations of video or textual recordings of police interviews or giving of the caution to determine defendants' proficiency levels and decided on the admissibility of the interview in question. For example, in one of the cases where the interview evidence was excluded (see Table 7.1), Hall J. determined that his observation of Gibson's 'very limited understanding of English' in the interview meant he could not be confident Gibson had understood what the police said to him (*Gibson* [84]). Likewise, in *Natale*, after reading the interview transcripts and viewing the recorded interview several times, Bell J. found that the defendant had insufficient knowledge of English to understand police questioning. Philippides J. was also not satisfied that Trinh understood his right to silence on reviewing the recorded interview in that case [21], while in *Bastos De Frietas*, Wall J. did not think the defendant was capable of understanding or effectively communicating his answers to all of the questions asked in the interview [39].

Judges likewise relied on their observations of defendants' English language proficiency in recorded interviews in cases where they decided to admit the interview evidence. In *Tupou*, Barr J. found that Tupou 'generally appeared to understand the questions asked of him by police; his answers to questions were appropriately responsive' [65], while the trial judge in *Cho* observed that Cho's 'comprehension and command of English were … adequate for elementary communications' [20]. Herron D. C. J. was also 'satisfied' in *Talib*, after viewing the video-recorded police interview that Talib could 'sufficiently understand and communicate in spoken English' [45]. In *Lawrence*, Grant C. J. was even confident on viewing the recorded interview that there was no suggestion that Lawrence's answers resulted from gratuitous concurrence [50]. Gratuitous concurrence is a well-documented phenomenon in Australian Indigenous people, referring to the act of a speaker appearing to agree with questions put to them even when they do not understand what is being asked (Eades 2016; Gray 2022).

These observations highlight the critical role that judges play in determining the admissibility of interview evidence using their own assessment of the defendant's English language proficiency. To gain a better understanding of judges' decision-making about language proficiency in contested interviews, we mapped judicial evaluations of defendants' English language proficiency in the Table 7.1 cases against the part 4 factors of the JCDI test described earlier. These are represented in Table 7.2, which shows that several factors considered by the judges feature in the JCDI test. The cases where police interviews were admitted are highlighted in the Table. Notably, two or more part 4 factors were present in 40% of these cases: *Tupou*; *HS*; *Narrier*; and *Talib*.

As the last column in Table 7.2 indicates, judges in 10 cases considered that police needed to repeat or simplify questions to assist defendants' understanding. Rather than indicating a struggle for defendants to understand matters put to them by the police, as the JCDI Part 4 factors suggest, some judges appeared to accept repetition of questions by police as adequate to address misunderstandings. For instance, in *Mohammed*, Kaye J. found it became clear during Mohammed's interview with police that on numerous occasions, 'he did not understand the thrust of questions that were put to him and they had to be repeated or clarified' [59]. And in *Lem*, Nyland J. observed that the repetition of questions and statements by police reflected their attempt to ensure that the accused understood what was being put to him [99].

7.6.1 Demeanour and Non-verbal/Monosyllabic Responses

While some judges viewed the repetition and simplification of questions as sufficient for ensuring defendants' understanding, other judges relied on their perceptions of defendants' demeanour and non-verbal responses during video-recorded interviews to gauge comprehension (e.g., *Lawrence*, *Stojakovic*, *Liu*, *Deng*, *Gibson*). Porter J. in *Stojakovic* explained that the recorded interview provided a 'good insight in that the flow of the questions and answers could be closely followed, as could the behaviour and mannerisms of the accused' [80]. On appeal in *Deng*, James J. drew from observations of how Deng 'acted' in the video interview in concluding that the 'relevant understanding' was communicated to the defendant [18]. Similarly in *Lawrence*, Grant C. J. stated that it was apparent from viewing the recorded interview that Lawrence made 'various nonverbal responses' capable of conveying his understanding of the police caution [56]. Judges' confidence in their abilities to accurately assess a person's English language competence from their demeanour reflects research suggesting that judges are similarly confident in assessing witness credibility from demeanour (Porter & Ten Brinke 2009).

Monosyllabic or very short responses to questions were also considerations in determining English language competence in five cases. In *Durilla*, Armitage S. M. stated: 'I am not persuaded that Mr Durilla's single word answers demonstrated an understanding of the caution. His subsequent silence was equally unenlightening. Mr Durilla may have been silently exercising his right or he may have been silent because he did not understand the question or because he did not have sufficient command of the English language to respond' [25].

Table 7.2 *Mapping judicial evaluations of English language proficiency against the JCDI Part 4 factors (based on reported cases)*

	Case	*Difficulty articulating back*	*Very short sentences or monosyllabic*	*Consistent agreement*	*Unclear meaning*	*Frequent. inappropriate answers*	*Unaware of contradictions*	*Limited vocabulary*	*Grammatical errors***	*Need to frequently repeat or simplify*
1	*Weston & Anor*							✓		✓
2	*BL*		✓		✓			✓	✓	✓
3	*Cotchilli*		✓					✓		✓
4	*Tupou*							✓	✓	✓
5	*Lawrence*							✓		
6	*Durilla*		✓					✓		
7	*Deng*									
8	*HS*			✓					✓	✓
9	*Karalasingham*	✓		✓	✓			✓		
10	*D Bastos De Frietas*			✓	✓			✓		
11	*Cho**									
12	*Trinh*	✓	✓	✓				✓		✓
13	*Lem*									✓
14	*Stojakovic*								✓	
15	*Liu*									
16	*Mohammed*				✓	✓		✓	✓	✓
17	*Natale*				✓			✓	✓	✓
18	*Gibson*		✓		✓	✓	✓	✓	✓	
19	*Narrier*							✓		✓
20	*Talib*				✓			✓	✓	
21	*George*									

*Insufficient information available about factors considered by judges on evaluating language proficiency.
**This factor is assumed from the defendant's limited ability to speak English.

Similarly, Blokland J. in *BL* pointed to 'the lengthy silences, the many monosyllabic answers and some acknowledged miscommunication' as factors indicating that 'this is not a record of interview that can be relied upon' [48]. The court in *Gibson* also took the defendant's monosyllabic responses into consideration in determining the admissibility of his police interview, commenting: '[m]any of his responses are single words which do not necessarily indicate an understanding of the questions' [83].

7.6.2 English Fluency and Responsiveness

English language fluency was another consideration in assessing English language competency. Fluency tended to be described either in terms of the presence or absence of 'broken English' (*BL*, *Cho*, *Gibson*, *Talib*) or in terms of 'reasonable fluency' (*Lawrence*, *BL*, *Bastos De Freitas*, *Tupou*), which is the term used in section 139(3) of the UEA concerning the giving of the caution.

The cases suggest that judges may have inconsistent approaches to assessing English language fluency. For example, in *Cho*, McKenzie J. for the Queensland Court of Appeal observed that while the defendant's record of interview suggested Cho's English was 'far from perfect and fits the description of broken English', Cho's responses suggested 'he understood the questions and was able to give appropriate answers' [10]. The trial judge had reached the same conclusion. Grant C. J. in *Lawrence* also considered Lawrence's non-verbal responses capable of conveying that he understood the caution [56]. Blokland J. in *BL*, however, found that BL should have been provided with an interpreter. He noted that while BL's spoken English might 'appear to be reasonable for social conversations', it could not be described as 'standard English. He … is perhaps better described as a partial English speaker' [37].

Judges also had different interpretations of 'fluency'. In *Bastos De Frietas*, Wall D. C. J. found that while the defendant 'generally appeared to understand many of the questions … [u]nderstanding some, or key words, is not the same as understanding and appreciating or comprehending issues, concepts, meanings and nuances associated with questions which I consider to be part of fluency in a language' [39]. In *Tupou*, Barr J. was satisfied that the defendant 'demonstrated reasonable fluency and comprehension' as Tupou 'gave responsive and coherent answers to most if not all relevant questions asked' by the police [95]. Blokland J. in *BL*, however, found it was evident from the record of interview that BL was not a fluent English speaker 'particularly the silences in response to important but seemingly simple questions, the large number of monosyllabic answers and occasional examples of obvious miscommunication' [37]. It should be noted, however, that Blokland's assessment of Tupou's language fluency was also influenced by additional protections applying to young offenders.

The defendant's responsiveness to police questions was a significant factor in eight cases: *Cho, Tupou, Weston & Anot, BL, Lawrence, HS, Stojakovic, and Narrier*. For instance, Porter J.'s assessment of Stojakovic's understanding of English was influenced by the defendant's 'relatively prompt and responsive answers' despite his 'difficulties with pronunciation, grammar and syntax' [85]. In *Narrier*, Jenkins J. was satisfied that, although Narrier only understood 'basic English', he 'usually understood what questions that were asked of him [sic] and that he gave responsive answers which are able, in the main, to be understood' [41].

7.7 Evidence of English Language Ability

Few judges in our dataset accepted evidence on defendants' English language abilities when considering whether to admit police interviews, other than the evidence of interviewing police officers professing some expertise or experience (e.g., *Deng, HS, Stojakovic, Lem*). For instance, in *Lawrence*, Grant C. J. accepted a police officer's assessment that the defendant did not require an interpreter [87] based on her assessment of her previous interactions with Aboriginal people who had varying degrees of English fluency [18].

Expert linguistic evidence was only received in *Gibson*, where the trial judge accepted evidence of English language testing and linguistics experts, revealing Gibson's proficiency to be at a 'very basic level of English comprehension and speaking ability' [83]. In *Cotchilli*, Mildren J. accepted evidence of a psychologist with extensive experience in assessing the intellectual and educational capacity of Indigenous Australians about the defendant's 'very limited English skills' and was 'not persuaded' Cotchilli understood his right to silence [42] [51].

We applied the JCDI part 4 factors to the cases in this study to understand how judges were approaching their evaluations of language proficiency. We found that interviews were admitted into evidence in four cases where multiple JCDI part 4 factors appeared to be present, despite the absence of interpreters in those interviews. The presence of the JCDI part 4 factors suggests that any doubts about the English competence of those defendants should have been resolved through expert assessment. We argue that judges should consider the JCDI standards when deciding on the admissibility of police interviews where language capacity is in doubt and no interpreter was present. Incorporating the JCDI standards at the gatekeeping point would encourage decisions about a defendants' language proficiency to be informed by expert assessments rather than ad hoc evaluations by police officers or judges.

The JCDI standards are intended to ensure procedural fairness by providing quality interpretation in proceedings in Australian courts and tribunals for people with limited English proficiency. The standards recommend an expert

English proficiency assessment as part of a voir dire if doubt remains about a person's level of English competence and that an interpreter should be arranged where two or more of the criteria in Table 7.2 applied (JCDI 2022: 51, 95–97).

7.8 Conclusion

Our research underscores the phenomenon of judicial exceptionalism. When judges assess defendants' linguistic competence during police interviews, they make assumptions about their own competence to decide matters that usually fall to experts and overestimate the role of common sense in determining matters that relate to culture, language and demeanour (Guthrie et al. 2000). Judges' interpretation of factors such as limited vocabulary, monosyllabic responses, and non-verbal engagement impinge on areas of linguistic science that are beyond their legal expertise, as they generally lack the necessary training and expertise to interpret these indicators of English language capacity. Expert evidence was only received in two cases in this study, and only one gave linguistic evidence, while judges in five cases deferred to previous language assessments made by police, potentially undermining the gatekeeping role.

Judges in this study had inconsistent approaches to evaluating language proficiency, which would be resolved through the adoption of expert forensic language assessments. Porter and Ten Brinke (2009) urged that education and expert evidence were essential in improving credibility assessments and reducing the problem of wrongful convictions. The same must clearly be argued about improving the accuracy of English language competence assessments, particularly when determining the admissibility of police interviews in which language proficiency is an issue.

Part 4 of the JCDI test recommends that an interpreter is advisable where two or more factors are present. In four cases in this study, however, interview evidence was admitted despite the absence of interpreters at those interviews and the presence of two or more JCDI part 4 factors. Given the powerful impact of police interview evidence, particularly those containing confessions, it seems extraordinary that judges' 'common sense' evaluations of English language proficiency should be made on less stringent considerations. We strongly urge that judges consider the JCDI methodology when assessing an accused's English language ability in determining whether to admit the police interview. This practice would ensure that language assessments are reliable, and the judiciary is better equipped to fulfill its gatekeeping role. Inconsistencies in assessing linguistic competence further highlight the need for expert forensic language assessment in legal proceedings. Recognising the complexities of language proficiency and the limitations of lay assessments is crucial for ensuring fairness in criminal proceedings. Integrating expert opinions on language proficiency can help mitigate biases and improve the accuracy of judicial decision-making.

References

Alceste, F. and Kassin, S. M. (2021). 'Perceptions of custody: Similarities and disparities among police, judges, social psychologists, and laypeople'. *Law and Human Behavior*, 45(3), 197–214.

Australian Department of Home Affairs. (2024). *English Language Visa Requirements*. Home Affairs. Retrieved 03/03/2024 from https://immi.homeaffairs.gov.au/help-support/meeting-our-requirements/english-language.

Australian Law Reform Commission (ALRC). (2021a). *Judicial Impartiality: Background Paper J16 Cognitive and Social Biases in Judicial Decision-Making*. Brisbane QLD (Australia): Australian Government.

Australian Law Reform Commission (ALRC). (2021b). *Review of Judicial Impartiality, Consultation Paper and Background Papers*. Brisbane QLD (Australia): Australian Government.

Australian Law Reform Commission (ALRC). (2021c). *Without Fear or Favour: Judicial Impartiality and the Law on Bias, Final Report*. Brisbane QLD (Australia): Australian Government.

Barnett, M. (2006). 'Mind your language – Interpreters in Australian immigration proceedings'. *University of Western Sydney Law Review*, 10, 109–138.

Conway, V., Daly, Y. and McEvoy, G. (2021). 'Interpretation in police stations: Lawyers' perspectives on rights and realities'. *Journal of Human Rights Practice*, 13(3), 606–628.

De Jongh, E. M. (2008). 'Court interpreting: Linguistic presence v. linguistic absence'. *Florida Bar Journal*, 82(7), 20–30.

Dissake, E. M. K. (2022). 'Assessing litigant's language proficiency: The case of the Bafoussam Court of First Instance'. *Language Policy*, 21(2), 217–234.

Eades, D. (2016). 'Judicial understandings of Aboriginality and language use'. *Judicial Review (Sydney, N.S.W.)*, 12(4), 471–490.

Edmond, G. and Martire, K. (2019). 'Just cognition: Scientific research on bias and some implications for legal procedure and decision-making'. *Modern Law Review*, 82, 633–664, http://dx.doi.org/10.1111/1468-2230.12424.

English, F. (2020). 'Non-native speakers in detention: Assessing the English language proficiency of non-native speakers in detention: An expert witness account'. In Coulthard, M., May, A., and Sousa-Silva, R. (eds.), *The Routledge Handbook of Forensic Linguistics*. London/New York: Routledge, 465–484.

Fallon, L. and Snook, B. (2020). 'Beyond common sense and human experience: Lay perceptions of witness coercion'. *Criminal Justice and Behavior*, 47(2), 208–221.

Fraser, H. (2018). 'Forensic transcription: How confident false beliefs about language and speech threaten the right to a fair trial in Australia'. *Australian Journal of Linguistics*, 38(4), 586–606.

González, R. D., Vásquez, V. F. and Mikkelson, H. (1991). *Fundamentals of Court Interpretation: Theory, Policy and Practice*. Durham, NC: Carolina Academic Press.

Gray, P. (2022). 'Language matters: Gratuitous concurrence: When "yes" might not mean "I agree"'. *Victorian Bar News*, 172, 81–82.

Grimes, B. (2021). 'Judicial reliance on the executive: Tensions, discrepancies and recommendations for court interpreter service delivery models across Australian jurisdictions'. *Griffith Law Review*, 30(1), 71–96. https://doi.org/10.1080/10383441.2021.2014773

Guthrie, C., Rachlinski, J. J. and Wistrich, A. J. (2000). 'Inside the judicial mind'. *Cornell Law Review*, 86, 777–830.

Guthrie, C., Rachlinski, J. J. and Wistrich, A. J. (2002). 'Judging by heuristic-cognitive illusions in judicial decision making'. *Judicature*, 86, 44–50.

Guthrie, C., Rachlinski, J. J. and Wistrich, A. J. (2009). 'The "hidden judiciary": An empirical examination of Executive Branch justice'. *Duke Law Journal*, 58(7), 1477–1530.

High, A. (2021). 'The exclusion of prison informant evidence for unreliability in New Zealand'. *The International Journal of Evidence & Proof*, 25(3), 217–238.

Judicial Council on Diversity & Inclusion. (2022). *Recommended National Standards for Working with Interpreters in Courts and Tribunals*. Judicial Council on Cultural Diversity. Retrieved 1st February 2024 from jccd.org.au/wp-content/uploads/2022/05/JCDD-Rec-ommended-National-Standards-for-Working-with-Interpreters-in-Courts-and-Tribunals-second-edition.pdf

Kassin, S. M., Drizin, S. A., Grisso, T., Gudjonsson, G. H., Leo, R. A. and Redlich, A. D. (2010). 'Police-induced confessions: Risk factors and recommendations'. *Law and Human Behavior*, 34(1), 3–38.

McClellan, P. (2009). 'Admissibility of expert evidence under the Uniform Evidence Act.' Emerging Issues in Expert Evidence Workshop, Judicial College of Victoria, Melbourne.

Mikkelson, H. (2014). *Introduction to Court Interpreting*. London: Routledge.

Nir, E. and Liu, S. (2021). 'What do the gatekeepers see? Perceptions and evaluations of scientific evidence among State Court judges'. *Criminology, Criminal Justice, Law & Society*, 22(1), 20–35.

Porter, S. and Ten Brinke, L. (2009). 'Dangerous decisions: A theoretical framework for understanding how judges assess credibility in the courtroom'. *Legal and Criminological Psychology*, 14(1), 119–134.

Prescott, D. E. (2020). 'Bending the light of social science in Family Court: Epistemic injustice and epistemic exceptionalism matter'. *Journal of the American Academy of Matrimonial Lawyers*, 33(1), 99–136.

Rachlinski, J. J., Guthrie, C. and Wistrich, A. J. (2007). 'Heuristics and biases in bankruptcy judges'. *Journal of Institutional and Theoretical Economics (JITE)/Zeitschrift für die gesamte Staatswissenschaft*, 163(1), 167–186.

Rachlinski, J. J., Johnson, S. L., Wistrich, A. J. and Guthrie, C. (2008). 'Does unconscious racial bias affect trial judges'. *Notre Dame Law Review*, 84, 1195–1246.

Ross, S. (1998). 'Self-assessment in second language testing: A meta-analysis and analysis of experiential factors'. *Language Testing*, 15(1), 1–20.

Ross, M. and Sicoly, F. (1979). 'Egocentric biases in availability and attribution'. *Journal of Personality and Social Psychology*, 37(3), 322–366.

Sagiv, M. (2015). 'Cultural bias in judicial decision making'. *Boston College Journal of Law & Social Justice*, 35, 229–256.

Schweitzer, N. and Saks, M. J. (2009). 'The gatekeeper effect: The impact of judges' admissibility decisions on the persuasiveness of expert testimony'. *Psychology, Public Policy, and Law*, 15(1), 1–18.

Sheldon, J. C. (2016). 'Common sense and the law of voluntary confessions: An essay'. *Maine Law Review*, 68, 119–160.

Shifton, J. J. (2019). 'How confession characteristics impact juror perceptions of evidence in criminal trials'. *Behavioral Sciences and the Law*, 37(1), 90–108.

Shuy, R. W. (2002). 'To testify or not to testify'. In Cotterill, J. (ed.), *Language in the Legal Process*. Basingstoke: Palgrave Macmillan, 3–19.
Steiner-Dillon, J. R. (2019). 'Epistemic exceptionalism'. *Indiana Law Review*, 52, 207–256.

Cases Cited

State *v*. Natividad (1974). Supreme Court of Arizona http://law.justia.com/cases/arizona/supreme-court/1974/2854-0.html

8 Interpreting for Jurors and Defendants' Right to a Fair Trial

Eva N. S. Ng

8.1 Interpreting in the Legal Process

One of the key safeguards of the right to a fair trial, as specified in the International Covenant on Civil and Political Rights (ICCPR) (United Nations 1966) is the provision of free interpreting services for defendants who do not speak the language used in criminal proceedings. Interpreting is therefore by and large a standard service provided for defendants facing criminal charges in jurisdictions which have ratified the ICCPR. This is to ensure defendants' linguistic presence and meaningful participation in the judicial process, and thus to avoid compromising their right to a fair trial.

However, interpreting for jurors, who determine defendants' guilt or innocence in jury trials, has hitherto been limited to sign language interpreting with a view to enabling deaf people's civil right to serve on juries, which has been shown to enable deaf jurors to perform just as well as their hearing peers (Napier & McEwin 2015; Napier & Spencer 2017; Napier et al. 2018; Spencer et al. 2017). Unfortunately, even across the ICCPR compliant jurisdictions, equivalent interpretation services are not available for jurors who are not L1 speakers of the language of the proceedings.

In the United States, for instance, allowing deaf jurors to serve on juries whilst denying non-English-speaking (NES) people or those with limited English proficiency (LEP) the same right has been criticised as inconsistent with the promotion of equality and justice (Chávez 2008; Chavez 2012; Duffy 2017; Gonzales-Rose 2011, 2014, 2020; Johnson 2016). Excluding NES/LEP individuals from the jury pool is also considered a violation of the principle of trial by one's peers and the defendant's right to a trial by an impartial jury drawn from a fair cross-section of the community under the Sixth Amendment of the US Constitution (U.S. Const. amend. VI) (Chávez 2008; Chavez 2012; Duffy 2017; Gonzales-Rose 2011, 2014, 2020; Johnson 2016). It is suggested that providing an interpreter for the deaf but not for NES/LEP individuals is 'a distinction without a difference' (Johnson 2016: 973).

Funding statement: The study was part of a project funded by the Research Grants Council (RGC) of Hong Kong under the General Research Fund (GRF) 2022/23 (Project number: 17600822).

This chapter contributes to the debate by exploring interpreting for NES/LEP jurors in the bilingual legal context of Hong Kong. The data come from two appellate courts' conflicting views and rulings about an appeal (*HKSAR* v. *Chan Hon Wing* 2020, 2021), which contested the trial judge's permission for jurors to access interpretation services (*HKSAR* v. *Chan Hon Wing* 2015). Drawing on the larger research project examining judicial opinions about appeals advanced on interpretation-related grounds, this single-case study seeks to demonstrate that interpreting for jurors in Hong Kong not only enhances equal participation and upholds the principle of trial by one's peers but also fulfils a practical need to improve jurors' comprehension, thereby ensuring defendants' right to a fair trial.

This chapter lends further support to the broader discussion on the contention that consistency should be applied to permit NES/LEP persons to serve on juries, assisted by interpreters to promote equal participation and uphold the principle of trial by one's peers (Brown 1994; Gonzales 2014; Johnson 2016; Kisor 2001). In the United States, this plea for consistency is strengthened by the fact that the state of New Mexico allows NES/LEP persons to serve on juries under Article VII, Section 3 of the New Mexico Constitution (NM Const., 1910, art. VII, § 3). Gonzales-Rose (2014) suggests that allowing NES/LEP citizens to participate in jury service with the help of an interpreter is appropriate given that over one third of the population of New Mexico speaks a language other than English at home. It was found that the participation of NES/LEP jurors and their interpreters did not influence the final verdicts or compromise the integrity of jury deliberations (Chavez 2012). This chapter adds to the growing body of literature focusing on Hong Kong, where around 90% of the populace speak Cantonese at home (Census and Statistics Department 2022: 54). To provide context for this study, the following section offers an overview of the unique Hong Kong courtroom where common law is practised, discussing the implementation of the jury system, issues of jury comprehension and the practice of court interpreting.

8.2 The Hong Kong Courtroom

8.2.1 Hong Kong Juries and Their Representativeness

Hong Kong has inherited the common law system from the British colonial rule and its key institution of trial by jury. The colonial rule brought not only the legal system to Hong Kong but also the use of English as the official language in which trials were held for well over a century (see also Leung, this volume). It was not until 1974 that Chinese gained the status as the other official language, and in December 1995 the High Court heard its first civil case in Chinese (*Sun Er-jo* v. *Lo Ching and others* 1995). Despite the increasing use of Chinese as a trial language in lower courts since the changeover of Hong Kong's sovereignty in 1997, English remains the dominant language of criminal trials held in the High Court to this day, due to the ongoing presence of expatriate judges and counsel. In 2023, for instance, only 21.1% of the criminal trials in the High Court were conducted in Chinese (Department of Justice 2023). The Jury Ordinance (1999) specifies that jurors must be able to understand the proceedings, so given the high proportion of criminal trials held in English, proficiency in English is obligatory.

The English language requirement in a Chinese society where the majority of the local population speaks Cantonese necessarily excludes the linguistic majority from the jury pool, currently consisting of 795,262 people as per the List of Common Jurors which came into force in February 2021 (accessed in person on 26 May 2022). This represents slightly over 10% of a population of 7.41 million (Population Census Office 2021). The law does not specify how linguistic competence in English is measured, but the administrative practice has been to include in the jury pool only those who have completed High School education (Law Reform Commission of Hong Kong 2010). As pointed out by Duff et al. (1992: 123), the language requirement means juries in Hong Kong are mostly made up of English-speaking expatriates and well-educated professionals, whereas defendants are mostly working-class Chinese people with low educational levels and LEP. This calls into question the representativeness of the Hong Kong juries, as well as the principle of trial by one's peers.

8.2.2 Jury Comprehension Issues

In addition to the issue of representativeness, another concern regarding Hong Kong juries is the ability of jurors to understand court proceedings conducted in English, which most of them speak only as a foreign language (L2). Studies on jury comprehension have largely focused on Anglo-American courtrooms, revealing that the complexity of legal discourse poses challenges to the comprehension of jurors who are laypersons unversed in legal language (Charrow & Charrow 1979; Dumas 2000; Gibbons 2017; Heffer 2005, 2018; McKimmie et al. 2014; Steele & Thornburg 1991; Thomas 2010). The standard legal-lay comprehension issues are further exacerbated by jurors' language proficiency challenges in Hong Kong. Comprehending a foreign legal language can be particularly difficult for Chinese jurors, as it involves not only intra-lingual legal-lay comprehension but also inter-lingual communication barriers. Despite the language proficiency requirement, jurors selected during the jury empanelling process occasionally expressed concerns about their ability to understand court proceedings (Ng 2016, 2018, 2022). In some cases, jury comprehension problems were raised as a ground for appeal. *HKSAR* v. *Lai She Hung* (2005) is an example of this. In this case, the appellate court expressed concerns over the jury's ability to understand the trial judge's instructions about the verdicts to be returned in relation to the three charges facing the defendant. While the trial judge indicated in his instructions to the jury that the three charges should stand or fall together, the jury convicted the defendant on one charge, but acquitted him of the other two. The appeal was allowed and the conviction was quashed (see Ng 2016, 2018 for a detailed discussion of this case).

The earliest research to shed light on the jury comprehension issue in Hong Kong is a survey study by Duff et al. (1992), which examined jurors' experience in court and their comprehension levels of court proceedings. The study revealed that a significant proportion of the jurors had some difficulty in understanding the English language and legal terminology, and in following the evidence (Duff et al. 1992: 84–85). One native English-speaking respondent also reported that he had a problem holding a simple conversation with two of his fellow jury members and wondered how much of the proceedings they had understood (Duff et al. 1992: 72). Another respondent expressed surprise over the Cantonese-speaking jurors' limited understanding of English and had to explain to them the meaning of words not limited to legal terms (Duff et al. 1992: 84).

It must be noted that Duff et al.'s (1992) study was based on the respondents' subjective evaluation of their comprehension levels of court proceedings. To further explore the jury comprehension issue in Hong Kong, Ng's study (2022, 2025) adopted an objective comprehension test method. The study involved 53 participants who were invited to take part in a listening comprehension test of authentic audio clips recorded from two jury trials and a reading comprehension test of a short transcript excerpted from one of the trials. All the participants were local Chinese eligible for jury service, some with actual jury experience and others without. The results showed that the average comprehension rate was 45.9%, and that participants' comprehension problems were not limited to technical legal terminology. Plain and ordinary English were found to be equally challenging to L2 jurors, especially when the speakers did not articulate the message clearly and slowly. The study revealed a genuine need for juror language assistance in English-medium trials, as L2 jurors in Hong Kong face both an interlingual and an intralingual comprehension problem arising from the need to comprehend legal language uttered in a foreign tongue.

8.2.3 *Interpreting in English-Medium Trials and Jurors' Access to Interpretation*

Given that Hong Kong is a predominantly Cantonese-speaking society, local defendants and witnesses appearing in court mostly speak Cantonese, irrespective of whether the trial is conducted in Chinese (meaning Cantonese in

Hong Kong) or English. In the case of an English-medium trial, interpretation between English and Cantonese is almost a *sine qua non* service. The ubiquity of the court interpreter in an English-medium trial creates a misconception that court proceedings are fully bilingual. Somewhat concerningly, this misconception could be held even by presiding judges. For instance, in a rape trial (the audio recordings of which the author was given rare permission to access), a selected juror expressed concerns about her ability to follow the trial in English. The juror was, however, persuaded to stay by the judge reassuring her that everything said in court would be interpreted and that she would be able to hear the interpretation provided, including the interpretation of his instructions and summing-up (see Ng 2016, 2018). The judge was, unwittingly, telling only part of the truth, but not the whole truth. He was right in saying that everything said in court would be interpreted, but wrong in claiming that jurors would be able to hear all the interpretation provided in court. Whether jurors are able to access the interpretation depends on the mode of interpreting used.

The two common modes of interpreting used in court are consecutive interpreting (CI) and *chuchotage*. CI is provided in open court with the speaker and the interpreter taking turns to speak, whereas *chuchotage* is simultaneous interpreting (SI) in a whisper, delivered as the speaker goes on without pausing for interpreting. Interpretation provided in *chuchotage* is audible only to the person (usually the defendant) for whom it is provided. This means jurors can hear interpretation provided in the consecutive mode, but not in *chuchotage*. By default, interpretation provided in *chuchotage* is not part of the court record and is not captured even if a recording system is in place. In a typical English-medium trial in Hong Kong with the defendant and witnesses speaking Cantonese, CI is usually used for dialogic communication between counsel and witnesses, as in witness examination. This way, both the witness testifying in Cantonese in the witness stand and the Cantonese-speaking defendant in the dock are able to hear the Cantonese interpretation of counsel's questions asked in English. On the other hand, *chuchotage* into Cantonese is used for interpreting English monologues, such as jury instructions, summings-up and counsel opening and closing addresses, for the defendant in the dock. It can also be used to keep the defendant informed of non-interpreter-mediated dialogic communication, such as testimony given in English. Note that interpreters are not used to assist with jurors' comprehension, as jurors are considered to possess the required English proficiency to understand the court proceedings conducted in English. Therefore, although jurors experiencing problems with their comprehension of questions asked in English are able to benefit from the Cantonese interpretation provided in open court, they have no access to the interpretation provided in *chuchotage*, which is exclusive to the defendant. This explains why a special arrangement had to be made in the trial of *HKSAR* v. *Chan Hon Wing* (2015) for jurors to access the *chuchotage* interpretation, leading to an appeal to the two levels of appellate courts in Hong Kong. This case forms the data source of the current study and will be discussed in detail in the rest of this chapter.

8.3 Grounds of Appeal for Jurors' Access to Interpretation and Courts' Rulings

In *HKSAR* v. *Chan Hon Wing* (2015), the defendant was tried for three drug-related offences. The trial was conducted in English, but evidence was presented in Cantonese, and CI and *chuchotage* were used for interpretation at different stages of the trial. At a later stage of the trial, the jury requested access to the Cantonese interpretation of counsel's closing addresses and the judge's summing-up. Headphones were subsequently provided for some jurors to listen to the Cantonese interpretation provided in *chuchotage*, while others listened to the original speech in English. The defendant was ultimately found guilty of all three counts and sentenced to 26 years in prison.

An appeal was filed to the Court of Appeal (CA) in *HKSAR* v. *Chan Hon Wing* (2020), arguing that the special arrangement allowing jurors to access the Cantonese interpretation was unprecedented, and constituted a material irregularity in the conduct of the trial. It was argued that the arrangement potentially deprived the defendant of a fair trial, as *chuchotage*, conducted in the simultaneous mode, could compromise the quality of interpretation. It was further submitted that the lack of a record of the *chuchotage* interpretation rendered it impossible to ascertain any misinterpretation problems and thus the verdict was unsafe and unsatisfactory.

The CA dismissed the argument of possible misinterpretation as speculative, noting that the appellant failed to prove a real or substantial risk of misinterpretation. The CA pointed out that the interpreter was experienced and competent, having worked in the Judiciary as a full-time interpreter for almost 25 years at the time of trial. The court concluded that the arrangement, though unprecedented, was constitutional, as English and Chinese have equal status under section 3 of the Official Languages Ordinance (1995) and dismissed the appeal.

The CA's rejection of the appellant's argument regarding possible misinterpretation is consistent with the 'predominant pattern' observed by Berk-Seligson (1990: 200), where appellate judges tend to uphold rulings of lower courts when appeals are based on alleged interpreter errors or inaccuracies. Berk-Seligson (1990) noted that this pattern exists because the interpretation from the language of the court into a foreign language is often not entered into the court record. Likewise, before the installation of a digital recording system in the mid-1990s in Hong Kong, interpretation out of English into Cantonese or any other dialects or foreign languages was never part of the court record, making it difficult to substantiate any claim about misinterpretation. However, with court proceedings being audio recorded at all court levels in Hong Kong, interpretation into and out of English provided in the consecutive mode is both recorded and can be transcribed to become a written court record. Interpretation provided in *chuchotage*, however, remains an exception, as that cannot be captured by the recording system as noted above, which is the subject of the appeal in this case.

Following the dismissal of the initial appeal, a further appeal was filed with the Court of Final Appeal (CFA) and was unanimously allowed, with the convictions quashed and a trial *de novo* ordered (*HKSAR* v. *Chan Hon Wing* 2021).[1] This represents a departure from the appellate courts' predominant pattern of upholding lower court rulings on appeals related to interpreter errors or inaccuracies. The CFA's ruling focused on the limitations of the *chuchotage* mode of interpreting used in this case. The court accepted the appellant's argument that the absence of a record of the *chuchotage* interpretation rendered it impossible to ascertain what the jurors following the interpretation had heard, which raised a concern about whether the arrangement was consistent with the principle of open justice. The CFA suggested that CI should have been used instead, as it would allow any mistakes to be spotted and an audio record of the interpretation to be kept for later verification.

While the CFA's concerns about the possibility of misinterpretation and the lack of a record associated with *chuchotage* are not without merit, the court's ruling and reasoning raise interesting legal and linguistic questions that will be discussed further in Section 8.4.

8.4 Implications and Possible Ramifications of the CFA's Ruling and Reasoning

Chuchotage has long been one of the common modes of interpreting used in court, with the interpretation typically not being entered into the court record. This lack of a record was the basis for the CA's dismissal of the initial appeal, as the claim of potential faulty interpretation was deemed speculative without any record to substantiate it. Ironically, the CFA's subsequent ruling in favour of the appellant was also based on the absence of a record of the *chuchotage* interpretation. The CFA held that this lack of a record gave rise to concerns about the principle of open justice and potentially compromised the defendant's right to a fair trial. This raises questions about the suitability of *chuchotage* for the defendant, whose meaningful participation in the trial hinges on effective interpretation. It stands to reason that accuracy and the

[1] At the retrial, the defendant pleaded guilty and was sentenced to a total of 18 years' imprisonment (*HKSAR* v. *Chan Hon Wing* 2022).

principle of open justice matter for the defendant as a key stakeholder in the trial, just as much as for the jurors who determine the outcome of the trial.

There have been appeals contesting the accuracy or adequacy of *chuchotage* interpretation provided for defendants. In the case of *HKSAR* v. *Moala Alipate* (2019), the court allowed the appeal on inadequate interpretation provided in the *chuchotage* mode and concluded that the defendant had been deprived of a fair trial. In the case of *HKSAR* v. *Gutierrez Alvarez* (2020), however, a similar claim was advanced but was dismissed by the court, which opined that the appellant failed to prove that the interpretation was inadequate in the first place and how the alleged inadequacy had compromised her right to a fair trial. In both cases, there was no record of the interpretation provided to support or reject the claim. In *Gutierrez*, the court also ruled that the appellant had no right to demand a record of the interpretation, as most courts do not maintain a record of interpretation provided in *chuchotage*, including courts in the United States, the United Kingdom and Singapore. It can be inferred that the absence of a record inherent in the adoption of *chuchotage* can be used by the appellate court to either dismiss an interpreter-related appeal as speculative or otherwise to allow it based on the principle of open justice. This inconsistency in rulings on similar grounds may pose challenges for the application of the principle of *stare decisis*, which binds courts to follow legal precedents (see Ng 2023 for a detailed discussion of these two cases). In *HKSAR* v. *Chan Hon Wing* (2021), the CFA referenced the CA's views in *Gutierrez*, regarding the quality of *chuchotage* and its dismissal of the appellant's contention about the lack of a record of the *chuchotage* interpretation. The CFA, however, argued that the standard of *chuchotage* intended for a defendant should be distinguishable from the *Chan Hon Wing* case, where the interpretation was provided for some members of the jury as the decision-making body, and thus the absence of a record of the interpretation was a concern. The CFA's view in this regard suggests that the quality of interpretation and the lack of a record of the interpretation are less of a concern for the court where interpretation is provided for defendants, highlighting a concerning double standard and potential ramifications.

The CFA's remark in *Chan Hon Wing* that CI should be the preferable mode of interpreting in court is likewise problematic, as it sends an ambiguous message to the court about the future use of *chuchotage* in court. A further suggestion made by the CFA in this regard is that whether CI or *chuchotage* should be used would depend, in part, on the length of the speech. This view is equally concerning: if the implementation of the open justice principle is crucial to safeguard the defendant's right to a fair trial, why should the length of the speech matter at all? If *chuchotage* is to continue as a mode of interpreting for defendants, this seems to reinforce the inference of a double standard being applied regarding interpreting for defendants versus interpreting for jurors.

Similarly, the CFA's concerns regarding the potential for misinterpretation in *chuchotage* leading to jurors receiving varying interpretations of the same speech can give rise to significant issues. It is worth noting that the possibility of jurors relying on different versions of the same testimony can also arise even when CI is used. As discussed earlier in this study, in CI settings, jurors are able to hear both the original utterance and its interpretation. In the United States, bilingual jurors are instructed to ignore testimony given in a foreign language and to consider only the English interpretation (Office of the Executive Secretary 2023). Following the Supreme Court's decision in *Hernandez* v. *New York* (1991), jurors bilingual in English and Spanish may even be removed from juries in cases involving Spanish and English evidence (Rich 2021). However, this approach would not work in Hong Kong. Excluding jurors bilingual in Cantonese and English would make it extremely difficult to empanel juries in Hong Kong, as most jurors in Hong Kong are nowadays bilingual in English and Cantonese to varying degrees. Thus, bilingual jurors in Hong Kong are neither removed nor instructed to ignore Cantonese testimony in English-medium trials. Therefore, in witness examination, it is likely that some jurors are listening to the original testimony given in Cantonese, while others are following the English interpretation. Similarly, while some jurors are able to fully understand counsel's questions asked in English, others may have to follow their Cantonese interpretation. This means that even in the consecutive mode of interpreting, there is no way to prevent jurors from receiving different versions of the evidence.

As noted earlier, court interpreters have long been instrumental in the administration of justice in trials involving litigants who do not speak the language of the court. Until the contrary is proved, speculating on the possibility of misinterpretation has grave implications for all past and future interpreter-mediated trials and casts unjustified aspersions on the skill of the interpreter. As the US Court of Appeals notes: 'When any non-English speaking witness (including a defendant) testifies, the entire jury, the judge, the attorneys, the court reporter and, consequently, all future appellate courts, are dependent on the English record made by that interpreter. If we do not trust the skills of that person then we have no trial at all' (*People* v. *Guzman* 1984; cited also in Brown 1994: 23).

Indeed, if the skills of the court interpreter cannot be trusted, there should never be interpreter-mediated trials. That misinterpretation might be a possible result does not mean jurors have to access only unmediated evidence or legal instructions for justice to be done. As Leung (2019: 236) observes, '[i]f unmediated access to evidence is where the bar is set, then many defendants (such as immigrants and other aliens) can never be said to have a fair trial'. Leung (2019: 239) suggests that the risk of L2 jurors' misunderstanding evidence is presumably higher than that of mistranslation by professional interpreters.

While the CA's dismissal of the appeal in *HKSAR* v. *Chan Hon Wing* (2020) could have set a legal precedent for interpreting for jurors, the CFA overruled this potential precedent. The CFA's ruling and reasoning not only discourage the full extension of this service to jurors but also raise questions about the existing practice of court interpreting – a longstanding service in the courts of Hong Kong. Specifically, the CFA's concerns about possible misinterpretation during *chuchotage* and about the lack of a record for verification challenge what has long been legitimately practised – the provision of *chuchotage* for defendants. These concerns suggest a tacit acknowledgement that the adoption of *chuchotage* is not desirable, but tolerable until jurors sought to access it.

8.5 Conclusion

Trial by jury is a crucial safeguard for defendants' right to be tried by their peers drawn from a cross section of the community. Ensuring jurors' comprehension of legal discourse is as important as the representativeness of juries. As suggested by Tiersma (2009: 1), defendants' right to trial by jury 'has little meaning if jurors do not properly understand the law that governs their decisions'.

This study has highlighted both inclusivity and comprehension issues with juries in Hong Kong. To address these challenges, this study argues for language assistance to be provided for jurors who lack the proficiency in English to enable their participation in English-medium trials. Interpreting for defendants who are not conversant in the language of the court is a standard practice, which ensures their effective participation in criminal proceedings and their right to a fair trial. In the case of Hong Kong, interpreting between English and Cantonese in English-medium trials has long been a day-to-day service, though it is currently only partially accessible to jurors. Making the service fully accessible to jurors can be easily implemented with the use of appropriate equipment (e.g., headphones), as demonstrated in the case of *HKSAR* v. *Chan Hon Wing* (2015). Therefore, unlike in the United States, where the cost associated with providing interpretation for jurors is a major concern (Chávez 2008; Duffy 2017), extending the full existing interpretation service to jurors in Hong Kong would have minimal financial implications. However, the CFA's ruling and reasoning have effectively vetoed what would otherwise be a significant legal precedent for interpreting for jurors in Hong Kong.

This study argues that the need for interpreting for jurors in Hong Kong is evident and long overdue. Ignoring this need would be at the expense of justice and would compromise defendants' right to a fair trial as well as the principle of trial by jury. Studies in interpreting for jurors revealed that competent and professionally trained interpreters were able to effectively facilitate the communication of deaf and NES/LEP jurors in court proceedings. What is important is that the court should make every effort to ensure the highest possible quality of interpreting services to avoid compromising the delivery of justice and defendants' fundamental right to a fair trial.

To mitigate disputes and speculation regarding potential misinterpretation in *chuchotage*, the court might consider transitioning the *chuchotage* mode of interpreting to a fully electronic SI system. With the adoption of an electronic SI system, interpretation and the original speech can be simultaneously recorded on separate tracks as in conference interpreting, or in court proceedings in the International Criminal Court (ICC) (Stern 2012). Findings of empirical research support the adoption of such an SI system to minimise the impact of the interpreter on the proceedings (Hale et al. 2017, 2024) and more importantly, for a full record of the interpretation to be kept. The retention of a record of interpretation is not only consistent with the principle of open justice but also has the advantage of preventing misinterpretation from being used as a convenient ground for appeal and the interpreter from being scapegoated. In the interests of justice and to uphold the principle of trial by jury, it is equally important for both jurors and defendants who require language assistance to be provided with interpreting services. Last but not least, the quality of interpretation matters just as much for jurors as it does for defendants.

References

Berk-Seligson, S. (1990). *The Bilingual Courtroom: Court Interpreters in the Judicial Process*. Chicago: University of Chicago Press.

Brown, C. L. (1994). 'A challenge to the English-language requirement of the juror qualification provision of New York's Judiciary Law'. *New York Law School Law Review*, 39(3), 479–510.

Census and Statistics Department. (2022). '2021 Population Census', Hong Kong Special Administrative Region. www.census2021.gov.hk/doc/pub/21c-main-results.pdf

Charrow, R. P. and Charrow, V. R. (1979). 'Making legal language understandable: A psycholinguistic study of jury instructions'. *Columbia Law Review*, 79(7), 1306–1374. https://doi.org/10.2307/1121842

Chávez, E. L. (2008). 'New Mexico's success with non-English speaking jurors'. *Journal of Court Innovation*, 1, 303–327.

Chavez, H. L. (2012). 'Examining the effects of the inclusion of non-English speaking jurors on jury verdicts and juror experiences'. Unpublished PhD thesis, University of Nevada, Reno.

Department of Justice. (2023). 'Key Figures and Statistics – Percentage of Criminal Cases Conducted in Chinese'. www.doj.gov.hk/en/about/stat.html

Duff, P., Findlay, M., Howarth, C. and Chan, T. F. (1992). *Juries: A Hong Kong Perspective*. Hong Kong: Hong Kong University Press.

Duffy, K. P. (2017). 'Lost in translation: New Mexico's non-English speaking jurors and the right to translated jury instructions'. *New Mexico Law Review*, 47(2), 376–400.

Dumas, B. K. (2000). 'US pattern jury instructions: Problems and proposals'. *Forensic Linguistics*, 7(1), 49–71. https://doi.org/10.1558/sll.2000.7.1.49

Gibbons, J. (2017). 'Towards clearer jury instructions'. *Language and Law / Linguagem e Direito*, 4(1), 142–160.

Gonzales Rose, J. B. (2011). 'The exclusion of non-English-speaking jurors: Remedying a century of denial of the Sixth Amendment in the Federal Courts of Puerto Rico'. *Harvard Civil Rights*, 46, 497–549.

Gonzales Rose, J. B. (2014). 'Language disenfranchisement in juries: A call for constitutional remediation'. *Hastings Law Journal*, 65(3), 811–864.

Gonzales Rose, J. B. (2020). 'Color-blind but not color-deaf: Accent discrimination in jury selection'. *New York University Review of Law and Social Change*, 44(3), 309–354.

Hale, S. B., Martschuk, N., Ozolins, U. and Stern, L. (2017). 'The effect of interpreting modes on witness credibility assessments'. *Interpreting. International Journal of Research and Practice in Interpreting*, 19(1), 69–96. https://doi.org/10.1075/intp.19.1.04hal

Hale, S., Martschuk, N., Goodman-Delahunty, J. and Lim, J. (2024). 'Juror perceptions in bilingual interpreted trials'. *Perspectives*, 33, 1–24. https://doi.org/10.1080/0907676X.2024.2343772

Heffer, C. (2018). 'When voices fail to carry: Voice projection and the case of the "dumb" jury', in Leung, J. and Durant, A. (eds.), *Meaning and Power in the Language of Law*. Cambridge: Cambridge University Press, 207–235.

Heffer, C. (2005). *The Language of Jury Trial: A Corpus-Aided Analysis of Legal-Lay Discourse*. New York: Palgrave Macmillan.

Johnson, L. (2016). 'What does justice have to do with interpreters in the jury room?' *UMKC Law Review*, 84(4), 941–985.

Jury Ordinance. (1999). Cap 3, Laws of Hong Kong. www.elegislation.gov.hk/hk/cap3.

Kisor, C. A. (2001). 'Using interpreters to assist jurors: A plea for consistency. *Chicana/o Latina/o Law Review*, 22(1), 37–54. https://doi.org/10.5070/C7221021137

Law Reform Commission of Hong Kong. (2010). Report: Criteria for Service as Jurors. www.hkreform.gov.hk/en/docs/rjurors_e.pdf.

Leung, J. H. C. (2019). *Shallow Equality and Symbolic Jurisprudence in Multilingual Legal Orders*. New York: Oxford University Press.

McKimmie, B. M., Antrobus, E. and Baguley, C. (2014). 'Objective and subjective comprehension of jury instructions in criminal trials'. *New Criminal Law Review*, 17(2), 163–183.

Napier, J. and McEwin, A. (2015). 'Do deaf people have the right to serve as jurors in Australia?' *Alternative Law Journal*, 40(1), 23–27. https://doi.org/10.1177/1037969X1504000106

Napier, J. and Spencer, D. (2017). 'Jury instructions: Comparing hearing and deaf jurors' comprehension via direct or mediated communication'. *International Journal of Speech Language and the Law*, 24(1), 1–29. https://doi.org/10.1558/ijsll.30878

Napier, J., Spencer, D., Hale, S., Roque, M. S., Shearim, G. and Russell, D. (2018). 'Changing the international justice landscape: Perspectives on deaf citizenship and jury service'. *Sign Language Studies*, 19(2), 240–266. https://doi.org/10.1353/sls.2018.0034

New Mexico Constitution. (1910). NM Const art VII § 3. In JUSTIA US Law. https://law.justia.com/constitution/new-mexico/article-vii/section-3/.

Ng, E. N. S. (2016). 'Do they understand? English trials heard by Chinese jurors in the Hong Kong courtroom'. *Language and Law / Linguagem e Direito*, 3(2), 172–191.
Ng, E. N. S. (2018). *Common Law in an Uncommon Courtroom: Judicial Interpreting in Hong Kong*. Amsterdam/Philadelphia: Benjamins Publishing.
Ng, E. N. S. (2022). 'Trials heard by a foreign ear: A study of Chinese jurors' comprehension of English trials in Hong Kong'. *International Journal of Speech, Language and the Law*, 29(2), 172–200. https://doi.org/10.1558/ijsll.23248
Ng, E. N. S. (2023). 'The right to a fair trial and the right to interpreting: A critical evaluation of the use of *chuchotage* in court interpreting'. *Interpreting*, 25(1), 87–108. https://doi.org/10.1075/intp.00082.ng
Ng, E. N. S. (2025). *Linguistic Disadvantage in Jury Trials: Lessons from Hong Kong and Beyond*. Edinburgh: Edinburgh University Press.
Office of the Executive Secretary. (2023). Virginia Language Access Plan Manual. Department of Judicial Services. www.vacourts.gov/courtadmin/aoc/djs/programs/interpreters/manuals/lep/guidelines.pdf
Official Languages Ordinance. (1995). Cap 5, Laws of Hong Kong. www.elegislation.gov.hk/hk/cap5
Population Census Office. (2021). Main Results. Census and Statistics Department, Hong Kong Special Administration Region. www.censtatd.gov.hk/en/scode600.html
Rich, A. (2021). 'Bye, bye, bilinguals: The removal of English-Spanish bilinguals from the criminal jury and Latino discrimination'. *Chicago-Kent Law Review*, 95(3), 697–717.
Spencer, D., San Roque, M., Napier, J. and Hale, S. (2017). 'Justice is blind as long as it isn't deaf: Excluding deaf people from jury duty – An Australian human rights breach'. *Australian Journal of Human Rights*, 23(3), 332–350. https://doi.org/10.1080/1323238X.2017.1392479
Steele, W. and Thornburg, E. G. (1991). 'Jury instructions: Persistent failure to communicate'. *Judicature*, 74(5), 249–254.
Stern, L. (2012). 'What can domestic courts learn from international courts and tribunals about good practice in interpreting?: From the Australian war crimes prosecutions to the International Criminal Court'. *T&I Review*, 2, 7–30.
Thomas, C. (2010). Are Juries Fair? UK: Ministry of Justice. www.justice.gov.uk/downloads/publications/research-and-analysis/moj-research/are-juries-fair-research.pdf
Tiersma, P. M. (2009). 'Communicating with juries: How to draft more understandable jury instructions'. *Loyola-LA Legal Studies* Paper No. 2009–44. http://papers.ssrn.com/sol3/papers.cfm?abstract_id=1507298
United Nations. (1966). International Covenant on Civil and Political Rights. www.ohchr.org/en/professionalinterest/pages/ccpr.aspx
U.S. Const. amend. VI. https://constitution.congress.gov/constitution/amendment-6/

Cases Cited

Hernandez *v*. New York [1991] 500 U.S. 352, 358
HKSAR *v*. Chan Hon Wing [2015] HCCC 210/2015 https://legalref.judiciary.hk/lrs/common/search/search_result_detail_frame.jsp?DIS=104975&QS=%2B&TP=RS
HKSAR *v*. Chan Hon Wing [2020] HKCA 938 https://legalref.judiciary.hk/lrs/common/ju/ju_frame.jsp?DIS=131891

HKSAR *v*. Chan Hon Wing [2021] HKCFA 45 https://legalref.judiciary.hk/lrs/common/ju/ju_frame.jsp?DIS=141159&currpage=T
HKSAR *v*. Chan Hon Wing [2022] HKCFI 2426 https://legalref.judiciary.hk/lrs/common/search/search_result_detail_frame.jsp?DIS=146278&QS=%2B&TP=RS
HKSAR *v*. Chan Hon Wing [2022] HKCFI 2426 3174 https://legalref.judiciary.hk/lrs/common/search/search_result_detail_frame.jsp?DIS=146278&QS=%2B&TP=RS
HKSAR *v*. GUTIERREZ ALVAREZ Keishu Mercedes [2020] HKCA 184. https://bit.ly/42EVJHp
HKSAR *v*. Lai She Hung [2005] HKCA 46 https://legalref.judiciary.hk/lrs/common/search/search_result_detail_frame.jsp?DIS=46390&QS=%2B%7C%28CACC%2C46%2F2005%29&TP=JU
HKSAR *v*. Moala Alipate [2019] HKCA 537 https://bit.ly/42F89im
People *v*. Guzman [1984] 125 Misc.2d 457, 478 N.Y.S.2d 455 https://casetext.com/case/people-v-guzman-66
Sun Er-jo *v*. Lo Ching and others [1995] HCA003283 https://legalref.judiciary.hk/lrs/common/ju/ju_frame.jsp?DIS=29421

Part II

Communication and Legal Profession

9 'Being Sure'

Judicial Practices in Directing Juries on the Criminal Standard of Proof

Chris Heffer and Malcolm Coulthard

9.1 Introduction

The fairness of criminal jury trial is predicated on the jury being able to clearly understand and accurately apply the criminal standard of proof. If the threshold for conviction is set too low or too high in jurors' minds, this might lead, respectively, to an unjust conviction or unjust acquittal, both of which ultimately undermine confidence in the criminal justice system. Among legal scholars, there is a strong international consensus on the essential properties of the criminal standard of proof as a legal concept: that it is a very high standard but does not require absolute certainty; that it must maintain the overall burden of proof on the prosecution; and that it is a subjective rather than objective standard arrived at after hearing and assessing all the evidence (Clermont & Sherwin 2002; Keane & McKeown 2019). It has long been established in psychological (e.g., Horowitz & Kirkpatrick 1996; Kagehiro & Stanton 1985), linguistic (e.g., Heffer 2006, 2007, 2013, 2026; Solan 1999) and legal (e.g., Keane & McKeown 2019) research that the traditional formula *beyond (a/any/all)*[1] *reasonable doubt* is now a legal term that is no longer comprehensible to jurors without careful explanation. However, some jurisdictions (such as New South Wales and Victoria in Australia, and Oklahoma and Kentucky in the US) have dogmatically held on to the belief that the term is ordinary language that is easily understood by jurors and so needs no explanation.

That jurors had difficulty with an unexplained *beyond reasonable doubt* direction was known by judges long before any academics took an interest in the question. In England and Wales, Lord Chief Justice Goddard, in *R* v. *Summers* (1952), remarked that it would be better to tell jurors that they had to be 'satisfied so that you are sure'. At the time, his suggestion was laudable both for implicitly recognising that *beyond reasonable doubt* is a legal term and

[1] It is generally *beyond reasonable doubt* in Commonwealth jurisdictions (England and Wales, Scotland, Australia, New Zealand, etc.) but *beyond **a** reasonable doubt* (or sometimes *any* or *all reasonable doubt*) in US jurisdictions.

for trying to find an everyday alternative (*sure*) that would be understood by lay jurors (Heffer 2006, 2007). Goddard's *obiter* became authoritative when approved by the Privy Council in *Walters* v. *R* [1969: ¶30] and English and Welsh judges have subsequently been strongly advised to use *sure* rather than *beyond reasonable doubt* in their proof directions. However, the use of *sure* has been fiercely resisted by many in the legal community, particularly by the authors of the 'Barrister's Bible' *Archbold* (Archbold & Lucraft 2025), who would prefer to return to an undefined *beyond reasonable doubt* instruction (Darbyshire, Maughan & Stewart 2001, Heffer 2007). This opposition to *sure* supposedly gained empirical support from two legal studies at the turn of the century (Montgomery 1998; Zander 2000), which appeared to show that jurors would have to be absolutely certain (i.e., too high a standard) before they convicted. However, Heffer (2007) argued both that the studies were riddled with methodological issues and that they fundamentally misunderstood the ordinary meaning of *sure*, which indicates a level of practical conviction ('after hearing the evidence we're sure he did it') rather than evidentiary certainty ('there is not the remotest possibility in the evidence that he might not have done it').

Our involvement as linguistic experts in a more recent Court of Appeal case involving the use of *sure* in the criminal standard (*R* v. *Mohammad* 2022), though, led to the realisation that the simple everyday word *sure* has, in the context of the judge's directions, become a technical legal term with a quite distinct meaning from its ordinary language meanings (McKeown 2022). In essence, this derives from the avowed legal synonymy between *sure* and *beyond reasonable doubt* and from a series of Court of Appeal judgments relating to judges' attempts to explain the meaning of *sure* when asked to do so by the jury, which then established legal precedent for a certain construction of the term (the argument and evidence for how and why *sure* has become a legal term are discussed in a publication in preparation by the authors). Furthermore, since the judicial authorities fail to recognise that it has indeed become a legal term, judges do not perceive the need to give juries clear assistance in understanding its meaning in this specific context.

In keeping with the theme of this collection, though, in this chapter we take as given that *sure* has become a legal term and focus instead on a set of legal and judicial discursive practices that result in the apparently clear and ordinary *sure* standard becoming functionally opaque in English and Welsh courts. We first outline and exemplify these five discursive practices: legal synonymisation, legal formularisation, adversarial framing, judicial silencing and judicial distortion. We then apply this framework to a key case in the jurisprudence of *sure*: the trial judge's direction and subsequent 'clarification' in *R* v. *Majid* [2009].

9.2 Legal Synonymisation: '*Sure* Means the Same as *Beyond Reasonable Doubt*'

By legal synonymisation, we mean the active process of making an ordinary language word synonymous with an existing legal term. This synonymisation may be explicitly stipulated ('x means the same as y') or it may be implicit in the co-option of an ordinary word or phrase to serve a specific legal purpose previously conveyed with another term (e.g., the replacement of *beyond reasonable doubt* with *sure*). In the case of *sure* in the criminal standard of proof, we see both processes.

9.2.1 Explicit Legal Synonymisation

The synonymisation of *sure* with *beyond reasonable doubt* is often made explicit to both judges and juries. The main reason is that the traditional formula has refused to go away. Even though judicial authorities in England & Wales have been advocating the use of *sure* rather than of *beyond reasonable doubt* for over seventy years, there are at least three reasons for the survival of *beyond reasonable doubt*. Firstly, at no point have barristers ever been prevented from using the traditional formula in their speeches to the jury, and they frequently do so. The *Crown Court Compendium* (Judicial College 2023) states that where 'an advocate has referred to "beyond reasonable doubt", the jury should be told that this means the same thing as being sure' (5-3). This must seem very odd to jurors since they are superficially such different terms. Secondly, many judges (along with *Archbold*) still prefer the traditional term and some, like the trial judge in *R* v. *Majid* [2009] discussed later, keep using it despite the decades-old explicit recommendation not to use it. Finally, jurors are not blank slates. Many, if not most, will be familiar with the term *beyond reasonable doubt* as the term used to convey the threshold for guilt in criminal trials because they will have heard it being used, for example, in courtroom dramas. Many will thus be *expecting* the judge to use this term and they might even use it themselves in a lay sense to mean 'beyond *all* doubt' (as indicated in some general dictionaries) (Heffer 2006, 2007).

9.2.2 Implicit Legal Synonymisation

Nevertheless, since *sure* in the summing-up is being used in an attempt to convey the criminal standard of proof and since this legal concept is necessarily fixed, the very fact of using *sure* to convey the standard implicitly makes it a legal synonym of *beyond reasonable doubt*. Once *sure* becomes a legal synonym of the traditional formula, it not only ceases to be the everyday word understood by all jurors and takes on the specific technical meaning (a meaning considerably narrowed from the ordinary meaning of *sure* used in everyday life by the jurors to express confidence and/or certainty), but it also incorporates a number of specialised elements that diverge from its ordinary meaning. These elements are discussed in detail in a forthcoming article but can be briefly summarised here.

Firstly, while ordinary *sure* can refer to both a point on a scale ('I'm sure') and to the scale itself ('How sure are you?') and therefore derives its exact meaning in each instance of use from the context in which it is uttered and the surrounding linguistic co-text (the words preceding and following it), legal *sure*, by contrast, refers to a fixed point on a legal 'Satisfaction' scale: a point between the US legal standard *clear and convincing evidence* and the legal fictional standard *beyond a shadow of a doubt* or *absolutely certain*. Consequently, the common jury question 'How sure do we have to be?' makes no more sense than 'How much beyond a reasonable doubt do we have to be?'

Secondly, given that legal *sure* must represent a fixed point on a scale, it cannot, unlike ordinary *sure*, be a gradable adjective. Ordinary *sure*, when it is conveying 'certainty and confidence' (OED 'sure' III.9), is gradable across quite a large range and can be modified by adverbs such as *pretty*, *fairly* and *entirely*. However, in its legal use, *sure* cannot be more or less because that would necessarily move the intended meaning up or down a scale from its legally defined and fixed position. Just like the verdict itself (Guilty/Not Guilty), legal *sure* is a binary option (Sure/Not Sure).

Thirdly, while both ordinary and legal *sure* represent a psychological state of conviction, for legal *sure* that conviction needs to have been arrived at through reasoning about the evidence adduced at trial, rather than through prejudice, conjecture, overconfidence and so on. In everyday life, on the other hand, we are often 'sure' without firm evidential grounding (e.g., 'I'm sure you'll win the award', 'I'm sure the election was stolen'). Legal *sure*, then, cannot allow for the different psychological profiles of an underconfident or overconfident juror.

Finally, while ordinary *sure* generally indicates a subjective state of confidence, it can also indicate more objective forms of certainty (e.g., 'a sure sign'), particularly in negative constructions ('Scientists can't be 100% sure of anything'). Legal *sure*, on the other hand, can never indicate objective certainty. Legal *sure* lies on a subjective scale of satisfaction rather than an objective scale of probability. This is why it is legally possible to be 100% sure while not removing all possible doubt (Heffer 2007).

So simply by co-opting *sure* for use into the direction on the criminal standard of proof, the word has taken on a specific legal meaning that cannot be assumed to be understood by lay jurors.

9.3 Legal Formularisation: 'Satisfied So That You Are Sure'

By legal formularisation, we mean the tendency of the law to develop specific formulaic phrases in which all or most of the individual words are ordinary language, but where the overall phrase as a communicative unit is unique to legal language and serves a specific legal function. For example, while judges often insist that the phrase *beyond reasonable doubt* is ordinary language because each of its component terms is 'ordinary' or 'plain' (Heffer 2013), yet the empirical evidence shows that it is very much a legal term that is not understood by jurors (Horowitz and Kirkpatrick 1996) and partly this is because the collocation 'reasonable doubt' is not found outside the law, let alone the trigram 'beyond reasonable doubt'[2] (Heffer 2006).

Sure was always intended to replace the legal formulaic phrase *beyond reasonable doubt* with a plain English term. However, by embedding *sure* in a difficult legal formula, *satisfied so that you are sure*, the result was not to make the standard more transparent for jurors but to encourage juries to seek clarification of the term from the judge (e.g., *R* v. *Stephens* 2002, *R* v. *Mohammad* 2022). The Judicial Studies Board (now the Judicial College) eventually came to recognise the legal formulaic nature of the phrase and consequently recommended a simpler, plain English wording of the standard of proof in their *Specimen Directions*: simply 'the prosecution must make you sure' (Judicial Studies Board 1999). While this rightly places the burden of proof on the prosecution and is certainly composed of ordinary English words (Heffer 2006), it also implicitly accepts that the *sure* legal formula itself is one with which juries might struggle.

9.4 Adversarial Framing: 'You Must Be Absolutely Sure'

A judge's summing-up does not occur in isolation and needs to be seen in the context of a trial that is fundamentally adversarial. While judges set out the law for the jury and communicate the criminal standard as clearly, accurately and impartially as they can, barristers, working in an adversarial context, will exploit any chance to slant the meaning of *sure* in their favour. This is achieved by exploiting two rhetorical openings:

1. the lack of prohibition on the use of *beyond reasonable doubt* in opening and closing speeches; and
2. the fact that *sure*, and even the formula *satisfied so that you are sure*, are still considered ordinary language terms.

[2] 'Beyond doubt' is a common collocation, but it means a very different thing from the legal formula.

With regard to the first, barristers can exploit the fundamental lack of understanding of *beyond reasonable doubt* to make it sound like it is beyond **all** doubt (defence) or beyond a **sensible amount of** doubt (prosecution). This is helped by the resistance of the judicial authorities to defining *beyond reasonable doubt*. If there is no formal definition, there is considerable leeway for barristers to give an impression of the formula that makes it more favourable to the prosecution or defence.

With regard to the second, the lack of recognition that *sure* and *satisfied so that you are sure* have become legal terms with specific legal meanings allows barristers to exploit the many ordinary meanings of *sure* that judges themselves must expressly avoid. Thus, it is not uncommon, in their closing speeches, for barristers to exploit the ordinary language gradability of *sure*, with the prosecution telling the jury that 'you don't need to be 100% sure' and the defence responding that 'you need to be absolutely 100% sure' (Heffer 2007), while judges often appear to be reluctant to intervene to correct these legally wrong formulations.

So gradable understandings of *sure* become mixed with the legal stipulation of *sure* as non-gradable. While the reluctance to recognise *sure* as a legal term means that judges perhaps feel similarly reluctant to prevent barristers from modifying *sure* adversarially in their closing speeches, at the same time they feel the need to rectify the misconception by saying things like 'the prosecution need to make you sure. No more or less,' or 'sure cannot be modified,' without specifying 'in this particular legal context' (Heffer 2005).

9.5 Judicial Distortion: 'Sure Beyond Reasonable Doubt'

'Pathological distortion' occurs when 'the speaker has unintentionally misrepresented a state of affairs because he has not made a sufficient investigative investment in establishing and/or conveying the facts' (Heffer 2020: 189). In the absence of a clear legal definition of *sure*, judges can believe they are treading safely while actually distorting the meaning of the standard. Often these distortions come when trying to respond to the jury's 'dreaded questions' (McKeown 2022) on the standard of proof. One of the worst examples of distortion (Heffer 2017, *R v. Mohammad* 2022) is use of the unapproved, *ad hoc* legal formula 'sure beyond reasonable doubt.' This formula distorts the legal meaning of *sure* in several ways: it uses *sure* as the denominator of a particular confidence scale rather than as a point on the scale ('sure'); it qualifies *sure* and thus makes it gradable like *pretty sure* or *not entirely sure*; and, by making *sure* scalable and gradable, it fails to show that *sure* and *beyond reasonable doubt* are legal synonyms. Instead, *sure* represents the scale of satisfaction and *beyond reasonable doubt* the required point on that scale. The result is effectively an undefined *beyond reasonable doubt* instruction with the added complication of adding *sure* as a scale denominator. This could not be further from the intention of Lord Goddard to replace the traditional formula with an ordinary language term, and to understand it the jury must understand perfectly the meaning of *beyond reasonable doubt*.

Extraordinarily, to our knowledge, this particularly grievous and evidently common distortion – it occurs in both the infamous 'incompetent jury' *Vicky Pryce* case (Heffer 2017) and *R* v. *Mohammad* – has not been picked up by Court of Appeal judges. Other distortions of the criminal standard that *have* been discussed at Appeal include a trial judge explaining 'reasonable doubt' as 'the kind of doubts which you may have when trying to make up your minds what kind of motor car to buy' (*R* v. *Yap Ching* 1976: ¶10). *Yap Ching* discusses many such distortions, but rather than concluding, as one might expect, that there was a real need for judicial guidance on a clear and accurate explanation, it instead insisted that judges should stop trying to explain the legal formulae at all.

9.6 Judicial Silencing: 'I Can't Tell You More'

Our final legal discursive practice is judicial silencing. By judicial silencing we mean the tendency of higher courts to have a chilling effect on what trial judges feel they can safely say when directing the jury. As we have seen, the Court of Appeal has shown a notable resistance to permitting judges to explain the standard. Yet, it is difficult to see how lay jurors can arrive at the legal meaning of *sure* without careful explanation by the judge. It is clear that jurors are often aware that *sure* has a specific legal sense because otherwise they would not ask the judge, as they frequently do, 'How sure do we have to be?' And by asking that question, they must surely be making the judge aware that they need further explanation. Such questions to the judge were precisely what led Lord Goddard to intervene with respect to *beyond reasonable doubt*.

The effects of this judicial silencing are evident in actual judges' directions. For example, the only legally safe way of responding to the question 'How sure do we have to be?', like the question 'Can you define reasonable doubt?' in non-defining jurisdictions, is to refuse to answer the question at all (Heffer 2013, 2017). There are various ways in which this can be done. Some judges will explicitly say that the law does not allow them to help. Others claim that there is no *need* to explain because *sure* is an ordinary word. Still others will draw attention to *sure*'s legal synonymy with *beyond reasonable doubt*. And some will simply repeat the instruction: 'you just have to be sure.'

9.7 An Example of What Can Go Wrong: *R* v. *Majid* [2009]

An example of the combined dangers of legal synonymisation, legal formularisation, adversarial framing, judicial silencing and judicial distortion can be seen in the case of *R* v. *Majid* [2009]. The case facts are that the appellant drove his car into three men after an altercation and was found guilty, by a majority of 10 to 2, of dangerous driving and grievous bodily harm with intent. The grounds for the appeal related to the part of the judge's summing-up concerned with the standard of proof. The three specific issues were: whether the judge's initial 'beyond reasonable doubt' direction to the jury was appropriate; whether his subsequent clarification to the jury, which relied on the (legal) synonymy between *beyond reasonable doubt* and *sure*, was sufficient; and whether the distinction drawn by the judge between 'being sure' and 'being certain' was valid.

Regarding the first issue, the trial judge in his summing-up directed the jury, using a formulation he claimed he had always used, that 'You must be satisfied of guilt beyond all reasonable doubt' (*R* v. *Majid* 2009: ¶11). This direction is predicated on the erroneous assumption that jurors understand the legal term and Lord Justice Moses noted in his Appeal Court judgment that it 'not only does not comply with the Judicial Studies Board standard direction, but led to the very problem that the Judicial Studies Board direction is designed to avoid' (¶11), namely a question from the jury.

With respect to the second issue, the judge's erroneous direction led to the following very specific jury question:

> Q. If the evidence supports possible but very unlikely scenarios, which themselves would lead to a 'not guilty' verdict, does this exclude a 'beyond reasonable doubt' conclusion? There are concerns over how to interpret 'beyond reasonable doubt' — does this need to exclude all possible scenarios associated with 'not guilty'? (¶14)

What the jury were asking (perhaps not with legal clarity, but with the legal nous to standardise the formula, as we have done in this chapter, by removing the determiner *all*) is whether the defendant needs to be proven guilty with absolute certainty. They had clearly found themselves in precisely the situation of being satisfied beyond reasonable doubt envisioned by Lord Denning in *Miller* v. *Minister of Pensions* (1947), that is, one in which the jury are entertaining 'not guilty scenarios' that are technically 'possible but very unlikely' given the weight of the evidence. The judge simply needed to point out that they did not need to be absolutely certain to the point that they had no doubts whatsoever, but that if one of the scenarios they were considering seemed to be a reasonable one given the evidence, then in that case the prosecution would not have made them sure or proved the case beyond reasonable doubt.

Yet the judge, in discussing the question with counsel, said that 'he did not understand altogether what the jury meant,' as if they were asking something quite peculiar [*R* v. *Majid* 2009: ¶12]. When the jury returned to court, the judge delivered the following direction relating to legal synonymy:

> We have had further discussions about your question and both counsel are at one in asking me to add to what I said before in relation to the other meaning of 'beyond any reasonable doubt'.

> Juries are often directed by the judge during the course of the summing-up that they have to be satisfied of guilt so that they are sure of guilt. I chose not to give that direction but to give you the direction that you must be satisfied beyond any reasonable doubt. I think the three of us agreed that those two directions, 'satisfied so that you are sure' and 'satisfied beyond any reasonable doubt', *mean the same* but I am asked to tell you and direct you that you have to be 'satisfied so that you are sure' in the sense of being satisfied beyond any reasonable doubt of guilt before you can find the defendant guilty because 'sure' is easier to understand perhaps than 'being satisfied beyond any reasonable doubt.'
>
> But the two *mean the same*. 'Sure' and 'satisfied beyond any reasonable doubt' *mean the same*. [*R v. Majid* 2009: ¶14. Our emphasis]

We can see in this clarification four of the five legal-discursive practices identified in this chapter. Firstly, the judge explicitly establishes the **legal synonymy** between *sure* and *beyond reasonable doubt*. Unfortunately, though, repeating the mantra 'mean the same' three times does not actually magically convey the meaning of either legal formula. Secondly, he uses the **legal formulae** *satisfied so that you are sure* and *beyond (all/any) reasonable doubt* rather than trying to explain them in plain English, but he is also inconsistent in using these formulae. He uses 'sure' and 'satisfied so that you are sure' interchangeably and, while failing to use the recommended wording 'beyond reasonable doubt', he uses 'beyond *all* reasonable doubt' in his original direction and then 'beyond *any* reasonable doubt' here. The direction has a clear **adversarial framing**. The judge makes it clear that he is only providing the clarification because 'both counsel are at one in asking me to add' and, subsequently, 'I am asked to tell you and direct you that'. The pragmatic implication is that it would be better were he not to give this direction at all. The crucial legal synonymy itself is also framed in adversarial terms: not that the two terms legally mean the same, but 'I think the three of us agreed that those two directions [...] mean the same', as if the legal synonymy were contentious rather than being established almost sixty years earlier and reiterated in legal materials and judgments.

Finally, the judge manages to **distort** rather than clarify the direction. Firstly, it is an utter mystery what, in the first sentence, 'the other meaning of "beyond any reasonable doubt"' could possibly be. If *satisfied so that you are sure* and *beyond reasonable doubt* are legal synonyms, then, as the judge keeps saying, they 'mean the same'. The former is not the *other* legal meaning of *beyond reasonable doubt*: it is another way of expressing the *same* legal meaning. Secondly, while he subsequently states accurately that the legal synonymy is between the two legal formulae 'satisfied so that you are sure' and 'satisfied beyond any reasonable doubt,' by the end of this section of his response, he is equating the single word *sure* with the latter formula: '"Sure" and "satisfied beyond any reasonable doubt" mean the same'. But by only using the single word *sure*, he is increasing the likelihood that the jury will see this word as the ordinary language *sure* rather than legal *sure* with its specific set of meanings.

While the judge shows at the end of his clarification that he is aware that he might not have been as clear as he could have been – 'So I do not know whether that helps or whether that is more confusing but I hope that it is of further assistance' – Moses LJ, in his Appeal Court judgment, sees no problem whatsoever with the judge's 'clarification': 'It is plain that the judge was being astute to direct them, as he repeated on many occasions, that being satisfied beyond a reasonable doubt meant the same as being sure' (¶15).

On the other hand, Moses LJ *does* see a problem with the way the judge clarified with respect to the third issue, the distinction between being sure and being certain:

> The prosecution do not have to prove the case so that you are certain of guilt, and the reason I do not usually at all direct juries that they have to be sure of guilt is because, to my mind, juries can then become confused and think that 'sure' is the same as 'certain'. So I prefer to direct juries that they are to be satisfied beyond any reasonable doubt which is the same as being satisfied so that you are sure. [*R* v. *Majid* 2009: ¶14]

The real issue here is not that the judge uses the word *certain*, but that he fails to explain what he means by 'certain' in this context (i.e., the removal of any doubt whatsoever, however fanciful the scenario). He has not even indicated, as many judges used to do before it was frowned on by the Court of Appeal, that '*sure* is less than *certain*.' And he is still too focussed on the validity of his own practice ('the reason I do not', 'to my mind', 'I prefer') rather than conveying the standard clearly to the jury. However, Moses LJ is not concerned with such issues of clear communication. Instead, he is only exercised by the very fact that the judge attempted to draw a distinction between being sure and being certain. And it is here that we see our fifth legal-discursive practice: **judicial silencing**. Moses LJ's judgment is damning: '*This is not a direction that a judge should give* to the jury. It is likely only to confuse and it is difficult for anyone to articulate, in a clear and helpful manner, the difference between being sure and the difference between being certain (sic). *The distinction should therefore be avoided*'. (¶16. Our emphases)

The focus is entirely on the need *not* to direct in a certain way and to *avoid* making a distinction, rather than on how to communicate the crucial distinction between absolute certainty and beyond reasonable doubt. So, the Court of Appeal has **judicially silenced** a possible avenue for clearer explanation rather than risk potential misdirections. Yet it is somewhat puzzling that the judge's long 'mean the same' response to the jury's question, with its focus on his procedural struggles rather than on clarifying his direction, is not considered a misdirection, while it *is* considered a misdirection to point out (however ineffectively) that the standard does not require (absolute) certainty.

In summary, the jury asked the judge to clarify the meaning of *beyond reasonable doubt* and accurately identified the precise issue in interpreting the legal term in context, but the judge singularly failed to address the question and most likely further confused the jury. This was then exacerbated by the Court of Appeal judgment, which failed to recognise these issues but instead focussed on silencing judges with respect to a possible avenue for explanation. Unfortunately, this case of obfuscating the standard of proof through either *sure* or *beyond reasonable doubt* or both is by no means unique and has been discussed in relation to cases in both Australia (Heffer 2013) and the UK (Heffer 2017).

9.8 Conclusion

In this chapter, we have provided evidence of some everyday legal-discursive practices in England & Wales that work to obfuscate rather than clarify the meaning of the criminal standard of proof for the jury. This results in some clear practical conclusions.

Firstly, it is not sufficient simply to *stipulate* that henceforth an ordinary language word – here *sure* – will have a technical legal meaning and then expect a lay jury to understand that legal meaning without receiving any explanation except the drawing of attention to its synonymy with another difficult and equally unexplained legal term, here *beyond reasonable doubt*. There needs to be greater awareness within the legal community that by incorporating ordinary words and phrases into specific patterns of legal discourse, they will become legal formulaic phrases, the overall meaning of which is different from the meaning of their once-ordinary parts.

One should similarly not recommend legal directions without considering the overall adversarial context in which jury instruction takes place: if advocates are permitted to use the traditional term or are allowed to distort the legal meaning of *sure* so that it conforms better with the ordinary meanings of *sure*, then the judge's task in trying to clarify the legal meaning of *sure* while denying that it has a technical legal meaning is virtually impossible. If we have criticised judges' discursive practices, it is with the sympathetic understanding that they are in an invidious position.

Next, with regard to judicial silencing, as has been recognised by others (e.g., Keane & McKeown 2019), it is somewhat bizarre to conclude from a few misdirections resulting from judges' sincere attempts to clarify the meaning of these legal terms for jurors, that it is better not to try to assist the jury at all. Educators do not have the privilege of being able to say, when struggling to explain a complex concept to their students, that given that it is difficult to explain, it is better not to even try. Nor would a barrister adopt such an attitude with respect to expert evidence. There is almost universal acceptance, outside very limited legal circles in the UK, Australia and some US jurisdictions, that the criminal standard of proof needs to be explained as clearly as possible to juries.

Finally, given the evidence of unwitting judicial distortion of the standard, the time has perhaps come for a template explanation of the criminal standard that truly explains in simple terms the essential elements of this fundamental legal concept that underlies the rule of law (Heffer 2006; Keane & McKeown 2019). *Sure* is currently failing to serve its purpose of communicating the criminal standard of proof clearly to juries, with potentially grave consequences for defendants and for society at large, but the solution is not to return to an unexplained *beyond reasonable doubt* direction but to formulate a direction that can genuinely be understood by all.

References

Archbold, J. F. and Lucraft, M. (2025). *Archbold Criminal Pleading, Evidence and Practice*. London: Sweet & Maxwell.

Clermont, K. M. and Sherwin, E. (2002). 'A comparative view of standards of proof'. *The American Journal of Comparative Law*, 50, 243–276.

Darbyshire, P., Maughan, A. and Stewart, A. (2001). 'What can the English legal system learn from jury research published up to 2001'. *New Law Journal*, 150, 1439–1507.

Heffer, C. (2005). *The Language of Jury Trial: A Corpus-Aided Analysis of Legal-Lay Discourse*. Basingstoke: Palgrave Macmillan.

Heffer, C. (2006). 'Beyond "reasonable doubt": The criminal standard of proof instruction as communicative act'. *The International Journal of Speech, Language and the Law*, 13(2), 159–188.

Heffer, C. (2007). 'The language of conviction and the convictions of certainty: Is "sure" an impossible standard of proof?' *International Commentary on Evidence* 5(1): Art.5.

Heffer, C. (2013). 'Communication and magic: Authorized voice, legal-linguistic habitus and the recontextualization of "beyond reasonable doubt", in Conley, J. M., Heffer, C. and Rock, F. (eds.), *Legal-Lay Communication: Textual Travels in the Law*. New York: Oxford University Press, 206–225.

Heffer, C. (2017). 'When voices fail to carry: Voice projection and the case of the "dumb" jury', in Leung, J. and Durant, A. (eds.), *Meaning and Power in the Language of Law*. Cambridge: Cambridge University Press, 207–235.

Heffer, C. (2020). *All Bullshit and Lies? Insincerity, Irresponsibility and the Judgment of Untruthfulness*. New York: Oxford University Press.

Heffer, C. (2026). 'The golden rule and the golden thread: The ethics of communicating the criminal standard of proof', in Nick, I. and Blewitt, K. (eds.), *The Routledge Handbook of Ethics in Forensic Linguistics*. London: Routledge, 206–224.

Horowitz, I. A. and Kirkpatrick, L. C. (1996). 'A concept in search of a definition: The effects of reasonable doubt instructions on certainty of guilt standards and jury verdicts'. *Law and Human Behavior*, 20(6), 655–670.

Judicial Studies Board. (1999). *Crown Court Benchbook: Specimen Directions*. London: Judicial Studies Board.

Judicial College. (2023). *Crown Court Compendium Part 1: Jury and Trial Management and Summing Up*. Judicial College. Accessed 12 August 2025.

Kagehiro, D. K. and Stanton, W. C. (1985). 'Legal vs. quantified definitions of standards of proof'. *Law and Human Behavior*, 9(2), 159–178.

Keane, A. and McKeown, P. (2019). 'Time to abandon "Beyond Reasonable Doubt" and "Sure": The case for a new direction on the criminal standard and why and how it should be used'. *Criminal Law Review*, 2019(6), 505–527.
McKeown, P. (2022). 'Dreaded questions, doubtful answers and the trouble with "sure"'. *New Law Journal*, 13–14 (29 July), 7989.
Montgomery, J. W. (1998). 'The criminal standard of proof'. *New Law Journal*, 148(6837), 582–585.
Solan, L. M. (1999). 'Refocusing the burden of proof in criminal cases: Some doubt about reasonable doubt'. *Texas Law Review*, 78(1), 105–147.
Zander, M. (2000). 'The criminal standard of proof: How sure is sure?' *New Law Journal*, 150(6596), 1517–1524.

Cases Cited

Miller *v*. Minister of Pensions [1947] 2 All E.R. 372 at 373; 63 T.L.R. 474
R *v*. Majid [2009] EWCA Crim 2563
R *v*. Mohammad [2022] EWCA Crim 380
R *v*. Stephens [2002] EWCA Crim 1529
R *v*. Summers [1952] 36 Cr. App. R. 14
R *v*. Yap Chuan Ching [1976] 63 Cr App R 7
Walters *v*. R [1969] 2 AC 26

10 Signposting Topics in the Cross-Examination of Vulnerable Witnesses

David Wright, John Jackson, Jonathan Doak, Candida Saunders and Debbie Cooper

10.1 Introduction

Cross-examination is regarded as 'beyond doubt the greatest legal machine ever invented for the discovery of the truth' (Wigmore 1940: §1367). Generally, cross-examination is seen to have two main aims: 'to weaken the case for the other side and to establish facts which are favourable to the case for the cross-examiner' (Du Cann 1964: 95). Questioning during cross-examination can be challenging for witnesses, and this is particularly the case for vulnerable witnesses. The Criminal Practice Directions, which govern the procedure to be followed in criminal courts, specify that accommodating the needs of vulnerable people 'may require a radical departure from traditional cross-examination' (CrimPRC(23)90(b), section 6.1.8). Recent research in law, linguistics, psychology and criminology has highlighted that cross-examination can be detrimental to truth-finding and to the rights and interests of vulnerable victims and witnesses (Doak et al. 2021: 35), and there have been calls for cross-examination to shift away from its traditional adversarial roots and towards a more reliable 'forensic' tool for testing a witness's evidence (e.g., Henderson 2014). One such change that is recommended by professional guidelines for advocates is the need to clearly introduce new and changing topics during questioning, to avoid any confusion caused by rapidly shifting topics. Drawing on transcripts of cross-examinations in criminal trials in the UK and Ireland, this chapter provides the first linguistic analysis of how this signposting is performed by advocates when questioning vulnerable witnesses and reveals some of the interactional issues that arise as a result of this signposting. The chapter shows how linguistic theory, methods and analysis can shed light on cross-examination in practice and demonstrates the value of linguistic research in providing evidence-based professional guidance for improving the experiences of vulnerable witnesses.

Funding statement: The research reported in this chapter was undertaken as part of a project funded by the Nuffield Foundation between 2020 and 2024.

10.2 Cross-Examination of Vulnerable Witnesses

It has been increasingly acknowledged that the rigour and combative nature of traditional cross-examination can be bruising and distressing for vulnerable witnesses (Jacobson 2017: 15). Vulnerability is not a condition inherent only to certain groups or individuals but is a condition to which we are all subject (Jackson et al. 2024: 22). However, legislation across UK jurisdictions designates the term 'vulnerable' to particular categories of witness who are eligible for 'special measures' (Youth Justice and Criminal Evidence Act 1999 ss 16–17, Criminal Evidence (NI) Order 1999 arts 4–5, Criminal Procedure (Scotland) Act 1995 s271(1)). Special measures are procedural adjustments to enable witnesses to give their 'best evidence' (UK Ministry of Justice 2022) and include screening the witness from the accused in court, witnesses giving evidence by live link or evidence being video-recorded and played to the court, examination of a witness through an intermediary and the use of communication aids (see Marchant 2017). Under such statutory definitions, 'vulnerable' witnesses include children under 18; elderly and frail witnesses; witnesses with a mental or physical disability, or significant impairment of intelligence and social functioning; and witnesses who may suffer fear and distress such as victims of sex offences.

Forensic and legal linguistics research has analysed the strategies used by lawyers to control cross-examination, such as the use of specific question types (Woodbury 1984; Gibbons 2003; Tkačuková 2010), reformulation of witnesses' words (Cotterill 2004), quoting witnesses' earlier testimony back to them (Johnson 2013) and manipulating witnesses' responses until they give a response preferred by the cross-examiner (Matoesian 2005). Various elements of traditional cross-examination are problematic when cross-examining vulnerable witnesses, including a difficulty in understanding legal terminology (Crawford & Bull 2006), suggestive, tagged or structurally complex questions (Andrews & Lamb 2017), or questions that relate to abstract concepts or aim to elicit memory reports (Morrison et al. 2021). The aspect of cross-examination that this chapter is chiefly concerned with is topic management and in particular the explicit changing of topics. Conversation analysis research in institutional contexts has long shown that topic control and unilateral changes of topic characterise power-asymmetric interactions (e.g., Ainsworth-Vaughn 1992). Although it is acknowledged by forensic linguists that topic control is a major tool available to cross-examiners in exerting interactional power over witnesses in legal settings (Conley et al. 2019: 30; Grieshofer 2024: 10), the discursive mechanisms by which this is achieved have received little linguistic attention (although see Heydon 2005 on police interviewing).

Topic management and rapid topic changes can be used strategically by advocates to exercise interactional power over the witness and to restrict the time that the jury has to process the details of an ongoing narrative (Aldridge & Luchjenbroers 2007: 95). However, sudden switching from one topic to another can easily confuse and disorientate a vulnerable witness (Davies et al. 2010: 353). One possible safeguard against this is for counsel to 'signpost' the topics that they are going to ask questions about and to signal when they are changing topics (Henry et al. 2021: 1395). The Inns of Court College of Advocacy national training guide to cross-examining vulnerable people and children (The Council of the Inns of Court 2022) outlines '20 principles of questioning', one of which (Principle 8) implores advocates to signpost a new topic, stating that 'signposting is important to help vulnerable people and children focus attention and remain focused'. Similarly, The Advocate's Gateway, which produces good practice toolkits for advocates when questioning witnesses or defendants with communication needs, encourages the signalling of topic changes as this gives the witness transition time to focus on the upcoming topic and questions (The Advocate's Gateway 2023: 7). This study aims to find out whether this guidance is being followed in practice, to examine the linguistic means by which counsel signpost topics and topic shifts and to discuss some potentially unforeseen consequences of signposting.

10.3 Metadiscourse

This chapter adopts the discourse-analytic concept of *metadiscourse* as a means by which to understand and interpret the signposting identified in cross-examination. 'Metadiscourse' refers to how people use language out of 'consideration for our readers or hearers based on our estimation of how best we can help them process and comprehend what we are saying' (Hyland 2017: 17). In his model of metadiscourse, Hyland (2005) distinguishes between *interactive* and *interactional* dimensions. The interactive dimension of metadiscourse is concerned with linguistic resources that are used to help guide the listener or reader through the text and includes features such as *transitions* (e.g., 'in addition'), *frame markers* (e.g., 'finally'), *endophoric markers* (e.g., 'noted above'), *evidentials* (e.g., 'according to X') and *code glosses* (e.g., 'in other words'). The interactional dimension, meanwhile, relates to language that aims to involve the reader in the text and make the writer/speaker's views explicit. It includes *hedges* (e.g., 'perhaps'), *boosters* (e.g., 'definitely'), *attitude markers* (e.g., 'unfortunately'), *self-mentions* (e.g., 'I', 'we') and *engagement markers* (e.g., 'you can see that'). Previous linguistic studies of metadiscourse in legal contexts have examined interactive and interactional features in international legislation (Orts Lopis 2017), opening statements (Chaemsaithong 2014) and court judgments (McAuliffe & Trklja 2019). The analysis of metadiscursive practices in the examination of witnesses in court has received comparatively less attention in the literature, though Cavalieri (2011) analyses metadiscourse in the questions asked of witnesses in UK public inquiries. The current study therefore breaks new ground by analysing metadiscourse in the questions put to (vulnerable) witnesses during cross-examination in criminal trials. The findings of this analysis have the potential to impact and inform professional guidance, court practice and the experience of vulnerable witnesses in court.

10.4 Data and Approach

The corpus analysed in this chapter contains 56 cross-examinations from 23 trials that took place across 6 Crown Court Centres in the UK and Ireland between 2020 and 2023. It includes the cross-examination of 29 complainants, 18 defendants, 8 prosecution witnesses and 1 defence witness. There are 40 advocates represented in the data, most of whom (*n* = 28) appear only once; 9 advocates appear in 2 cross-examinations, 2 cross-examine 3 witnesses and 1 cross-examines 4. The trials all involve serious offences including assault, child sexual abuse, murder and rape. Of the 56 witnesses, 34 are vulnerable witnesses and 22 are 'non-vulnerable' witnesses. Witnesses with a range of vulnerabilities are represented in our data, including child witnesses (under 18), witnesses with significant impairment of intelligence and social functioning, complainants in sexual offence trials, victims of serious crime and relatives of victims of serious crime. Most of the vulnerable witnesses are complainants (*n* = 29), but there are 3 other vulnerable prosecution witnesses and 2 vulnerable defendants in the data. The transcripts used in this corpus are the official transcripts provided by the relevant Crown Court Centre and produced by professional transcribers and can therefore be considered accurate accounts of what was said in court (see Tkačuková 2015: 151; although see Walker and Haworth, this volume). The full corpus contains 10,553 cross-examination questions and 189,757 words.

This analysis applies a corpus-assisted approach to discourse study (CADS). This approach involves the use of specialist computer software and processes to analyse large bodies of language use to uncover quantifiable linguistic patterns (see Baker 2023: 1) and has been fruitfully applied in previous socio-legal research (e.g. Tkačuková 2020). The first step in this process was to compute the most frequent 3-word 'n-grams' (3-word strings) in the questions posed to all witnesses in our corpus, generated by the corpus software *SketchEngine* (Kilgarriff et al. 2014). The next stage involved identifying those n-grams that act as 'lexical bundles' (Biber et al. 2021: 982), which 'help language users carry out particular discourse functions' in a given context (Gray 2016: 33). Although they are often not complete structural units, 3-word lexical bundles essentially reflect 'extended

Table 10.1 *Distribution of 'to ask you', 'i want to' and 'going to ask' across the corpus*

	Frequency	Cross-examinations (n = 56)	Advocates (n = 40)
to ask you	162	38 (67.86%)	32 (80.00%)
i want to	92	28 (50.00%)	25 (62.50%)
going to ask	82	27 (48.21%)	10 (25.00%)

collocational association' and are much more common than longer sequences (Biber et al. 2021: 984). The top 20 most frequent n-grams in the corpus contained 3 lexical bundles that serve signposting functions in questions: *to ask you, I want to* and *going to ask*, which were found to be used in most cross-examinations and by most advocates in our data (Table 10.1). There is overlap between the 3 bundles; namely, *to ask you* is part of the longer sequences *I want to ask you* (n = 35) and *I am/I'm going to ask* (n = 80).

It should be noted that there are instances in the data where advocates signpost changing topics in other ways that do not rely on these bundles, saying things such as 'moving onto a different topic', 'the next topic is …' or simply just 'new topic'. However, these explicit references to 'topic(s)' are much less common. There are only 22 instances of the word 'topic' used in this way in the data, and only 5 advocates use such signposts more than once. Therefore, the metadiscursive lexical bundles analysed in this chapter are the most common way in which signposting is performed by lawyers in our data. The analysis focuses on the lexical bundles: *to ask you, I want to* and *going to ask*. It begins by demonstrating the ways in which advocates use these metadiscursive devices to signpost topics in the questioning of vulnerable witnesses before moving to examine some of the interactional problems that arise from doing so.

10.5 Analysis

10.5.1 Metadiscursive Signposting in Cross-Examination

In our data, signposting sequences are more common in the questions to vulnerable witnesses than they are in the questions to non-vulnerable witnesses (Table 10.2). This indicates a recognition from advocates that they serve a particular function in helping vulnerable people during cross-examination and is in line with the recommendations from The Inns of Court College of Advocacy and The Advocates Gateway.

Examples 10.1 and 10.2 show how these sequences are used to signpost (new) topics.

Table 10.2 *Signposting sequences in the corpus (freq ≥ 2)*

Lexical bundle/signposting sequence	Frequency	Vulnerable witnesses	Non-vulnerable witnesses
I'm going to ask you	53	45	8
I want to ask you	35	21	14
I'd like to ask you	10	1	9
I'm now going to ask you	7	7	0
I now want to ask you	5	5	0
I just want to ask you	4	2	2
I'm just going to ask you	4	3	1
I wanted to ask you	4	2	2
I am going to ask you	4	3	1
me to ask you	3	1	2
I just wanted to ask you	3	3	0
I'm not going to ask you	2	2	0
have to ask you	4	4	0
questions to ask	2	2	0
I need to ask you	2	0	2
Total	**142**	**101**	**41**

Example 10.1 Cross-examination of a complainant in a rape trial

1 Q. *I want to ask you* a little bit about drugs.
2 A. Okay.
(transcript ref: A035a)

Example 10.2 Cross-examination of a complainant in a historical sexual abuse trial

1 Q. Well you know *I'm going to ask you* some questions on behalf of
2 [defendant name] and hope to deal with them in order of topics so that
3 you know beforehand the kind of area I am going to ask you about. It's
4 very important if you're confused by a question or you don't understand
5 it, please say so and I'll just rephrase it
6 A. Okay
(transcript ref: A040a)

These lexical bundles have a discourse-organising function as 'topic introduction/focus' bundles reflecting relationships between prior and coming discourse (Biber et al. 2004: 391). First and foremost, they serve an *interactive* function, intending to guide the witness through the interaction and to point the witness in the direction that the questions are heading (cf. Hyland 2005: 75). They show counsel's awareness of the witnesses' interactional needs and 'shape and constrain' the discourse to meet those needs (cf. Hyland 2005: 49). More specifically, these signposts are *frame markers* that 'signal text boundaries or elements of schematic text structure' (Hyland 2005: 51). Frame markers are oriented towards the listener and explicitly sequence the interaction, order stages and shift topics and can be used to *preview* 'things that will immediately happen as well as things that will follow later' (McKeown 2021: 226). Their scope is reflected in the extracts earlier; whereas in Example 10.1 counsel signals that they are imminently about to embark on questions on the topic of drugs, in Example 10.2 the signposting occurs at the beginning of the questioning and sets out a preview for the full cross-examination.

Although the frame markers in counsel's questions are ostensibly used to signpost topics and topic shifts, they also 'signal an interactive relationship' with interlocutors, 'indicating that their text processing needs are being taken into account' (Hyland & Zou 2020: 32). By involving the witness in the discourse in this way, frame markers reach into the *interactional* dimension of metadiscourse. 'I'm going to ask you' and 'I want to ask you' might both be considered *engagement markers* (Hyland 2005: 151). Counsel explicitly address the witnesses as participants in the questioning (through the pronoun 'you'), acknowledge their expectations of inclusion in the discourse and, in doing so, build a relationship with them. Engaging in interpersonal work with vulnerable witnesses can create the conditions that allow for the elicitation of the best evidence while minimising the stressfulness of the courtroom experience. These lexical bundles are therefore not only used by counsel to signpost new and changing topics but also give the impression of mutual engagement with witnesses, 'pulling them along' (Hyland 2005: 52) as the questioning unfolds.

10.5.2 Issues with Signposting in Practice

Examples 10.1 and 10.2 are both from cross-examinations of vulnerable adult witnesses. The same signposts are also used in the cross-examination of child witnesses, as in Example 10.3, which is taken from the opening exchange in a cross-examination of a 12-year-old complainant. Note that the transcription conventions used in the examples are those of the official transcribers. The double dash mark (--) indicates an incomplete turn.

Example 10.3 Cross-examination of a child complainant (12 years old) in a grooming case

Q. Another thing I'm going to do is I'm going to tell you what topic *I want to ask you* about before I ask the questions, and I'll try and give you a reminder of what was happening at the time in case it helps you to remember to answer the questions, okay. So, *I'm going to ask you* questions in four different topics, and all of the questions are about things that happened in [year]. The topics are, firstly, how you and [defendant] met; secondly, a police chase; thirdly, a visit from your social

8 worker; and then, finally, the contact that you had with [defendant], all
9 right. Good. So, the first topic is how you and [defendant] met. So, think back --
10 A. It was in (Inaudible) --
11 Q. I'll ask you the question, and then you answer it, and then that's how,
12 hopefully, we will move forward. So, think back, please, to [year] when all
13 of this happened when you were [age], all right. First of all, *I'm going to*
14 *ask* questions about how you and [defendant] met, and I want to start
15 with a few questions about social media, okay. What types of social
16 media did you use in [date]?
17 A. Facebook and Snapchat

(transcript ref: A006a)

This extract shows a lengthy introduction in which counsel previews the full cross-examination, outlining the topics that they are going to ask questions about and the order in which those topics are going to be covered. Following the preview, counsel explicitly signposts the first topic (line 9), and the witness begins to respond before counsel has asked a question. Although we cannot be sure, we might presume that the witness was going to tell counsel when or where they met the defendant ('It was in --'). The witness is offering an answer to the *signpost*, rather than a *question*. This causes counsel to interrupt the witness, emphasising the question-answer sequence that must be followed, and then repeat the signpost. Here, the witness follows the turn-taking conventions of everyday conversation (giving a desired response to an albeit indirect request for information), rather than the interactional expectations of cross-examination (waiting for counsel to ask a question). In this example, counsel could have allowed the witness to cooperate in the way that she tried to, being somewhat more flexible in the strict question-answer sequence they enforce. Alternatively, or additionally, it may be that listing all of the topics to be covered in the cross-examination, which leads to a lengthy preamble and repetition of signposts, may in fact not be of help to the witness who cannot predict the lawyer's agenda (see Henderson's (2014: 13) criticism of enumerating topics in this way). It might be argued that if this 'previewing' of topics imposes rigidity at the expense of the witness, as in Example 10.3, then it is best avoided. After all, the purpose of signposting is to ameliorate, not exacerbate, the challenges of cross-examination for vulnerable witnesses.

Furthermore, one of the assumptions built into the notion of signposting is that one topic is signposted at a time. This is to avoid confusing the witness and will 'help vulnerable people and children focus attention and remain focused' (The Council of the Inns of Court 2022: 10). The previewing of all of the topics at once at the outset of questioning would seem to flout this assumption. Similarly, Example 10.4 presents an example in which more than one topic is signposted as the cross-examination unfolds.

Example 10.4 Cross-examination of a child defendant (12 years old) with ADHD in a GBH with intent case

Q. You can probably tell, [defendant name], that I'm moving on to the topic of asking you about the clip and the incident, all right
A. Yes
Q. That's what *I'm going to ask you* about. So, we're getting into what happened on [date], all right
A. Yeah
Q. While that's being set up, I can ask some other questions. Did you lose your temper badly?
A. Yes
Q. You completely lost it.
A. Yes.
Q. When you were looking at [complainant name], you could see that you'd hurt him.
A. Yes.
(Nine questions and answers removed for space)
Q. Did you mean to hurt him?
A. Not to this extent, no.
Q. Did you mean to hurt him at all?
A. (Pause). Yes.
Q. Did you mean to injure him at all?
A. (Pause). It wasn't -- yes.
Q. Why did you go so far then?
A. I didn't realise how far I went.
Q. Who was doing the kicking and the stamping?
A. Me
(six questions and answers removed for space)
Q. Thank you very much, we're ready.
Judge: [Defendant name], do you want to look at the screen that's closest to you. Tell me if you can see it properly and, if you can't, let me know and we'll pick another screen, all right.
(Video footage played)
Q. Thank you. You watched that at the start, but not throughout. Is that fair?
A. I don't want to watch it.
(transcript ref: A001)

At the start of this extract, which occurs about a quarter of the way through the cross-examination, counsel clearly signposts a change of topic, but in doing so they mention two topics: (1) 'the clip' and (2) 'the incident'. To make matters (more) confusing, counsel follows up this signpost by stating, 'That's what I'm going to ask you about'. It is unclear here whether 'that', a demonstrative pronoun usually used with singular nouns, refers to the clip or the incident. This is a potential source of difficulty for the witness, who is a child defendant with ADHD (Attention Deficit Hyperactivity Disorder). However, the witness responds positively to both signposts and does not appear to signal any difficulty.

The 'clip' here refers to footage of the assault that the defendant was accused of committing and that was recorded on a mobile phone. This footage was to be played to the court, but, as can be seen in Example 10.4, the playback caused some technical difficulties, and counsel decided to carry on asking questions 'while that's being set up'. There are 22 questions asked and answered between the signpost and the video footage being played, all of which are evidentially significant questions about the defendant's intention to hurt the complainant, some of which are shown in Example 10.4. When the footage was eventually played, the defendant watched the start of the video but then turned away and when asked about it, said 'I don't want to watch it' (line 31). We might assume that upon first mention of the video, the defendant knew that he did not want to see what it showed. It is therefore fair to deduce, perhaps, that the child defendant's attention may be divided when answering highly evidentially significant questions about one signposted topic (the incident) as they anticipate questions about another signposted topic (the clip that they do not want to watch). That is to say, rather than counsel *focusing* the child witness' attention on a single topic, the signposting of two topics at once may in fact *distract* them at a key point in their evidence, undermining their ability to give their best evidence.

Example 10.5 presents a separate issue in which counsel signposts a topic but then asks a question that is not explicitly related to that topic.

Example 10.5 Cross-examination of a complainant in a rape case

Q. *I'm going to ask you* about leaving the club now
A. Okay
Q. Do you agree that there is a big difference between remembering something and consenting to something happening?
A. (Pause). I'm not -- I'm not sure what you mean.
Q. Putting it another way, just because you don't remember something, you can still have been capable of making a free choice to do it, can't you?
A. I'm not sure I agree because if you're not in a state to control your body, or your actions, or your decisions, then you're not in a state to consent.
Q. So, if you can't control your body or your actions.
A. I couldn't even walk.

(transcript ref: A035a)

One of the fundamental points underpinning the usefulness of topic signposting is that the questions that follow should relate to the topic signposted. That does not happen in Example 10.5, where the topic that counsel signposts is about leaving a nightclub, but the leading question asked is an evidentially significant one about the nature of consent. The question itself, 'do you agree…', is highly suggestive and coercive, restricting the witnesses' answer to 'yes' or 'no' and strongly favouring a compliant response (Henry et al. 2021: 1400). 'Do you agree' questions are challenging for witnesses due to the amount of pressure that they place on them to agree with the proposition of the question (Gibbons 2008: 123). Preceding this question with a signpost that does not signal the topics of consent or memory may have a disarming effect on the witness. In turn, following this signpost with a question directly related to the topic that was signposted may exacerbate the question's suggestiveness; its unexpectedness may amplify the pressure on the witness to agree. Indeed, this sequence does cause a problem for the witness who becomes confused (line 5) and this is followed by a more combative exchange on the important difference between remembering and consenting. Signposting a topic and then asking a question that is seemingly unrelated to that topic, particularly significantly evidential ones (such as about the nature of consent), may have the same effect as suddenly shifting topics, a practice that confuses witnesses and which signposting is supposed to avoid.

Finally, there are instances in the cross-examinations wherein an ostensibly frame-marking lexical bundle is used, but it does not serve a discourse-organising function, as shown in Example 10.6.

Example 10.6 Cross-examination of a complainant in a historic child sexual abuse case

Q. *I'm going to ask*, [witness name], when you say grazed on your hands and your knees, do you accept that you told the police you only had grazes on your knees? You never mentioned grazes on your hands?
A. If you're telling me that I didn't say on my hands…
Q. Sorry, sorry, I want … sorry, [witness name], I want be, I want to be fair to you. Sorry, you did mention your hands, okay, so you did mention your hands. Now, as far as any medical treatment is concerned, you didn't receive any medical treatment for that?
A. No

(transcript ref: C012)

In this case, the lexical bundle *I'm going to ask* does not signpost a topic shift. Rather, it simply serves as a preface to a restrictive and suggestive 'do you accept' question. Because it does not serve its signposting frame-marking function as we have seen elsewhere in the analysis, it is rendered an unnecessary part of an already lengthy leading question. Questions become more complex when they are 'padded with redundancies' (Plotnikoff & Woolfson 2015: 194), and so instead of making questioning easier to follow for witnesses by signposting topics, attempts to give the *impression* of signposting can actually lead to questions becoming more complex, convoluted and confusing.

10.6 Conclusion

Both academic literature and recent professional guidance on cross-examining vulnerable witnesses have recommended that advocates should clearly signpost topics and topic changes during questioning. This moves away from the strategy in traditional cross-examination where sudden changes of topic can be used to confuse or 'trip up' a witness. This chapter has identified that there are recurring metadiscursive lexical bundles that advocates use to perform this signposting function, namely, *I'm going to ask you* and *I want to ask you*. These sequences are more common in the cross-examination of vulnerable witnesses than non-vulnerable witnesses, suggesting that advocates are aware of their usefulness in guiding the vulnerable person through the questioning. However, this analysis has also revealed issues that can arise in the interaction as a result of ineffective or inconsistent signposting and some important considerations that should be made regarding their use:

- Counsel's intentions to signpost topics should not unduly interfere with questioning, should not place extra restrictions on witnesses or come at the expense of cooperative witness responses.
- Signposting more than one topic at a time can distract a witness. Rather than focusing their attention, this leads to witnesses answering questions about one topic while anticipating questions about another. This includes previewing several or all of the different topics to be covered at the start of a cross-examination, from which witnesses may derive no assistance whatsoever (Henderson 2014: 13).
- Asking questions that are not obviously or explicitly related to the topic that has just been signposted can exacerbate the effect of already difficult questions and can cause interactional problems for the witness.
- In some instances, phrases (or lexical bundles) typically associated with topic signposting are used but serve no organising function. In these cases, they instead 'pad' questions with 'redundancies' (Plotnikoff & Woolfson 2015: 194), making them longer and more complex for the witness than is necessary.

This analysis has been the first to closely examine the way(s) in which advocates signpost topics when they are cross-examining vulnerable witnesses. It is hoped that the analysis presented here can inform more specific and nuanced guidance and recommendations for practitioners and can demonstrate the potential for incorporating linguistic theory and analysis into training and court practice. Examples such as those shown here can be used to provide an empirical evidence base for professional good practice guidance. At the very least, this analysis has shown that simply recommending to advocates that 'topics should be signposted' is not enough.

References

Ainsworth-Vaughn, N. (1992). 'Topic transitions in physician-patient interviews: power, gender, and discourse change'. *Language in Society*, 21(3), 409–426. https://doi.org/10.1017/S0047404500015505

Aldridge, M. and Luchjenbroers, J. (2007). 'Linguistic manipulations in legal discourse: framing questions and "smuggling" information'. *International Journal of Speech, Language and the Law*, 14(1), 85–107. https://doi.org/10.1558/ijsll.v14i1.85

Andrews, S. J. and Lamb, M. E. (2017). 'The structural linguistic complexity of lawyers' questions and children's responses in Scottish criminal courts'. *Child Abuse & Neglect*, 65, 182–193. https://doi.org/10.1016/j.chiabu.2017.01.022

Baker, P. (2023). *Using Corpora in Discourse Analysis* (2nd ed.). London: Bloomsbury.

Biber, D., Conrad, S. and Cortes, V. (2004). 'If you look at…: lexical bundles in university teaching and textbooks'. *Applied Linguistics*, 25(3), 371–405. https://doi.org/10.1093/applin/25.3.371

Biber, D., Johansson, S., Leech, G. N., Conrad, S. and Finegan, E. (2021). *Grammar of Spoken and Written English.* Amsterdam/Philadelphia: John Benjamins.

Cavalieri, S. (2011). 'The role of metadiscourse in counsel's questions', in Wagner, A. and Cheng, L. (eds.), *Exploring Courtroom Discourse: The Language of Power and Control.* London: Routledge, 79–110.

Chaemsaithong, K. (2014). 'Interactive patterns of the opening statement in criminal trials: a historical perspective'. *Discourse Studies*, 16(3), 347–364. https://doi.org/10.1177/1461445613508900

Conley, J. M., O'Barr, W. M. and Conley Riner, R. (2019). *Just Words: Law, Language, and Power* (3rd ed.). Chicago: Chicago University Press.

Cotterill, J. (2004). 'Collocation, connotation, and courtroom semantics: lawyers' control of witness testimony through lexical negotiation'. *Applied Linguistics*, 25(4), 513–537. https://doi.org/10.1093/applin/25.4.513

Crawford, C. and Bull, R. (2006). 'Teenagers' difficulties with keywords regarding the criminal court process'. *Psychology, Crime & Law*, 12(6), 653–667. https://doi.org/10.1080/10236190500489970

Davies, E., Henderson, E. and Hanna, K. (2010). 'Facilitating children to give best evidence: are there better ways to challenge children's testimony?' *Criminal Law Journal*, 34(6), 347–362.

Doak, J., Jackson, J., Saunders, C., Wright, D., Gómez Fariñas, B. and Durdiyeva, S. (2021). *Cross-Examination in Criminal Trials towards a Revolution in Best Practice? A Report for the Nuffield Foundation.* Nottingham: Nottingham Law School, Nottingham Trent University. Available at: https://irep.ntu.ac.uk/id/eprint/44924/1/1497281_Doak.pdf

Du Cann, R. (1964). *The Art of the Advocate.* New York: Penguin.

Gibbons, J. (2003). *Forensic Linguistics: An Introduction to Language in the Justice System.* London: Wiley-Blackwell.

Gibbons, J. (2008). 'Questioning in common law criminal courts', in Gibbons, J. and Turell, M. T. (eds.), *Dimensions of Forensic Linguistics.* Amsterdam/Philadelphia: John Benjamins, 115–130.

Gray, B. (2016). 'Lexical bundles', in Baker, P. and Egbert, J. (eds.), *Triangulating Methodological Approaches in Corpus Linguistic Research.* Cambridge: Cambridge University Press, 33–56.

Grieshofer, T. (2024). *Legal-Lay Discourse and Procedural Justice in Family and County Courts.* Cambridge: Cambridge University Press.

Henderson, E. (2014). 'All the proper protections – the Court of Appeal rewrites the rules for the cross-examination of vulnerable witnesses'. *Criminal Law Review*, 2014(1), 93–108.

Henry, L. A., Crane, L., Millmore, A., Nash, G., Wilcock, R. (2021). 'Intermediaries and cross-examination resilience in children: the development of a novel experimental methodology'. *Applied Cognitive Psychology*, 35(6), 1387–1404. https://doi.org/10.1002/acp.3869

Heydon, G. (2005) *The Language of Police Interviewing: A Critical Analysis*. Basingstoke: Palgrave.

Hyland, K. (2005). *Metadiscourse: Exploring Interaction in Writing*. London: Continuum.

Hyland, K. (2017). 'Metadiscourse: what is it and where is it going'. *Journal of Pragmatics*, 113, 16–29. https://doi.org/10.1016/j.pragma.2017.03.007

Hyland, K. and Zou, H. (2020). 'In the frame: signalling structure in academic articles and blogs'. *Journal of Pragmatics*, 165, 31–44. https://doi.org/10.1016/j.pragma.2020.05.002

Jackson, J., Doak, J., Saunders, C., Wright, D. and Cooper, D. (2024). *Mapping the Changing Face of Cross-Examination in Criminal Trials*. Report for the Nuffield Foundation. https://doi.org/10.17631/rd-2024-0001-drep

Jacobson, J. (2017). 'Introduction', in Cooper, P. and Norton, H. (eds.), *Vulnerable People and the Criminal Justice System*. Oxford: Oxford University Press, 1–21.

Johnson, A. (2013). 'Embedding police interviews in the prosecution case in the Shipman trial' in Heffer, C., Rock, F. and Conley, J. (eds.), *Legal-Lay Communication: Textual Travels in the Law*. Oxford: Oxford University Press, 147–167.

Kilgarriff, A., Baisa, V., Bušta, J., Jakubíček, M., Kovář, V., Michelfeit, J., Rychlý, P. and Suchomel, V. (2014). 'The sketch engine: ten years on'. *Lexicography*, 1, 7–36. https://doi.org/10.1007/s40607-014-0009-9

Marchant, R. (2017). 'Special measures', in Cooper, P. and Norton, H. (eds.), *Vulnerable People and the Criminal Justice System*. Oxford: Oxford University Press, 333–362.

Matoesian, G. (2005). 'Nailing down an answer: participations of power in trial talk'. *Discourse Studies*, 7(6), 733–759. https://doi.org/10.1177/1461445605055424

McAuliffe, K. and Trklja, A. (2019). 'Formulaic metadiscursive signalling devices in judgments of the Court of Justice of the European Union'. *The International Journal of Speech, Language and the Law*, 26(1), 21–55.

McKeown, J. (2021). 'A corpus-based examination of reflexive metadiscourse in majority and dissent opinions of the U.S. Supreme Court'. *Journal of Pragmatics*, 186, 224–235. https://doi.org/10.1016/j.pragma.2021.10.019

Morrison, J., Bradshaw, J. and Murphy, G. (2021). 'Reported communication challenges for adult witnesses with intellectual disabilities giving evidence in court'. *The International Journal of Evidence & Proof*, 25(4), 243–263. https://doi.org/10.1177/13657127211031040

Orts Lopis, M. Á. (2017). 'Terror at home on the rhetoric of domestic violence legislation in the United Kingdom and Spain'. *Journal of Intercultural Communication*, 17(2), 1–15. https://doi.org/10.36923/jicc.v17i2.741

Plotnikoff, J. and Woolfson, R. (2015). *Intermediaries in the Criminal Justice System: Improving Communication for Vulnerable Witnesses and Defendants*. Bristol: Policy Press.

Tkačuková, T. (2010). 'Cross-examination questioning: lay people as cross-examiners', in Coulthard, M. and Johnson, A. (eds.), *The Routledge Handbook of Forensic Linguistics* (1st ed.). London: Routledge, 333–346.

Tkačuková, T. (2015). 'A corpus-assisted study of the discourse marker *well* as an indicator of judges' institutional roles in court cases with litigants in person'. *Corpora*, 10(2), 145–170. https://doi.org/10.3366/cor.2015.0072

Tkačuková, T. (2020). 'Changing landscape of advice provision: online forums and social media run by Mckenzie friends'. *Child and Family Law Quarterly*, 4, 397–420

The Advocate's Gateway. (2023). *Toolkit 12 – Planning to Question Someone with a Suspected (or Diagnosed) Mental Health Disorder* (online), available from: www.theadvocatesgateway.org/_files/ugd/1074f0_a1f896d74e30440f9ec8bac9ab27f642.pdf

The Council of the Inns of Court. (2022). *Advocacy for Vulnerable People and Children (Criminal Course) National Training Programme. The 20 Principles of Questioning: A Guide to the Cross-Examination of Vulnerable People and Children.* The Inns of Court College of Advocacy (online), available from: www.icca.ac.uk/wp-content/uploads/2023/03/20-Principles-of-Questioning.pdf

UK Ministry of Justice. (2022) *Achieving Best Evidence in Criminal Proceedings: Guidance on Interviewing Victims and Witnesses, and Guidance on Using Special Measures.* Available at: www.gov.uk/government/publications/achieving-best-evidence-in-criminal-proceedings

Wigmore, J. H. (1940). *Evidence in Trials at Common Law.* Boston, MA: Little, Brown & Company.

Woodbury, H. (1984). 'The strategic use of questions in court'. *Semiotica*, 48(3/4), 197–228. https://doi.org/10.1515/semi.1984.48.3-4.197

11 The Ambivalence of Judicial Interventions at the International Criminal Court

Fabio Ferraz de Almeida and Elena Barrett

11.1 Introduction

The International Criminal Court (ICC) is the first permanent international criminal tribunal. Located in The Hague, the Netherlands, it began operating in 2002 and prosecutes individuals charged with genocide, war crimes, crimes against humanity and the crime of aggression. As a purported global institution aiming to accommodate a broad spectrum of legal cultures (Ba 2023), ICC's trial procedure will not reflect pure forms of either adversarial or inquisitorial systems (Kress 2003). In fact, the court represents an unstable amalgamation of these major legal traditions (Wilson 2016). This unique compromise is visible, for example, in how testimonial evidence is presented in an accusatorial format, while judges hold the role of truth-finder and legal referee simultaneously. This chapter examines the active role of ICC judges in trials, illustrating how their questioning practices blend these distinct legal traditions by not only serving as neutral arbiters but also directly participating in witnesses' examination, altering the form or content of attorneys' questions and co-producing evidence.

The debate over this amalgamation has been mainly conducted on normative terrain, for example, how to correctly interpret the ICC legal framework as outlined in its core legal texts and to comment on judges' actions and obligations while presiding over trial hearings (see Ambos 2003; Kress 2003; Schmitt 2021). Discussion of judges' questioning intervening powers tends to lack a clear empirical account of these actions or simply offers the gist of the judges' conduct. Our aim in this chapter is to open the black box of this emergent form of adjudication and empirically examine ICC judges' questioning practices in action, through careful and repeated analysis of trial transcripts. After all, it is not what trial participants *should* do but instead what they *actually* do that constitutes courtroom behaviour (Dunstan 1980).

Funding statement: This research was funded by the Academy of Finland, project number 325535.

We are grateful to the student research assistants, Juuso Ohtonen, Sini Sydänmaanlakka and Terhi Niiti, for their help in identifying the judges' interventions.

In what follows, we first provide an overview of the functions and powers of ICC judges in conducting trial proceedings, especially related to testimony-taking, before examining actual ICC hearing transcripts and analysing a series of interventions performed by judges during witness examinations. By shedding light on the interactional accomplishment of these interventions, we point to unforeseen consequences of the ICC's amalgamation of procedural frameworks. Our analysis examines how the ICC's normative and procedural provisions are fleshed out *in action* and reveals emerging tensions associated with judges' dual role of referee and truth-finder.

11.2 The Role of the Judge at the ICC

Each ICC trial is presided over by three judges, who subsequently hear the Prosecution, the Defence, and the legal representatives of victims. The Rome Statute (RS) is relatively silent about the powers and functions of the judges at the trial stage, and the language of Article 64, 8(b) defines their role in broad terms: '(...) the presiding judge may give directions for the conduct of proceedings, including to ensure that they are conducted in a fair and impartial manner. Subject to any directions of the presiding judge, the parties may submit evidence in accordance with the provisions of this Statute'(Rome Statute of the international Criminal Curt, 1998). These general instructions are further elaborated in the Rules of Procedure and Evidence (RPE), which, among other matters, establishes who should question the witnesses and the order in which this should be conducted: judges have the right to question a witness before or after the witness is examined by the prosecution and the defence.

From a doctrinal perspective, an investigation about the role of ICC judges in questioning witnesses is limited to an interpretative analysis of these provisions, that is, positive law. This approach assumes that law consists of a body of written rules (*law in books*) that can be objectively examined to flesh out their implications, including specifically what judges should or should not do during witness examination (see Kress 2003; Schmitt 2021), eventually leading to proposing procedural modifications.

In contrast, from our perspective, rooted in *law-in-action*, legal provisions are not autonomous and should be examined in combination with the practical efforts made by legal practitioners to interpret these rules and the situated actions in and through which these rules are constantly negotiated. The RS and the RPE provide the framework and serve as a constraint for participants' actions – what witnesses, lawyers and judges can or cannot do while interacting in ICC hearings. These provisions offer general guidance for judges to intervene in witness examination, but they lack detail about how and when to do so. This provides presiding judges with significant discretion in designing their interventions.

11.3 Data and Methodology

Our data is comprised of transcripts from the trial of Dominic Ongwen, a former commander of the Ugandan rebel movement Lord's Resistance Army (LRA), who was convicted in 2021 of war crimes and crimes against humanity committed between July 2002 and December 2005. These transcripts are available online on a website sponsored by the ICC (ICC Legal Tools Database, 2024) and can be used for research.

As part of a larger project, we created an index of all the case's trial hearings and selected a representative sample of both prosecution and defence witnesses. For this study, we examined 34 hearing transcripts and identified all judge's interventions performed during witness examination. Although the examples presented here come from a single trial and our observations are limited to the interventions of an individual judge, our analysis illustrates the range of judicial transformative actions, highlighting the tension between adversarial and inquisitorial powers. The significance of these examples lies in the fact that they illustrate phenomena intrinsic to the ICC framework and the affordances it offers judges in courtroom interactions.

Our analysis draws upon ethnomethodology and conversation analysis (EMCA) as it (1) understands talk as a vehicle for *social action*; (2) focuses on how participants themselves *produce* and *interpret* each other's actions; and (3) approaches material as *anthropologically strange*, in that it draws analytic attention to familiar phenomena that scholars routinely take for granted (Pomerantz & Atkinson 1984). There is a wide range of EMCA studies on courtroom interaction (for an overview, see Drew & Ferraz de Almeida 2020), which specifically draws attention to the way testimonial evidence is interactionally co-produced. This includes research about the sequential management of accusations and defences (Atkinson & Drew 1979), strategic questioning in witness examination (Drew 1992) and the power of answers to control information (Ehrlich & Sidnell 2006). The majority of these studies were conducted in adversarial legal settings, where issues about the appropriateness and admissibility of questions and answers are an emic concern for trial participants, and the judge is responsible to rule on these (Licoppe 2021). Our chapter, in contrast, investigates interactions in a unique 'mixed' setting, in which judges play an active role but without clear guidance about how questioning should be conducted.

Working with pre-existing court records has intrinsic limitations (see Richardson, Haworth & Deamer 2022; also Haworth, this volume). First, these transcripts lack the prosodic and phonetical details that participants rely upon when interacting with each other. It is impossible to know whether the judge is emphasising certain words or talking in overlap with counsel, for example. Second, ICC transcripts erase the process of simultaneous interpretation that occurs when witnesses and legal professionals speak different languages (Swigart 2019; see Ng, this volume). Still, this is the type of material that legal professionals rely on when conducting most of their routine affairs. Also, the logocentricity of ICC transcripts is a realistic rendition of the logocentric character of multilingual ICC hearings, as simultaneous conference-style interpretation neutralises temporal, prosodic and multimodal features of testimony-taking (D'hondt 2021).

11.4 Judicial Interventions in Witness Examination

The role of the judges in questioning witnesses is a major dimension in the way that legal systems are designed and develop over time. In inquisitorial traditions, judges actively participate in witness examination and evidence production, while in adversarial systems, they assume a more passive role, mainly deciding as 'referees' whether the parties' actions conform to evidentiary and procedural rules (Ainsworth 2015). As the ICC represents an amalgamation of these two traditions, it is unsurprising to identify instances in which the presiding judge (J), while interacting with the defence counsel (DC) and the lead prosecutor (P), orients to their role either as referee or truth-finder, as in Examples 11.1 and 11.2, respectively:

Example 11.1 ICC-02/04-01/15-T-181-ENG

1 DC: Mr Adek, did you ever come to know about instances where some
2 community leaders would discourage people who had escaped – I mean,
3 discouraged people from escaping from LRA? And for those who – for some of
4 those who returned –
5 P: No, I'm sorry, **I object again**. The question is: Did
6 community leaders have a message for people who escaped? Or some such neutral
7 proposition. Not telling the witness what Mr Ayena thinks the message was.
8 J: I think there is no huge difference but,
9 simply, you can rephrase it a little bit.

(Ongwen, ICC-02/04-01/15-T-181-ENG, Transcripts, 2 October 2018, p. 28, lines 16–24, available at www.legal-tools.org/doc/75dc8f/, lines follow the official transcripts, but line numbers were adjusted here)

Example 11.2 ICC-02/04-01/15-T-123-Red2-ENG

1 DC: And from what you observed from the people around you that were
2 there witnessing the same event, did they believe that Joseph Kony was being
3 possessed by spirits?
4 W: People believe, yes, because the message that he passed from
5 Palutaka came to be, and for that matter believed it.
6 J: May I shortly.
7 DC: Yes, your Honour.
8 J: Mr Witness, did you continue to believe
9 this until you left the bush?

(Ongwen, ICC-02/04-01/15-T-123-Red2-ENG, Transcripts, 2 November 2017, p. 33, lines 3-11, available at www.legal-tools.org/doc/86518e/)

Each of these examples illustrates what is typically expected of courtroom hearings in a mixed legal system: a judge who at certain points in the interaction acts as a referee and decides on the appropriateness of the questions, as in an adversarial setting, but at others, orients to a more active role by posing questions to the witness, as in an inquisitorial setting. In the examples reviewed later, however, this distinction becomes blurred and the tension between the two judicial roles can be brought to the surface of the interaction by trial participants themselves.

11.4.1 Between Referee and Truth-Finder in Objection Sequences

ICC trial hearings are filled with objection sequences, a feature that reflects the influence of adversarial legal traditions in their proceedings. In such systems, objections are raised to prevent the introduction of inadmissible evidence and challenge the use of improper questions (Danet & Bogoch 1980). Objections are routinely placed after a question, once the opposing counsel has identified a potential 'objectionable' item (Atkinson & Drew 1979: 209–216), and before an answer, forestalling it (Matoesian 2018: 200). Hence, objections are a powerful resource for controlling testimony-taking as they enable the opposing party to influence, and the judge to decide, to a certain level, how facts and events are linguistically framed. In the case of ICC trials, this is particularly worth investigating since these objections are produced in the absence of clear rules over how questioning should be performed.

Typically, as in Example 11.1, these sequences involve a third party (prosecutor) interrupting a two-party exchange (defence counsel's examination of prosecution witness) by calling out the appropriateness of the prior question. In doing so, the third party initiates a remedy sequence that selects a fourth party (judge) who, after sustaining or overruling the objection, returns the floor to the examining party. In our data, however, this is frequently not the case, as in Example 11.3, which illustrates how the presiding judge takes over the questioner role during direct examination of a defence witness. The witness was abducted as a teenager and spent over 15 years in the LRA, the period in which he became familiar with Dominic Ongwen and Joseph Kony.

Example 11.3 ICC-02/04-01/15-T-192-Red2-ENG

1 DC: Now, Mr Witness, could you have learnt whether during the time he
2 was in the sickbay, around 2003, Dominic Ongwen fell into trouble with Joseph Kony
3 for attempting to contact, to contact a top UPDF –
4 P: Your Honour, I apologise yet again, but this is putting an
5 entire proposition.
6 J: Yes, yes, that's true.

7 P: It's leading.
8 J: This is a manner of questioning by the
9 non-calling party, I would say. I am much more indulgent since I am coming from
10 a system where we don't have any parties. But, nevertheless, you would have to
11 rephrase this. Formulate it openly so that the witness does not really know what
12 you want to hear. Let me put it.
13 Mr Witness, have you heard of any problems that Mr Ongwen had with Mr Kony?
14 DC: Yes.
15 W: (Interpretation) I did not hear any such thing. Even if it
16 was there, I am not part of their meetings, I do not attend – I don't get close to them to
17 attend what they talk about.
18 J: Thank you. I think that answers it.
19 You can move to another point.

(Ongwen, ICC-02/04-01/15-T-192-Red2-ENG, Transcripts, 6 November 2018, p. 43, lines 3-21, available at www.legal-tools.org/doc/55753e/)

The prosecutor objects mid-question, accusing the defence counsel of leading the witness, prompting the judge to decide whether to sustain or overrule the objection before allowing the defence to continue. The judge's response (lines 8–13), however, is far more complex and illustrates a progressive transition from referee to truth-finder. Instead of returning the floor to the examining counsel and closing the objection conference, the judge closes his turn by reformulating the question and addressing it directly to the witness (line 13).

In this example, we see how participants continuously calibrate their participation status (Goffman 1981) by rotating through different roles, which entail different activities. Here, the judge gradually shifts in orientation, from his position as an impartial referee, merely ruling on the previous question's appropriateness, to one of a participant in the activity of questioning. By reformulating the objected question and posing it directly to the witness, he extends his work beyond the ancillary task of responding to an objection and temporarily gains control over the main activity, that is, examining the witness.

That the judge shifts from a neutral role to one of far more active participation is also visible through the changes that he makes in reformulating the question. In the reformulated version, the judge neutralises the leading character of the original question by replacing the term 'fell into trouble' with 'any problem' and removing the motive that precipitated the alleged dispute between the defendant and his LRA superior ('for attempting to contact, to contact a top UPDF', line 3). In addition to that, the judge extends the changes beyond what the prosecutor disputed through his objection and rephrases the outset of the question, thereby transforming the nature of the evidence being elicited. Whereas 'have you heard' frames the testimony as hearsay, a form of evidence that is not disallowed in ICC trials (Acquaviva 2013: 111), 'could you have learnt' is more ambiguous and can encompass or exclude events the witness has seen, heard, heard *of*, and so on.

The tension between adversarial and inquisitorial features and the ambiguous, fluid role played by the judge are also visible in Example 11.4, in which the defence counsel questions a witness called by his own team. The witness is a cultural leader in Northern Uganda and testified about his participation in the peace negotiations with the LRA and his knowledge of Dominic Ongwen, Joseph Kony and other LRA commanders. The example refers to a section of the testimony in which the defence tries to substantiate the allegation that the defendant was almost executed by Kony for his involvement in the peace talks with Salim Saleh, general of the Ugandan armed forces and brother of President Museveni. The allegations included that Ongwen had received money from the general, a point the defence counsel is heading towards (line 2) when he is interrupted by the prosecutor, who raises an objection (line 3).

Example 11.4 ICC-02/04-01/15-T-181-ENG

1	DC:	There was an episode in 2003 when it is alleged that General
2		Salim Saleh – I mean, Dominic Ongwen received –
3	P:	I object. The counsel should ask a question to establish
4		whether the witness knows this. Not tell him.
5	J:	Yes. That's true. That's correct. What
6		you can do is perhaps simply, in a more general way, do you know of any incident
7		concerning Dominic Ongwen and Salim Saleh. That's the question.
8	DC:	Although it is on record.
9	J:	Yes, but we don't want to influence the
10		witness. Let me put the question, perhaps.
11	DC:	Very well.
12	J:	If you don't mind.
13		Mr Adek, do you have any knowledge, personal knowledge, not only from hearsay,
14		about an incident – and I word it very generally – allegedly concerning
15		Dominic Ongwen and Salim Saleh – and/or Salim Saleh?
16	W:	(Interpretation) Well, I didn't hear anything about
17		Salim Saleh. But after the collapse of the peace talks I heard that Kony and
18		Dominic Ongwen were not in good terms (…)

(Ongwen, ICC-02/04-01/15-T-181-ENG, Transcripts, 2 October 2018, from line 13 on p. 7 to line 5 on p. 8, available at www.legal-tools.org/doc/75dc8f/)

The objection (lines 3–4) is grounded on the normative expectation that a counsel should ask questions to the witness (Atkinson & Drew 1979: 61–65), without formulating their own statements. By objecting and pre-empting the question, the prosecutor leaves the judge in a position to decide whether the objection is sustained or overruled. The judge does so by assertively agreeing with the prosecutor's claim (line 5). His shift to more active participation surfaces when he instructs the defence counsel on how they might resolve the issue (lines 5–6). This time, however, the judge does not follow through with his instruction; instead, he immediately rephrases the question himself (lines 6–7) before asserting that 'that's the question' (line 7). The judge initially offers a hypothetical reformulation to resolve the issue, transforming the original statement, that is, about an alleged episode in 2003 in which Ongwen received money from General Salim Saleh, into an interrogative that asks if the witness has any knowledge about an incident involving the two actors mentioned. Despite some resistance from the defence counsel, who attempts to argue that the information about the incident involving the defendant and Salim Saleh was already on the record (line 8), the judge maintains control over the examination and reformulates the question himself (lines 13–15). In other words, this objection conference concludes with the judge directly addressing the witness. Nevertheless, this time the judge introduces further transformations to the question and as in Example 11.3, they are not directly connected to the prosecutor's objection. For example, the judge replaces the general term 'knowledge' with 'personal knowledge' (line 13), thereby specifying the nature of the evidence the witness should present in his answer, which must not be 'mere' hearsay. Notably, these transformations feature the use of hedging devices as a mitigation strategy (Caffi 1999), preceding both his proposed reformulation and his active reformulation of the question with a conditional frame ('what you can do is perhaps simply', lines 5–6; 'perhaps' and 'if you don't mind', lines 10 & 12). Although accepting his reformulations is certainly imperative, these hedging devices present them as optional and disguise their transformative character.

In Examples 11.3 and 11.4, the judge exploits the discretion given by the RPE, which does not prescribe how objections should be handled, and assumes the role of questioner. In reformulating the objected question, the judge not only attends to the problems indicated by the prosecutor but also extends his control over the testimony by making subtle but significant changes, often related to evidential weight, that transcend the original scope of the objection. The organisation and the design of the judge's talk display the equivocal character of his work in these proceedings: a referee who is responsible for enforcing the 'rules of the game' but who can also play an active role by reformulating questions and implementing changes not directly requested by the opposing party.

11.4.2 Ambiguity in Self-Initiated Question Reformulations

The equivocality that characterises judicial interventions extends beyond objection sequences to episodes in which the presiding judge intervenes and reformulates a question on his own initiative. Whereas in Examples 11.3 and 11.4, the judge's participation started as part of a time-out that had been initiated by the opposing party (see D'hondt et al. 2021), in Example 11.5 the judge self-selects and directly intervenes in the ongoing interaction between counsel and witness.

The defence case in *Ongwen* relied partially on the argument that it was virtually impossible for anyone to escape the LRA and that the defendant was acting under duress when he committed the alleged crimes. In Example 11.5, while questioning one of his own witnesses, the defence counsel attempts to elicit information to corroborate this argument. The witness responds to the counsel's second question with a request for clarification (line 14), which leads the judge to intervene.

Example 11.5 ICC-02/04-01/15-T-181-ENG

1 DC: Rwot Adek, from what you learnt as an elder and a person who
2 closely interacted with the LRA, can you please tell Court if it was easy to escape from
3 the LRA once you became an LRA soldier or commander.
4 W: I don't know how those soldiers were trained on how, whenever you
5 find yourself in trouble, how you would escape. Something like that. I don't know
6 how they were trained. But most times we would hear that they kept on killing
7 those who tried to escape and this was meant to scare those who were still in there
8 from escaping. But because we were not staying with them we are not aware of
9 what steps or actions they were taking to prevent their fighters from escaping. We
10 could only hear about that
11 DC: And according to what you heard, Mr Witness, was it any easier or
12 more difficult for somebody identified – I mean, for somebody who was identified by
13 Joseph Kony as a valuable fighter, courageous and successful in war?
14 W: Are you asking for my opinion or my observation?
15 J: Yes, that is correct. I also hesitated to
16 intervene. Perhaps we can rephrase it a little bit.
17 Do you know of any instances where Joseph Kony came to know that one of his
18 commanders wanted to escape? And if so, do you know how he reacted? And I
19 think then we leave it at that.

20 W: (Interpretation) One thing that I know is that I saw an
21 example in one of our areas (…)

(Ongwen, ICC-02/04-01/15-T-181-ENG, Transcripts, 2 October 2018, from line 9 on p. 24 to line 4 on p. 25, available at www.legal-tools.org/doc/75dc8f/)

Whilst asking for clarification about the type of information sought by the defence counsel (line 14), the witness relies on a distinction between 'opinion' (subjective domain: beliefs, attitudes, values, feelings, etc.) and 'observation' (objective domain: facts, first-hand experience, etc.), which he had already hinted at by contrasting hearsay and knowledge (lines 8–10). This is followed by an intervention from the judge, who treats the witness's turn as if it had been an objection, not a clarification question. Instead of letting the defence counsel answer the question and repair the problem, the judge reformulates the original question by unpacking it.

In his reformulated questions, the judge moves away from an evaluative claim about the escape of a commander and orients to eliciting a factual description of events involving Kony's awareness of and responses to the intention to escape. Note, for example, that the judge replaces 'from what you learnt' and 'according to what you heard', the expressions selected by the defence counsel to preface his questions, with 'do you know', which works to avoid establishing a direct connection with hearsay evidence (line 17). The reformulated version assists the witness in answering in a way that is legally more relevant, in terms of probative value. The witness demonstrates his understanding of it by, for example, displaying his orientation to provide first-hand knowledge about the events he is describing (e.g., 'I saw an example', lines 20–21). Equally relevant is how the judge prefaces his reformulated questions in this case: he displays the minimal character of his intervention by portraying his activity as 'rephrasing', which implies maintaining the meaning and goal of the original question.

This analysis contributes to the discussion about the equivocal role that ICC judges play in witness examination. First, it suggests that judges are constantly monitoring the talk by all participants in these hearings, and they exercise their discretion by intervening whenever they see necessary. Second, it shows that despite the judge's effort to display the minimal character of his participation – an orientation to the adversarial side of these proceedings – his intervention is rather transformative. By stepping in and reformulating the question, the judge provisionally takes control of the questioning and actively participates in evidence production – an orientation to the inquisitorial side of ICC trials.

Example 11.5 shows the judge navigating between his two functions: referee and truth-finder. Although he works to minimise and sometimes justify the disruptive and transformative character of his interventions, displaying an orientation to his role as referee, the changes performed through the reformulated questions suggest a far more active participation, more typical of his role as truth-finder. The leverage provided by the RPE for judges to monitor and intervene in witness examination creates the conditions for these rather ambiguous judicial interventions.

11.4.3 Resisting Reformulated Questions

In Examples 11.3, 11.4 and 11.5, the examining counsel has never disputed a question reformulated by the judge. However, in Example 11.6, the counsel contests the judge's reformulation and enters into a negotiation over how the question should be formulated. Example 11.6 may not be representative in a strictly quantitative sense, but it illustrates the underlying tension faced by ICC judges in combining adversarial and inquisitorial roles.

Earlier in the hearing, the witness had testified that the defendant, Dominic Ongwen, and LRA leader Joseph Kony were not on good terms after the collapse of the Juba peace talks. The example begins with the defence counsel returning to that topic (lines 3–4) and initiating a question.

Example 11.6 ICC-02/04-01/15-T-181-ENG

1 MR AYENA ODONGO:
2 Q. Let's relate it to what we discussed about what you came to learn
3 about his misunderstanding with Dominic Ongwen. In your – can you tell Court
4 what you think could have been –
5 PRESIDING JUDGE SCHMITT: No, I think 'what you think', calling for
6 an opinion, or something are like that. Do you have any information? Simply.
7 And I think it has been answered already, but okay, let's give it a second try.
8 Do you have any, any information, facts that might explain why there was
9 a disagreement or whatsoever between Joseph Kony and Mr Ongwen?
10 MR AYENA ODONGO: You know, that's not the way I wanted to put it.
11 Q. Do you have any information why, even after the misunderstanding,
12 Kony still kept Dominic Ongwen within his ranks?
13 PRESIDING JUDGE SCHMITT: Please, I think please answer both
14 questions: Do you have information why there was a disagreement? First question.
15 Second question: Do you have any information what happened afterwards and why
16 Mr Ongwen was still in the ranks after having a disagreement? But only if you
17 know something. But the whole two days you are here in the courtroom you always
18 have only related to things that you have really knowledge of. So, if you may, please
19 answer.
20 THE WITNESS: (Interpretation) Thank you for the question.

I request that we should understand well to, to know why they disagreed. It would only be possible if I was staying with them. I only heard about the quarrel. I was in Uganda and I heard that they were no longer in agreement. It is not possible to know why they disagreed if you are not living with them. I only heard, just like any other person heard, that they were no longer in agreement. Like I said earlier, that was why I was taken to speak on radio, a radio in Congo, so that those who can hear can surrender. I think that is a clear response I can give.

PRESIDING JUDGE SCHMITT: Indeed, and that is fair enough, and you would have simply to move to another point.

MR AYENA ODONGO: Yes.

PRESIDING JUDGE SCHMITT: So he has no direct information. And that speaks in favour of the witness, that he simply, simply makes clear what he has knowledge of. And this is also like yesterday, he differentiates clearly between own knowledge and hearsay and everything like that.

MR AYENA ODONGO: Yes.

(Ongwen, ICC-02/04-01/15-T-181-ENG, Transcripts, 2 October 2018, from line 4 on p. 13 to line 12 on p. 14, available at www.legal-tools.org/doc/75dc8f/)

As observed throughout the entirety of the data sample examined, the judge interrupts the counsel mid-question, determining it to be opinion-based rather than fact-based, and reformulates the question himself, displaying his control over the proceedings. Here, however, his task is far more intricate as he has no choice other than to infer what the question would have been.

Rather than letting the witness answer the judge's reformulation, the defence counsel contests it by tacitly relying on the fact that the judge did not wait until his question was completed (line 10). Next, he formulates a new question, in which he seems to agree with the epistemic change proposed by the judge (from 'what you think' to 'do you have any information') while disputing the presuppositional addition. For the counsel, the question should not be about the reasons that might explain the disagreement between the defendant and Kony, but about the possible explanations for Kony keeping the defendant within the LRA ranks despite their misunderstanding. The judge does not accept the change and intervenes again, proposing a solution that would apparently be a compromise between his and the defence counsel's interests: the witness should answer both questions. Despite having the option to conclude his intervention at that point and rely on the witness's recollection to answer both questions, the judge proceeds to reformulate each of them again. This provides the judge with an extra occasion to adjust the question according to his own preference. For example, the defence counsel's question (lines 11–12) presupposed that it was Kony who decided to keep Ongwen in the LRA ranks. The judge makes it more neutral by erasing Kony's agency over the defendant from the picture, that is, his question (lines 15–16) merely presupposes that Ongwen remained in the ranks after the disagreement.

Example 11.6 illustrates how the equivocal character of judges' work in ICC trials can rise to the surface of the interaction and become an issue for the participants themselves. In this case, the defence counsel orients to the tension between adversarial and inquisitorial modes of testimony-taking to contest and attempt to regain control over the examination. In his challenge, the counsel does not dispute the changes about 'how' the question was supposed to be designed but 'what' the question was about in the first place. In doing so, he recognises the judge as a referee, who ensures that questions are phrased in a proper manner but resists his truth-finder capacity. The ambiguous nature of the judge's intervention is also evidenced by the way he terminates the objection conference: with an evaluation of the witness's answer directed at the counsel (lines 28–29 and 31–34). The answer in this case is evaluated both regarding its probative value and efficiency. In other words, while the judge is clearly monitoring the production of testimony, he does so not only in terms of procedural rules but also in a more qualitative or aesthetic sense.

11.5 Conclusion

In a recent publication, Judge Bertram Schmitt, who presided over the Ongwen trial, offered his reflections about adjudicating in a court that represents such a unique compromise between common and civil law traditions. Combining his interpretation of the RS and the RPE and his professional experience, he argues that ICC judges must be cautious when questioning witnesses and prefer a restrained role during testimony-taking – an approach that, according to him, would lead the judges to be perceived as more neutral or impartial and prevent disputes between them and the parties (Schmitt 2021: 500–501). Despite clearly indicating his preference for moderate judicial participation, Schmitt added a caveat by granting that timely judges' interventions are necessary to neutralise the damaging effects of leading questions and streamline witness examination (Schmitt 2021: 502–503).

In practice, however, we observed that Schmitt's interventions were frequent and, more importantly, achieved substantially more than what he suggested in principle. The framework established by the ICC core legal texts gives the presiding judge a great deal of discretion in deciding when and how to intervene during testimony-taking. Our analysis of courtroom transcripts shows how they may use this leeway in objection sequences: they do not simply rule on the appropriateness of the questions but regularly assume control of the examination, shift their participation status and reformulate the questions themselves. In doing so, they shift away from their referee role and adopt a more proactive role in witness examination. While gradually occupying the role of questioner and rephrasing the counsel's questions, judges extend their control over the testimony with subtle changes that reconfigure the content and the nature of the evidence produced. In our study, we demonstrated that the latitude offered by the RPE for judges to monitor and intervene in witness examination creates the conditions for blurring the distinction between the functions of referee and truth-finder. This occurs, for example, when a judge corrects and reformulates a question previously posed by one of the parties: although working to minimise or obscure the transformative feature of such interventions, the changes carried out in the reformulated questions point to a substantially more active participation.

The ambivalence of judges' interventions discussed here is illustrative of the possibilities afforded by the RS and the RPE regarding the role of the ICC judges in witness examination. While our study may not be exhaustive, it makes a strong case that examining real-life instances of trial discourse is a fruitful avenue for understanding the tensions and procedural challenges presented by the ICC's amalgamation of inquisitorial and accusatorial frameworks for examining witnesses.

References

Acquaviva, G. (2013). 'Written and oral evidence', in Carter, L. and Pocar, F. (eds.), *International Criminal Procedure: The Interface of Civil Law and Common Law Legal Systems*. Cheltenham: Edgar Elgar, 99–124.

Ainsworth, J. (2015). 'Legal discourse and legal narratives: adversarial versus inquisitorial models'. *Language and Law/Linguagem e Direito*, 2(1), 1–11.

Ambos, K. (2003). 'International criminal procedure: "adversarial", "inquisitorial" or mixed?'. *International Criminal Law Review*, 3(1), 1–37.

Atkinson, J. M. and Drew, P. (1979). *Order in Court*. London: Macmillan.

Ba, O. (2023). 'Constructing an international legal order under the shadow of colonial domination'. *Journal of Human Rights*, 22(1), 4–15.

Caffi, C. (1999). 'On mitigation'. *Journal of Pragmatics*, 31(7), 881–909.

Danet, B. and Bogoch, B. (1980). 'Fixed fight or free-for-all? An empirical study of combativeness in the adversary system of justice'. *British Journal of Law and Society*, 7(1), 36–60.

D'hondt, S. (2021). 'Why being there mattered: staged transparency at the International Criminal Court'. *Journal of Pragmatics*, 183, 168–178.

D'hondt, S., Pérez-León-Acevedo, J. P. and Barrett, E. (2021). 'The indeterminacy of precedent: negotiating the admissibility of victim participant testimony before the International Criminal Court'. *International Criminal Law Review*, 22(5–6), 1068–1093.

Dunstan, R. (1980). 'Context for coercion: analyzing properties of courtroom questions'. *British Journal of Law and Society*, 7(1), 61–77.

Drew, P. (1992). 'Contested evidence in courtroom cross-examination: the case of a trial for rape', in Drew, P. and Heritage, J. (eds.), *Talk at Work*. Cambridge: Cambridge University Press, 470–520.

Drew, P. and Ferraz de Almeida, F. (2020). 'Order in court: talk-in-interaction in judicial settings', in Coulthard, M., May, A. and Sousa-Silva, R. (eds.), *The Routledge Handbook of Forensic Linguistics*, London: Routledge, 177–191.

Ehrlich, S. and Sidnell, J. (2006). '"I think that's not an assumption you ought to make": challenging presuppositions in inquiry testimony'. *Language in Society*, 35(5), 655–676.

Goffman, E. (1981). 'Footing', in Goffman, E. (ed.), *Forms of Talk*. Philadelphia: University of Pennsylvania Press, 124–159.

ICC Legal Tools Database (accessed 19 December 2024). Website: www.legal-tools.org.

Kress, C. (2003). 'The procedural law of the International Criminal Court in outline: anatomy of a unique compromise'. *Journal of International Criminal Justice*, 1(3), 603–617.

Licoppe, C. (2021). 'The politics of visuality and talk in French courtroom proceedings with video links and remote participants'. *Journal of Pragmatics*, 178, 363–377.

Matoesian, G. (2018). 'This is not a course in trial practice: multimodal participation in objections'. *Journal of Pragmatics*, 129, 199–219.

Pomerantz, A. and Atkinson, J. M. (1984). 'Ethnomethodology, conversation analysis and the study of courtroom interaction', in Muller, D., Blackman, D. and Chapman, A. (eds.), *Topics in Psychology and Law*. Chichester: Wiley, 283–297.

Richardson, E., Haworth, K., and Deamer, F. (2022). 'For the record: questioning transcription processes in legal contexts'. *Applied Linguistics*, 43(4), 677–697.

Rome Statute of the International Criminal Court (adopted 17 July 1998, entered into force 1 July 2002) 2187 UNTS 3.

Schmitt, B. (2021). 'Legal diversity at the International Criminal Court: Reflections of a Judge'. *Journal of International Criminal Justice*, 19(3), 485–510.

Swigart, L. (2019). 'Unseen and unsung: language services at the International Criminal Court and their impact on institutional legitimacy', in Baetens, F. (ed.), *Legitimacy of Unseen Actors in International Adjudication*. Cambridge: Cambridge University Press, 272–296.

Wilson, R. A. (2016). 'Expert evidence on trial: social researchers in the international criminal courtroom'. *American Ethnologist*, 43(4), 730–744.

12 Discourse and Contingency in International Criminal Justice

Sigurd D'hondt

12.1 Introduction

This chapter emphasises the inherent critical potential of linguistic analysis and its capacity to decentre or destabilise accepted views of the legal process as a self-contained, autonomous activity that can be exhaustively described in terms of its constitutive rules. The jurisdiction we will consider is that of the International Criminal Court (ICC), a permanent international tribunal based in The Hague, the Netherlands, charged with prosecuting and trying individuals accused of genocide, crimes against humanity, war crimes and the crime of aggression. Elsewhere in this volume, Ferraz de Almeida and Barrett describe the procedural uncertainty created by the ICC's amalgamation of inquisitorial and accusatorial systems, and they turn to conversation analysis for a detailed picture of how trial actors navigate the resulting tensions between the judge's truth-seeking and refereeing roles. This chapter takes a different perspective, away from the procedural level. It shows how the 'packaging' of law in language, the fact that the cases brought before the ICC are presented and processed in and through linguistic interaction, results in the inevitable entanglement of the legal process and its socio-political environment, a phenomenon that I will later refer to as radical contingency. This focus on language, discourse and contingency is particularly salient in the context of a novel, transnational legal institution such as the ICC, which must negotiate its legitimacy in a culturally diverse and geopolitically complex landscape.

In what follows, I will first elaborate on the notion of contingency and show how it draws on both linguistic anthropological work on intertextuality in the legal process and critical scholarship in international law. I then present samples of authentic courtroom discourse from two recently concluded ICC trials, that of Ugandan rebel commander Dominic Ongwen and Malian jihadist Ahmad Al Faqi Al Mahdi, to further illustrate how language intertwines the legal and the socio-political. I conclude with a suggestion for how scholars and practitioners might deal with this contingency.

Funding statement: This research was funded by the Academy of Finland, project number 325535.

12.2 The Contingency of Courtroom Talk

In its quest for legitimacy and transparency (D'hondt 2021a), the ICC website offers a wealth of information about past and ongoing cases, including submissions exchanged between the parties, transcripts of trial hearings and rulings by the Trial Chambers (all redacted to preserve the anonymity of vulnerable witnesses). Taken together, these documents offer a unique perspective on the nuts and bolts of international criminal justice and the language through which the law comes to life, going beyond the verdicts discussed in the media and in the academic literature and focusing on the (occasionally trenchant) live interactions among trial actors and the (often tedious) day-to-day routines of trials that can last several hundred hearing days. For critical scholars, they represent the 'black box' of courtroom talk, a metaphor borrowed from Actor Network Theory to draw attention to the often ignored interactional production of legal truth (Latour 2010).

Opening this black box is destabilising because it reminds us that criminal justice will always be more than the application of abstract rules to supposedly concrete facts, traditionally framed by legal scholars as a 'legal syllogism' with the applicable rule as the major premise and the relevant fact as the minor premise (see Dupret 2011: Chapter 6). This is not to deny that the formal study of the body of man-made, abstract rules applicable within a given jurisdiction (so-called positive law) constitutes a relevant object of study. It is illusory to assume that one could understand practices of adjudication without a thorough understanding of the formal rules that underlie the legal syllogism. However, doctrinal analysis is always only part of the story, and a careful examination of what is said and done in the courtroom reveals that the syllogistic reasoning enshrined in judicial decisions (case law) is intertwined with complex discursive and interactional processes that facilitate the coarticulation of rules and facts. It is through linguistically mediated practice that the law comes to life (Dupret 2011, Dupret et al. 2015, Mertz 2007). Criminal justice, then, is not exclusively a legal-doctrinal exercise that can be understood solely in terms of the law's constitutive rules. Instead, the discourses through which the law comes to life subject the legal process to radical contingency, that is, they infuse it with extrajudicial complexes of meaning and normativity. The notion of 'contingency' adopted here owes much to the poststructuralist discourse theory of Laclau and Mouffe (D'hondt 2013, Zienkowski 2024). This assigns a central role to the ways in which otherwise unconnected semiotic and material elements are fused or 'coarticulated' in discourse and argues that these *ad hoc* coarticulations reflect and sustain broader socio-political power arrangements. In this sense, contingency does not imply indeterminacy but stands for the entanglement of the law with the broader socio-political process, which is framed through linguistic means.

This chapter thus challenges formalist views of the legal process as a mere implementation of a limited number of fixed templates. Instead, it posits that legal decisions invariably possess a contingent character and reflect their socio-political context – a phenomenon all the more pronounced in a transnational jurisdiction like the ICC. To capture this contingency, it draws on a rich tradition of work in sociolinguistics and linguistic anthropology on intertextuality in the legal process. This work is concerned with issues such as de- and re-contextualisation, text trajectories and the vulnerability of supposedly stable texts as they move through the legal process, across speech and writing (Haworth 2018, Komter 2019) and across the realms of lay and professional discourse (Heffer, Rock & Conley 2013). Authors such as Matoesian (2001), Eades (2012), Ehrlich (2012) and others have extensively documented how oral testimony can undergo drastic shifts in interpretation as it is subsequently de- and recontextualised (Bauman & Briggs 1990), a process in which lay actors lose control over the meaning of their statements. These shifts, in turn, are facilitated and rendered invisible by deeply held beliefs ('language ideologies') about the transparency of referential meaning (Haviland 2003) and the infallibility of text and the written word (Mertz 2007).

This work on intertextuality will demonstrate the extent to which the legal syllogism depends on the *ad hoc* discursive processing of testimony to reconcile situated events in the lives of perpetrators and victims of international crimes with the abstract categories of positive law. Next, we show how this judicial fact-finding and its attendant discursive transformations in turn inscribe international criminal proceedings into broader theatres of (geo)political conflict. To this end, we turn to Koskenniemi's (2011 and elsewhere) critique of the liberal rule of law, based on the re-specification of international law as a 'language game' (Wittgenstein). According to this view, international law is primarily a discourse that allows actors to formulate multiple arguments and articulate contrasting positions. The selection of one position over another, however, is not dictated by the law as such, but is essentially a political one, and depends in crucial ways on the language in which cases and situations are presented.

Drawing on these two bodies of scholarship, we will elucidate how both the parties' submissions and the ICC judges' decisions depend on the situated coarticulation of legal doctrine with elements of common sense, extrajudicial normativity and occasional opportunistic *ad hoc* reasoning that elude legal definition. Moreover, this making sense of legal categories is always a two-way process, representing 'an unavoidably creative practice that constitutes the meanings that it purports to find' (Sander 2018: 304; see also D'hondt, Dupret & Bens 2021). This two-way process extends beyond narrow legal interpretation *per se* and almost automatically spills over into the domain of trial procedure, as the attribution of such meaning also depends on how evidence is handled, rules are interpreted and trials are conducted on the ground.

In principle, any form of adjudication can be considered a contingent discursive accomplishment, regardless of the nature or scope of its jurisdiction. Nevertheless, there are good reasons why language and discursive practice deserve special attention in international criminal justice settings. First, the situations and contexts that the ICC judges are called upon to review are often many thousands of kilometres away from The Hague, which is further complicated by cultural and institutional remoteness (for which Clark (2018) coined the term 'distant justice'). Second, the cases brought before the ICC typically involve crimes committed in a political context, and the judges' factual findings are therefore particularly vulnerable to political contestation (Koskenniemi 2011, Strandberg Hassellind 2021). Finally, it is important to remember that the Rome Statute, the multilateral treaty that established the ICC, was not adopted until 1998, and the Court did not become operational until 2002 (with a provisional total of 11 convictions at the time of writing). The aforementioned challenges should therefore be set against the backdrop of an emerging legal order that is not yet fully consolidated, an 'unstable amalgam' (Wilson 2016: 743) that faces uncertainties in substantive and procedural law (D'hondt et al. 2022, Ferraz de Almeida & Barrett, this volume) and is confronted with recurring legitimacy challenges (Clarke 2019, Vasiliev 2020; see D'hondt 2019, Barrett & Ferraz de Almeida forthcoming for how such challenges are interactionally managed). As the cases presented in this chapter illustrate, these specific circumstances have drastic implications for the conduct of ICC trials, making a focus on language use and contingency all the more relevant.

To illustrate these points, this chapter draws on previous work on two ICC trials in particular. First, we examine the production and assessment of evidence about Acholi spirituality in the ICC trial of Dominic Ongwen, a former brigade commander of the Ugandan rebel movement Lord's Resistance Army (LRA), to show the extent of the discursive processing that supports the legal syllogism. We then turn to the Office of the Prosecutor's (OTP) representation of Islamic legal institutions in the ICC trial of Ahmad Al Faqi Al Mahdi, a Malian jihadist found guilty of having directed the destruction of Sufi shrines during the 2012 jihadist occupation of Timbuktu. Here, we examine how the OTP's processing of the context of the case forces it to choose sides in a (political) theatre of competing narratives about the role of Islam in public life. For a full analysis of these cases, I refer the reader to D'hondt et al. (2025) and D'hondt, Dupret and Bens (forthcoming), from which the material for these empirical sections is drawn.

12.3 Ongwen, or a Legal Binary that Is Intertextually Accomplished

On 6 May 2021, after a 4-year trial with 234 hearings, ICC Trial Chamber IX sentenced Ugandan rebel commander Dominic Ongwen to 25 years in prison.

He was found guilty of 61 counts of war crimes and crimes against humanity, including attacks and atrocities against civilians, gender-based crimes and conscription and use of child soldiers. These were committed between July 2002 and December 2005 in the land of the Acholi (North Uganda), in the context of an armed conflict between the Ugandan government and the LRA rebel movement. A key defence argument was that Ongwen could not be held criminally responsible because he committed the alleged crimes under duress, an affirmative defence established by Article 31(1)(d) of the Rome Statute. To this end, Ongwen's counsel called several former LRA fighters to the stand (and cross-examined prosecution witnesses) to testify about the role of the supernatural in the LRA rebel movement and the prophetic powers attributed to LRA leader Joseph Kony. The latter acted as a medium for a host of spirits who had allegedly joined the rebel ranks, providing him with secret intelligence about impending betrayals and defections. The resulting climate of fear arguably made escape impossible, even for a senior commander like Ongwen.

Once this testimony about spirit beliefs was introduced, the judges had no choice but to examine it and assess whether it met the criteria for duress set forth in the Rome Statute. This presented Trial Chamber IX with a dilemma similar to that faced by the Special Court for Sierra Leone more than a decade earlier (Kelsall 2009: 145): how to determine the criminal liability of military actors who subscribe to a cosmology that attributes agency to supernatural entities, which is radically incompatible with the liberal legal tradition and its emphasis on individual responsibility. In the Judgment, the ICC judges wriggled out of this dilemma by stating that, according to the evidence, 'for many persons who stayed in the LRA longer their belief followed a pattern: it was stronger in the young, new and impressionable abductees and then subsided and disappeared in those who stayed in the LRA longer' (Trial Judgment, para. 2645). Moreover, much of the testimony they cited explicitly stated that senior LRA commanders deliberately manipulated belief in the supernatural to brainwash new recruits and instill fear in the rebel ranks. The resulting binary of (juvenile) 'true believers' versus (adult) 'impostors' effectively relieved Trial Chamber IX of the need to consider the supernatural in its decision-making, explicitly acknowledging the widespread nature of spirit beliefs and ritual practices among LRA rebels but preserving Ongwen's criminal liability under the Rome Statute. This way out of the dilemma has thus been essential to upholding the liberal legal paradigm. But it is questionable whether such a black-and-white perspective on belief, indoctrination and agency can do justice to the many shades of grey and ambiguity that characterise the struggle for survival in a protracted civil war, including the ways in which individual agency unfolds 'within local and global structures of violent constraint' (Branch 2017: 40).

The manner in which the judges of Trial Chamber IX arrived at this decision illustrates how legal interpretation merges into trial procedure, as their projection of this belief binary depended crucially on how the evidence was handled. As indicated earlier, linguistic anthropological work on intertextuality in the legal process provides a useful framework for this. Trial Chamber IX's projection of 'a pattern' of belief indeed appears to be a matter of a highly selective citation practice in which the judges picked those lines of testimony that supported their theory. In doing so, they took the referential content of the witnesses' statements at face value and ignored how these statements were embedded in their interactional context. The resulting 'pattern' is the result of the accumulation of cited instances in the Judgment, where coherence is established by the tacit metapragmatic instruction that they should be read as mutually elaborating (D'hondt et al. 2025: 382).

Take, for example, the testimony of Witness P-0205, a former LRA fighter who eventually escaped from the bush, who is quoted in the Judgment as saying, 'if I did believe strongly in the spirits, I would not have escaped' (Trial Judgment, para. 2650). However, in recontextualising this explicit disavowal of spirit belief as evidence of 'a pattern', the judges of Trial Chamber IX omitted that this statement was elicited during cross-examination by the defence, and that approximately five minutes later, Ongwen's counsel successfully elicited from the same witness an 'exhibition' of his belief in Kony's supernatural powers. In Example 12.1, P-0205 admitted that he had heard Kony make predictions that later came true, which at least partially contradicted his earlier disavowal of the supernatural (D'hondt et al. 2025: 377).

Example 12.1 Cross-examination of prosecution witness P-0205

Q. Now we are going to stay in the realm of the spirits a little bit longer, Mr Witness. The question is that: Did you ever hear Joseph Kony, hear him personally or be told about predictions that would come, predictions about the future that would eventually come to pass?
A. I heard them, I heard Joseph Kony talking about operations, operations that would take place and how the operation would end.
Q. Would these predictions sometimes come true?
A. On most times, yeah, the operations would actually take place.
(61 lines omitted, in which the witness described two prophesies made by Joseph Kony)
Q. Now, Mr Witness, you have just given us two examples of prophesies by Joseph Kony. And you said that he said others and after all of this you still do not believe at any time when you were in the LRA that Kony was actually possessed by

73 spirits; is that correct?
74 A. I said that I confirm with respects to the things that he prophesized
75 and the things that actually happened, I confirm in that regard.
76 Q. But you don't believe he was actually talking to spirits, do you?
77 A. I was always informed, the superior commanders would inform me.
78 They would tell us 'the spirits said', so I would also agree that the spirits said.

(from Ongwen, ICC-02/04-01/15-T-49-Red3-ENG, Transcripts, 8 March 2017, p. 20, line 22 to p. 22, line 20, available at www.legal-tools.org/doc/cbed47/pdf)

In addition to illustrating the judges' selectivity, Example 12.1 shows that, despite the self-evident appearance of the 'pattern' in the Judgment, the text trajectory that led to its formulation was not a unidirectional, teleological process. First, P-0205's testimony shows that binarism was already present in the entextualisation of lived experience, that is, in its interactional elicitation as 'quotable text' (Maybin 2017: 416). The questioning of P-0205 by Ongwen's counsel did not leave much room for grey either, and in this sense the counsel was complicit in the construction of the binarism (see D'hondt et al. 2025 for a detailed account). Second, it demonstrates that the entextualisation of spirit belief and the reconciliation of lived experience with the abstract binaries of positive law is not a straightforward process but is often actively contested by the parties and can have an unpredictable outcome. In the extract, for example, Ongwen's counsel indeed successfully elicited an 'exhibition' of belief from the witness but failed to obtain a quotable statement that could be easily extracted from its context of production and 'transported' to the Judgment.

In sum, the example of Acholi spirituality in Ongwen teaches us that the syllogistic reasoning found in judicial decisions is grounded in extensive discursive processing, both at the level of entextualising testimonial evidence and recontextualising it in the Judgment. Through this processing, the exigencies of the law, particularly the need to determine *individual* agency and responsibility, were coarticulated with a common sense 'anthropology' that assumes a binary perspective on belief in the supernatural.

Next, we will chart how this processing of facts to fit the legal syllogism and the tacit forms of extrajudicial normativity it projects, in turn, anchors legal reasoning in broader trajectories of conflict and reflexively inscribes proceedings in broader geopolitical theatres. This intertwining of international law and politics is evident, for example, in the recent debates over the arrest warrants issued by the ICC's Pre-Trial Chamber for war crimes and crimes against humanity committed in Ukraine and the State of Palestine. But it is equally present, perhaps more insidiously, in other ICC trials, such as the case against Al Mahdi for the destruction of Sufi shrines in the ancient city of Timbuktu.

12.4 Al Mahdi, or the Inescapability of Politics

On 27 September 2016, ICC Trial Chamber VIII found the Malian jihadist Ahmad Al Faqi Al Mahdi guilty of 'intentionally directing attacks against buildings dedicated to religion … and historic monuments' (nine shrines of Sufi scholars and the entrance door of a 15th-century mosque, destroyed in June and July 2012), punishable as a war crime under Article (8)(2)(e)(iv) of the Rome Statute. The trial, which lasted only three days, was widely perceived as an attempt by the Court to 'send a message' to other jihadist groups engaged in the 'performative' destruction of cultural heritage (Kersten 2016). In this sense, it demonstrated how the courtroom dialogues through which international criminal law unfolds are closely intertwined with translocal exchanges with audiences outside the ICC courtroom (D'hondt 2021b, D'hondt, Bens & Dupret 2021; cf. Sander 2019 on the expressivist turn in international criminal justice). Here, we explore an even more radical proposition, developed in critical legal studies by Koskenniemi (2011 and elsewhere), namely that international criminal law is not only brought to life in and through situated interactions but must also be understood as a form of discourse, a 'language game' (Wittgenstein) that allows actors to articulate particular arguments and positions. On the one hand, this view explains Jayyusi's (2015: 274) paradoxical observation that the corpus of international law (treaty law, human rights law, humanitarian law, etc.) 'is often invoked by both sides in a conflict at the same time [, … resulting in] disjunctive accounts that situate themselves in relation to a putatively shared body of principles and precepts'. The implication, however, is that international law alone is incapable of providing a normative ground for making a principled choice between the 'disjunctive accounts' articulated within the discursive space it opens. Overall, this perspective can be characterised as 'anti-foundational' because it regards the liberal rule of law not as a transcendent framework beyond politics but as an argument that actors use to buttress positions that are essentially political in nature.

This anti-foundationalism resonates strongly with Wittgenstein's argument that the applicability of a rule is never specified by the rule itself, as well as with our earlier remark that legal interpretation is essentially a two-way process. It additionally underscores that in international law, the discursive processing of a case to make the rule and the facts fit takes place in a context of political conflict. This further complicates matters, as political conflicts have a strong narrative component of their own and are often fuelled by divergent accounts of how the conflict came to be.

For Koskenniemi, this last point poses a fundamental challenge: in putting together a case, there is no escaping the fact that 'criminal law itself always consolidates some hegemonic narrative, some understanding of the political conflict which is a part of that conflict itself' (2011: 234). For an international tribunal like the ICC, the consequences are potentially devastating:

> as soon as the law tries to [...] evaluate the relevant contextual data, it will move onto an area of indeterminacy and political conflict. [...] A court cannot avoid taking judicial notice of a certain number of background facts. The moment it does this, however, it will seem to be conducting a political trial to the extent that what those facts are and how they should be understood is part of the conflict that is being adjudged. (Koskenniemi 2011: 195)

Let us now turn to an extract from Al Mahdi's confirmation of charges hearing, six months before the actual trial. Example 12.2 is part of the OTP's presentation of the context of the Timbuktu shrine destructions and gives a detailed account of the legal institutions established by the jihadist rebel authorities and Al Mahdi's role in them.

Example 12.2 Prosecution's submission at confirmation of charges hearing

1 À titre d'exemple, permettez-moi de vous montrer l'un de ces jugements rendus par
2 le tribunal islamique, qui est en langue arabe. Il s'agit d'une condamnation à une
3 peine de flagellation. Comme vous pouvez le voir à l'écran, ces jugements
4 observaient un certain formalisme. Ils étaient datés, numérotés, signés et portaient le
5 cachet du tribunal.
6 L'Accusation a divulgué à la Défense plusieurs dizaines de documents officiels
7 trouvés dans les locaux de la police islamique et du tribunal islamique, qui
8 observaient un formalisme similaire.
9 Il s'agissait d'un système répressif et coercitif organisé et structuré.

(from Al Mahdi, ICC-01/12-01/15-T-2-Red-FRA, Transcripts, 1 March 2016, p. 36, lines 2–10, available at www.legal-tools.org/doc/d3d6d7/)

My translation:

1 By way of example, allow me to show you one of these judgments handed down by
2 the Islamic Tribunal, which is in Arabic. It concerns a sentence of
3 flogging. As you can see on the screen, these judgments
4 observed a certain formalism. They were dated, numbered, signed and
5 stamped by the court.
6 The prosecution disclosed to the defence several dozen official documents
7 found on the premises of the Islamic police and the Islamic court, which
8 observed a similar formalism.
9 It was an organised and structured system of repression and coercion.

In the OTP's presentation, the act of visually displaying the document on the screen (and highlighting its formal-bureaucratic features in an 'ethnographic' manner) was accompanied by a refusal to engage with the judgments mentioned in the extract in terms of their legal content (e.g. by examining their compliance with human rights standards). Instead, the OTP opted for an 'exhibition mode' and de facto refused to recognise the Islamic Tribunal that produced these documents as a legitimate legal institution, casting it instead as part of a 'system of repression and coercion' with a mere pretense of legality. Elsewhere in the hearing, another OTP counsel showed footage of Al Mahdi engaged in an animated legal argument about the various sources of Islamic law used by the Tribunal (Al Mahdi, ICC-01/12-01/15-T-2-Red2-ENG, p. 44). Again, the OTP used audiovisual material to (literally) illustrate the 'kind of expertise' that Al Mahdi provided, but without discussing its legal content. This characterisation of the administrative and governmental structures established by the rebels in the territory under their control as 'not-legal' was not an isolated phenomenon but a recurring feature of the OTP's account of the political–historical context of the shrine destructions (D'hondt, Dupret & Bens forthcoming). The exhibition mode systematically highlighted the rebel institutions' claims to legality but also ironised them as mere pretence. Throughout the hearings, they were framed as part of a coercive apparatus installed by the jihadists to consolidate their power over the local population and impose their ideology, and the jihadists were consistently portrayed as external 'occupiers'.

This framing was not accidental, as recognising the legal aspirations of the rebel institutions (and, by extension, the legitimacy of jihadist rule) would have made it virtually impossible for the OTP to continue with the prosecution of the shrine destructions. The catch is that the destruction of cultural property is not included in the list of crimes against humanity in Article 7(1) of the Rome Statute, so the ICC's jurisdiction depended entirely on whether the destructions could be prosecuted as a war crime under Article 8. Recognising the incipient bureaucratisation of the jihadist regime and the successful establishment of a 'legal' order (even if it did not meet international human rights standards) would have made this impossible, since it would have meant that hostilities had ended and political governance had begun. In fact, Trial Chamber VIII's guilty verdict was indeed afterwards criticised because (1) the destructions took place after military operations had ended and (2) the jihadists' ties to the local community made their status as 'occupiers' questionable, leading the renowned international criminal law expert William Schabas to conclude that 'Al Mahdi was convicted of a crime he did not commit' (2017: 75).

Theoretically, it would also have been possible to construe the shrine destructions as a case of religious persecution under Article 7. However, it is doubtful whether such a charge based only on the shrine destructions would have met the threshold of gravity required for the OTP to open a case. Moreover, it would have required the Court to address the thorny issue of the right to alter cultural content 'from within' and the right to express this by physically removing monuments associated with the old regime from the landscape (Drumbl 2019: 92), as happened in many post-Soviet states.

The reasons for the OTP's decision to prosecute the Timbuktu shrine destructions as a war crime may have been of an internal legal nature, but the consequences reached deep into the real world. The destructions were part of a broader political conflict over the legitimacy of jihadist rule and the ownership of Mali's heritage sites and derived their performative character from their insertion into a trans-local 'dialogue' in which jihadists and representatives of the international community took successive 'turns' (D'hondt, Dupret & Bens 2021, Joy 2016). The OTP's decision to open a case on a relatively minor charge that could only be prosecuted as a war crime left it no choice but to venture into this political turmoil, since maintaining the necessary link to military conflict required rejecting the legitimacy of jihadist institutions. This, in turn, meant differentiating between acceptable and unacceptable expressions of Islam, taking a stance on the role of Islam in Sahelian society, and doing exactly what Koskenniemi warned against: unilaterally aligning oneself with the contextual narrative of one party to the conflict. According to Joy (2016), Islam in Mali has spread through a succession of jihads and counter-jihads. Inextricably linked to these recurring clashes, 'Islamic architecture in Mali has been the focus of violent contestation, both now and in the past' (67). By adopting the OTP's position on the non-legal character of the jihadist institutions that ordered the destructions, the ICC judges appear to have inscribed themselves in this cyclical movement.

As might be expected (see D'hondt 2009: 825), this political connection was never made explicit in the trial. In this sense, the example of the Islamic legal institutions in Al Mahdi illustrates at once how the discursive framing of the case was essential to prosecute the shrine destruction under Article 8 of the Rome Statute, while at the same time inscribing the trial into a broader political conflict.

12.5 Conclusion

In this chapter, opening the 'black box' of ICC courtroom talk has shown that the syllogistic reasoning that reconciles legal doctrine with the particulars of a case is always situated and subject to contingency. The practice of international criminal justice cannot be understood solely in terms of the law's constitutive rules, and the legal reasoning behind submissions and decisions also involves extrajudicial normative assessments that entangle the legal process with the broader social and (geo)political fabric. Thus, we have seen how ICC judges and counsel in the Ongwen case resorted to an *ad hoc* binarism in balancing the supernatural and individual agency, as they attempted to make sense of (testimony about) spirit beliefs in the context of the duress framework.

Finally, our brief foray into the OTP's representation of jihadist legal institutions in Al Mahdi demonstrated that, because the crimes were committed in a political context, this contingency may ultimately come to undermine the integrity of the judicial process itself.

This is not to say, of course, that we should necessarily share Koskenniemi's pessimism about the possibility of adjudicating political crimes within a criminal law framework. More than a decade ago, Nouwen and Werner (2010) called for the ICC to actively embrace its inherently political nature. More recently, Burgis-Kasthala and Sander (2024) have made the case for a 'post-critical' approach: in light of the fact that critical approaches to the international criminal law project have now gained widespread acceptance, it is time to look beyond its inherent limitations and biases and to harness the expressivist potential of a tribunal like the ICC to advance emancipatory political agendas. From this perspective, the contingency of the legal process is not something to be resisted but to be actively exploited. Understanding how the discourse of international criminal law works is a pivotal step in this direction.

References

Barrett, E. and Ferraz de Almeida, F. (forthcoming). 'From Timbuktu to the international community: Intertextuality, expressivism and legitimacy in the ICC's Al Mahdi trial'. *Journal of African Law*.

Bauman, R. and Briggs, C. (1990) 'Poetics and performance as critical perspectives on language and social life'. *Annual Review of Anthropology*, 19, 59–88.

Branch, A. (2017). 'Dominic Ongwen on trial: The ICC's African dilemmas'. *International Journal of Transitional Justice*, 11(1), 30–49.

Burgis-Kasthala, M. and Sander, B. (2024). 'Contemporary international criminal law after critique: Towards decolonial and abolitionist (dis-)engagement in an era of anti-impunity'. *Journal of International Criminal Justice*, 22(1), 127–150.

Clark, P. (2018). *Distant Justice: The Impact of the International Criminal Court on African Politics*. Cambridge: Cambridge University Press.

Clarke, K. M. (2019). *Affective Justice: The International Criminal Court and the Pan-Africanist Pushback*. Durham: Duke University Press.

D'hondt, S. (2009). 'Others on trial: The construction of cultural otherness in Belgian first instance criminal hearings'. *Journal of Pragmatics*, 41(4), 806–828.

D'hondt, S. (2013). 'Analyzing equivalences in discourse: Are discourse theory and membership categorization analysis compatible?' *Pragmatics*, 23(3), 421–445.

D'hondt, S. (2019). 'Humanity and its beneficiaries: Footing and stance-taking in an international criminal trial'. *Signs and Society*, 7(3), 427–453.

D'hondt, S. (2021a). 'Why being there mattered: Staged transparency at the International Criminal Court'. *Journal of Pragmatics*, 183, 168–178.

D'hondt, S. (2021b). 'One confession, multiple chronotopes: The interdiscursive authentication of an apology in an international criminal trial'. *Journal of Sociolinguistics*, 25(1), 62–80.

D'hondt, S., Dupret, B. and Bens, J. (2021). 'Weaving the threads of international criminal justice: The double dialogicity of law and politics in the ICC al-Mahdi case'. *Discourse, Context & Media*, 44, 100545.

D'hondt, S., Dupret, B. and Bens, J. (forthcoming). 'Islamic normativity and international criminal law: The colonial politics of recognition in the ICC Al Mahdi case'. Manuscript under review.

D'hondt, S., Pérez-León-Acevedo, J.-P., Ferraz de Almeida, F. and Barrett, E. (2022). 'Evidence about harm: Dual status victim participant testimony at the international criminal court and the straitjacketing of narratives about suffering'. *Criminal Law Forum*, 33(3), 191–232.

D'hondt, S., Pérez-León-Acevedo, J.-P., Ferraz de Almeida, F. and Barrett, E. (2025). 'Trajectories of spirituality: Producing and assessing cultural evidence at the International Criminal Court'. *Language in Society*, 54(2), 367–388.

Drumbl, M. A. (2019). 'From Timbuktu to The Hague and beyond: The war crime of intentionally attacking cultural property'. *Journal of International Criminal Justice*, 17(1), 77–99.

Dupret, B. (2011). *Adjudication in Action: An Ethnomethodology of Law, Morality and Justice*. Burlington: Ashgate.

Dupret, B., Lynch, M. and Berard, T. (eds.) (2015). *Law at Work: Studies in Legal Ethnomethods*. Oxford: Oxford University Press.

Eades, D. (2012). 'The social consequences of language ideologies in courtroom cross-examination'. *Language in Society*, 41(4), 471–497.

Ehrlich, S. (2012). 'Text trajectories, legal discourse and gendered inequalities'. *Applied Linguistics Review*, 3(1), 47–73.

Haviland, J. (2003). 'Ideologies of language: Reflections on language and U.S. law'. *American Anthropologist*, 105, 764–774.

Haworth, K. (2018). 'Tapes, transcripts and trials: The routine contamination of police interview evidence'. *International Journal of Evidence and Proof*, 22(4), 428–450.

Heffer, C., Rock, F. and Conley, J. (eds.) (2013). *Legal-Lay Communication: Textual Travels in The Law*. Oxford: Oxford University Press.

Jayyusi, L. (2015). 'Discursive cartographies, moral practices', in Dupret, B., Lynch, M. and Berard, T. (eds.), *Law at Work: Studies in Legal Ethnomethods*. Oxford: Oxford University Press, 273–298.

Joy, C. (2016). 'UNESCO is what? World heritage, militant Islam and the search for a common humanity in Mali', in Brumann, C. and Berliner, D. (eds.), *World Heritage on the Ground: Ethnographic Perspectives*. New York: Berghahn, 60–77.

Kelsall, T. (2009). *Culture under Cross-Examination: International Justice and the Special Court for Sierra Leone*. Cambridge: Cambridge University Press.

Kersten, M. (2016). 'Some thoughts on the Al Mahdi trial and the guilty plea'. *Justice in Conflict blog post*. https://justiceinconflict.org/2016/08/24/some-thoughts-on-the-al-mahdi-trial-and-guilty-plea/.

Komter, M. (2019). *The Suspect's Statement: Talk and Text in the Criminal Process*. Cambridge: Cambridge University Press.

Koskenniemi, M. (2011). *The Politics of International Law*. Oxford: Hart.

Latour, B. (2010). *The Making of Law: An Ethnography of the Conseil d'Etat*. Cambridge: Polity Press.

Matoesian, G. (2001). *Law and the Language of Identity: Discourse in the William Kennedy Smith Rape Trial*. Oxford: Oxford University Press.

Maybin, J. (2017). 'Textual trajectories: Theoretical roots and institutional consequences'. *Text & Talk*, 37(4), 415–435.

Mertz, E. (2007). *The Language of Law School: Learning to 'Think Like a Lawyer'*. Oxford: Oxford University Press.

Nouwen, S. M. and Werner, W. G. (2010). 'Doing justice to the political: The international criminal court in Uganda and Sudan'. *European Journal of International Law*, 21(4), 941–965.

Sander, B. (2018). 'History on trial: Historical narrative pluralism within and beyond international criminal courts'. *International & Comparative Law Quarterly*, 67(3), 547–576.

Sander, B. (2019). 'The expressive turn of international criminal justice: A field in search of meaning'. *Leiden Journal of International Law*, 32(4), 851–872.

Schabas, W. (2017). 'Al Mahdi has been convicted of a crime he did not commit'. *Case Western Reserve Journal of International Law*, 49(1), 75–102.

Strandberg Hassellind, F. (2021). 'The international criminal trial as a site for contesting historical and political narratives: The case of Dominic Ongwen'. *Social & Legal Studies*, 30(5), 790–809.

Vasiliev, S. (2020). 'The crises and critiques of international criminal justice', in Heller, K. J., Mégret, F., Nouwen, S. M. H, Ohlin, J. D. and Robinson, D. (eds.), *The Oxford Handbook of International Criminal Law*. Oxford: Oxford University Press, 626–651.

Wilson, R. A. (2016). 'Expert evidence on trial: Social researchers in the international criminal courtroom'. *American Ethnologist*, 43(4), 730–744.

Zienkowski, J. (2024). 'Poststructuralist discourse theory', in Vandenbroucke, M., Declercq, J., Brisard, F. and D'hondt, S. (eds.), *Handbook of Pragmatics 27th Annual Installment*. Amsterdam: Benjamins, 187–214.

13 The Politics of Official Language Rights in the Multilingual Courtroom

Janny H. C. Leung

13.1 Introduction: Universal and Official Language Rights

Language rights and the politics surrounding them often become focal points of legal contention within the courtroom. Key debates can revolve around issues such as whether the right to education includes the right to receive instruction in one's first language, as seen in cases such as the Belgian Linguistic Case (European Court of Human Rights), or what exactly constitutes linguistic discrimination, as illustrated by *Gajecki* v. *Surrey School District* (British Columbia Human Rights Tribunal). This chapter, however, focuses on a more specific set of contestations: those that centre on the contention over language use within legal proceedings. It delves into instances where individuals assert their right to use a particular language in courtroom settings, analysing the significance of their actions and the responses they elicit against the backdrop of broader political contexts. The chapter aims to unpack the intricate interplay between legal procedural norms and the politics of language, shedding light on how these realms influence and intersect with one another.

There are two primary types of language rights that pertain to legal proceedings. The first, rooted in the right to a fair trial, is based on principles of natural justice. It adopts a norm-and-accommodation approach, working with the assumption that a certain language is normally used as the medium of public communication and ensuring that accommodations are made for those who are not proficient in this language (as discussed by Patten & Kymlicka 2007). It aims to protect procedural fairness by ensuring that individuals are not placed at a communicative disadvantage due to their inability to speak the language used in court (see also Ng and Ruyters et al., this volume). As enshrined in Article 14 of the International Covenant on Civil and Political Rights, a criminal defendant who cannot understand the language of the proceedings is entitled to interpreter assistance. This type of language rights has broad application and can be referred to as universal language rights. The second type of language rights is usually derived from official language status granted by a legislative authority, often in a country's constitution. It provides recognition to languages, typically based on historical legacies and cultural identities. It is concerned with not only the communicative but also the symbolic function of an official language. These types of rights may be termed official language rights.

While universal language rights are subsumed under international human rights, official language rights are granted by individual jurisdictions. Although most governments serve a multilingual population, only a third of all states have granted official status to more than one official language. Leung (2019) offers a comprehensive survey of multilingual jurisdictions around the world and a theoretical framework to understand how official language rights work. The research reveals that mere conferral of official status does not necessarily guarantee the enactment of official language rights, and implementation of such rights is often sluggish. This chapter builds upon the insights gained from this foundational work and probes into the politics of official language rights as they are contested and negotiated in the courtroom. Legal proceedings from different jurisdictions, as detailed in court judgments and in media reports, will be compared and analysed through an interdisciplinary lens that crosses between legal and linguistic perspectives.

13.2 Seeking Official Recognition and Challenging Existing Language Practice

We will begin with a cluster of cases where trial participants sought to use local languages that did not have official status in their jurisdiction, but advocates contested that they should be recognised. In these instances, the pursuit of linguistic accommodation was not merely about overcoming a barrier to communication. Instead, it was aimed to contest the prevailing linguistic norms of the legal system. Such cases challenge the established order, bringing to light the cultural and identity conflicts embedded within the language policies of the legal regime (Leung 2019).

In the 1980s, a Breton defaced French road signs as part of a campaign for bilingual signage in Brittany, France. When prosecuted, he, along with his 12 witnesses, requested to testify in Breton, a language they used daily, which lacks official recognition in France. Their requests were denied by both trial and appellate courts on the basis that they were proficient in French. The United Nations Human Rights Committee later ruled that this did not constitute a violation of Article 14 of the International Covenant on Civil and Political Rights, noting that the defendant was not obstructed from expressing himself and had chosen not to participate in French (*Guesdon* v. *France*). Since the right to a fair trial treats language as nothing more than an instrument of communication, it does not entail the right to speak any language of one's choice in the courtroom, and the right to an interpreter is contingent on whether one can communicate in the language of the court. The Breton movement, on the other hand, is based on the assertion of cultural and linguistic identity and advocacy to strengthen minority language rights. Although the defendant lost every legal battle, the political campaign was not entirely futile. Bilingual road signs did arrive in Brittany (Vigers 2013), and the French suppression of regional identities has softened over time.

In 2008, a court application for an occasional liquor license, submitted in Irish, was rejected in Northern Ireland. The refusal was grounded in the Administration of Justice (Language) Act (Ireland) 1737, which stipulates that all court proceedings must be conducted in English (In re the Administration of Justice (Language) Act (Ireland) 1737). Originally intended to enhance court accessibility for individuals unfamiliar with Latin, French or court hand, this legislation inadvertently also excluded regional languages from use in legal settings. Although this act had been repealed across the rest of the United Kingdom, it remained in effect in Northern Ireland. Welsh could be used in Welsh courts after the Welsh Language Act 1993 came into force, and the use of Gaelic has been expanding in Scottish courts since the enactment of the Gaelic Language (Scotland) Act 2005. In the Republic of Ireland, both Irish and English hold official language status. Despite the British government recognising Irish as a minority language, its use in Northern Irish courts was restricted solely to individuals who could not speak English. The Queen's Bench dismissed the application for judicial review in this case, ruling that fairness was not compromised since the applicant was proficient in English. This situation bore similarities to the Breton case in France, with ongoing political advocacy for elevating the status of the Irish language in Northern Ireland. These efforts culminated in the recognition of Irish as an official language in 2022, following the passage of the Identity and Language (Northern Ireland) Act, which also saw the repeal of the 1737 Act. However, no positive legal right to use Irish in court proceedings has been established as a result of this change. In a historic moment in January 2024, the Irish language was spoken in the Royal Courts of Justice in Belfast for the first time in nearly three centuries, marking a significant milestone in the language's legal and cultural resurgence (McGovern 2024).

Language contestation in the courtroom is reflective of broader political struggles by language communities seeking status recognition. Such courtroom contestation could serve as catalysts for the conferral of official language status and the establishment of corresponding language rights. Canada serves as a prime example of how official bilingualism has evolved through a combination of constitutional changes, legislative acts and pivotal court rulings. A significant milestone in Canada's journey to legal bilingualism was the Supreme Court of Canada's decision in *R* v. *Dubois*, which established the equal authenticity of English and French texts in federal law. The equal authenticity principle then gained a statutory footing in the Official Languages

Act of 1969, which recognised English and French as the official languages of Canada, and was reaffirmed in the Canadian Charter of Rights and Freedoms of 1982. Judicial activism has played a crucial role in broadening the scope of official language rights in Canada. Initially, the Supreme Court had interpreted the right to 'use' an official language in legal proceedings as merely a speaker right. However, the court reversed its course in the landmark decision of *R* v. *Beaulac*. In this decision, the court applied a liberal interpretation of Section 530 of the Criminal Code, granting the defendant the right to be heard in an official language of their choice. This ruling drew a clear distinction between the general right to a fair trial and the specific rights associated with official language use. Justice Bastarache argues, 'Language rights are not subsumed by the right to a fair trial. If the right of the accused to use his or her official language in court proceedings was limited because of language proficiency in the other official language, there would in effect be no distinct language right'. Section 13.3 discusses jurisdictions where official language rights do appear to be subsumed by the right to a fair trial despite official recognition, and the contestations that have taken place in their courts.

13.3 Translating Status into Rights and Norm Creation

In a number of jurisdictions that have conferred official status to multiple languages, such as Canada, Finland, Ireland, Hong Kong and Wales, individuals participating in court proceedings are entitled to speak in an official language of their choice. However, in many other bilingual and multilingual jurisdictions, status recognition has not led to enforceable official language rights in the courtroom. A case in point is Hawaii, where, despite the Hawaiian language being officially recognised, individuals who are proficient in English do not have the right to testify in Hawaiian (*Tagupa* v. *Odo*). As a result, in legal settings, the Hawaiian language is effectively treated the same as any foreign language.

The South African Constitution, 1996, officially recognises 11 languages, but court proceedings take place almost exclusively in English and Afrikaans, languages historically linked to colonial rule. According to Section 35(3)(k) of the constitution, defendants are entitled to a trial in a language they understand, but they do not have a right to be tried in a language of their choice. The court in *Mthethwa* v. *De Bruin* thus rejected a teacher's desire to testify in IsiZulu, which is an official language with the largest number of speakers in the country. In a different case, a magistrate had used discretion to conduct an entire trial in IsiZulu, but his decision was deemed undesirable by a higher court (*S* v. *Damani*). Although advancing the use of indigenous languages is a constitutional imperative (Section 13.6), it is seen as a work in progress that requires the balancing of practicalities. In a significant move in 2017, the Chief Justice issued a directive mandating that English shall be the sole language of record in courts, replacing the previous requirement of English and Afrikaans as equal languages of record (The Judiciary Republic of South Africa 2017). Following this directive, the Western Cape High Court in *S* v. *Gordon* criticised a magistrate's court for using Afrikaans as the language of record. The court argued that the use of local languages allows litigants to unfairly shop for judges and the Department of Justice and Constitutional Development does not have the resources to promptly translate court records of proceedings from languages other than English. The court also pushed back against judicial activism concerning language rights, stating that while academics should be free to argue about what the law should be, judges do not have this luxury and are bound to resolve disputes within the framework of existing laws. In 2020, another departure from the norm took place in the case *Afriforum* v. *Unisa*, where Justice Maya wrote a bilingual judgment in English and her mother tongue, isiXhosa, challenging the dominance of English in South African courts. The bold experimentation met the requirement of the Chief Justice's directive by including English while simultaneously marking a historic moment by also adopting isiXhosa as a language of record. It makes the future creation of enforceable official language rights for indigenous languages more easily imaginable.

The Māori Language Act of 1987 (Section 13.4) in New Zealand empowers any participant in a legal proceeding, including members of the court, parties, witnesses, counsel or any individual granted permission by the presiding officer, to use te reo Māori. In 2018, an incident highlighted the practical application of this provision when a crown lawyer introduced herself to the court in te reo Māori. The presiding judge acknowledged her right to use the language but pointed out the necessity of providing advance notice for the arrangement of an interpreter. Their subsequent exchange, as reported in Gay (2018), has drawn media attention.

> JUSTICE BREWER: 'As a matter of curiosity, did you attribute to me an ability to speak Māori'
> JOHNSTON: 'No, sir. It's the convention of the Crown Law office to … '
> JUSTICE BREWER: 'Mystify judges'.
> JOHNSTON: 'To use one of the nation's languages'.
> Justice Brewer asked the lawyer if she was making a 'political point'.
> '… because you are not using it as a means of communication. You are using it as a means of making a point'.

Sociolinguist Olsen-Reeder (2019) interpreted the judge's reaction as a power play, arguing that it was actually Justice Brewer's language that was politically charged. Indeed, it is now not uncommon for judges in New Zealand to introduce themselves and open the court in te reo Māori, which – like English – can serve both symbolic and instrumental purposes. The entitlement to use an official language in court is not contingent upon the speaker's proficiency in another official language or their motivations for choosing a particular language. The perception that the use of a minority language in legal contexts is politically motivated may indicate that its utilisation has not yet been fully normalised within the legal system.

The formal recognition of a language's status bestows upon it a form of symbolic capital. For languages with a deep-rooted heritage in a region and for language communities that have experienced historical injustices, this recognition serves to honour their cultural significance and restore dignity to these communities. However, as illustrated by the aforementioned cases, the constitutional recognition of a language as official does not automatically guarantee swift legislative action to implement associated rights, nor does it ensure widespread usage of these languages in formal settings. The choice by court participants to use a less commonly employed official language, regardless of their underlying motives, serves as a practical test of the existing legal framework. Such actions can challenge the status quo and potentially expand the scope of official language rights, especially in contexts where the use of these rights is still being negotiated. The significance of such linguistic choices is magnified when made by individuals in positions of authority, like lawyers and judges, as their actions carry considerable weight and can set precedents for the normalisation of minority languages in legal settings.

13.4 Strategic Adoption of Language

As explored in Leung (2019), the adoption of official multilingualism expands the range of language options available, potentially offering advantages to bilingual individuals that are not accessible to monolingual speakers. This phenomenon underscores a complex dimension of language policy, where efforts to establish equality among different language communities might unintentionally lead to disparities within those communities.

It is no secret that a rich linguistic repertoire brings advantages in many contexts, from the workplace to social interactions. The courtroom is no different. Lawyers, in particular, have been known to adapt their communicative styles to better connect with their audience. For example, Fuller (2009) observed lawyers switching from Standard English to African American Vernacular English to strengthen solidarity with African American jurors. Similarly, in bilingual courtrooms in Malaysia, lawyers have been reported to alternate between Standard English and Malaysian English, tailoring their language use to the specific addressee (Powell & Hashim 2011).

Beyond the strategic use of language varieties for their emotional impact or rhetorical effectiveness, bilingual individuals may find unexpected advantages in legal contexts that may not have been anticipated by lawmakers supporting official multilingualism. For instance, litigants can deliberately involve interpreters to gain additional time to think, request document translations to delay proceedings or add to the stake of the trial (for example, for civil cases in Hong Kong, translation cost is a considered cost of proceedings, and the losing party may be liable for covering such costs, subject to judicial discretion; see Leung 2019). In regions where there is a scarcity of judges proficient in a certain official language, monolingual defendants might face extended pre-trial detentions. In contrast, bilingual defendants have the option to choose a language that could expedite their trial date (Wallace 2014). To some extent, bilingual defendants can also engage in judge-shopping. In Manitoba, defense counsels have reportedly chosen to have a trial conducted in English in order to avoid a certain francophone judge perceived as harsh on defendants (Standing Committee on Justice and Human Rights 2014).

The assertion of official language rights within the legal system does have its boundaries. This issue was brought to the fore in a notable Ontario case, where a monolingual motion judge dismissed a plaintiff's request for an adjournment until a bilingual judge became available. The judge's dismissal was based on the observation that the plaintiff had rejected over 16 judges for their lack of French proficiency, which led the judge to believe that the plaintiff was 'attempting to manipulate the bilingual obligation of provincial laws to his own purpose'. However, this decision was overturned in *Belende* v. *Patel*, where the appellate court affirmed that the right to a bilingual trial is fundamental and should not be subject to judicial discretion or withheld as a means to counter perceived abuses of process. The court clarified that this right could only be restricted if an individual is not proficient in the official language they choose for the proceedings. Such a restriction was applied in the cases *Ontario (Attorney General)* v. *Fleet Rent-a-Car Ltd.* and *Children's Aid Society of Toronto* v. *W.F.*, which involved applicants with limited French proficiency seeking trials in French, presumably to delay the legal process. These instances led to a nuanced understanding that while individuals are not required to demonstrate an inability to speak the other official language (English), there must be a genuine connection to the chosen official language to legitimately claim language rights. This framework aims to balance the protection of language rights with the need to prevent their misuse within the legal system.

While the benefits that bilingual individuals may gain from official multilingualism policies can be seen as an unintended side effect, these advantages are secondary to the broader objective of fully acknowledging and respecting the status of official languages. Such recognition should ideally occur without subjecting every instance of language use to judicial evaluation or discretion. The potential pitfalls of attempting to discern the motivations behind a participant's choice of language in legal proceedings are further explored in the subsequent Section 13.5.

13.5 Politicising Language Choice

This section examines instances where an individual's choice of an official language in legal proceedings has been either rejected or used adversely against them. Hong Kong, a former British colony with current status as a Special Administrative Region (SAR) of the People's Republic of China (PRC), recognises both English and Chinese as official languages (see also Ng, this volume). The SAR is governed under a One Country, Two Systems principle. However, the political landscape, especially following the large-scale protests in 2019 and the subsequent enactment of the National Security Law in 2020, has seen the choice of official language in trials, particularly those involving political activists, become a highly politicised issue.

Based on Cap. 5 of the Official Languages Ordinance, a party, witness or legal representative may use either or both of the official languages in court proceedings. However, the determination of the trial's language ultimately rests at the discretion of the presiding judge. There are at least three recent instances where the use, or the requested use, of an official language in the courtroom was questioned or denied. While these cases did not technically breach any official language rights – given the judge's discretion in determining the language of the trial – it is arguable whether these rights were genuinely respected.

In the case of *HKSAR* v. *Tam Tak Chi*, a sedition case which was conducted in Chinese, a notable interaction occurred during a pre-trial procedure concerning the language used in a report produced by the defence's expert witness. The expert, a university professor specialising in linguistics at an institution where English is the medium of instruction, had submitted her report in English. When questioned by the judge about this choice, the defence attorney explained that due to time constraints and the fact that English is the professor's professional language, the report was written in English. The judge expressed scepticism, suggesting that if the expert was ethnically Chinese and capable of speaking Chinese, it would have been more efficient for her to write the report in Chinese, especially under time pressure. He lamented that it was a waste of time to have to arrange for translation. The judge's comment falsely implies that the ethnicity of a speaker dictates the relative proficiency of their linguistic repertoire and overlooks the complexity of bilingual competence, which is sensitive to variables including the age of second language acquisition, the level of second language proficiency and the amount of first and second language exposure. Some bilinguals are known to be dominant in their second language. Bilingual competence is also known to vary according to discursive domains, resulting in a speaker being more proficient in everyday discourse in one language and professional discourse in another language (Birdsong 2014). Although the judge did not directly challenge the intention behind the choice of language in the expert report, the admonishment reflects misconceptions about language that have been long debunked.

In a significant case involving charges of conspiracy to commit subversion under the National Security Law – a law that stipulates life imprisonment as the maximum penalty – a language rights issue arose (*HKSAR* v. *Ng Gordon Ching Hang and Others*). The case featured 47 defendants, among whom was Ventus Lau, a defendant representing himself, who made a specific request for the trial to be conducted in Chinese, which is Lau's first language. It is also pertinent that the authoritative text of the National Security Law is in Chinese and the case involved evidence in Cantonese. Despite these factors, the trial was scheduled to be held in English, and Lau's request was denied by the judge without an explicit explanation (inmediahk.net, 2022). While the judge may have had valid reasons for this decision, possibly considering the rights and language proficiencies of the other defendants and their legal representatives, Lau's position as a self-representing litigant complicated the matter. Individuals who represent themselves in court are generally at a disadvantage due to their limited legal knowledge and unfamiliarity with legal language (see, e.g. Grieshofer, this volume). The added requirement to communicate via an interpreter further exacerbates these challenges, potentially impacting Lau's ability to effectively defend himself against a criminal charge that could lead to severe deprivation of his liberty.

In a third case, an activist and human rights lawyer, Chow Hang-tung, was self-representing in her trial for allegedly refusing to comply with a data request from the national security police (*HKSAR* v. *Chow Hang Tung and Others*). Despite the trial proceedings being conducted in English, Chow opted to give her testimony in Chinese. Considering that Chow is a bilingual barrister who was able to correct the court interpreter from time to time, the prosecutor challenged her decision to testify in Chinese, speculating whether her intention was to disseminate her political views to the court audience and to the media or to look for potential grounds for appeal through finding errors in court interpreting (The Witness, 2022). Chow countered these allegations by asserting her intention to present her evidence as precisely as possible and argued that it would be absurd for her to aim to testify in ways that the court audience did not understand. She added that since the nature of the trial was political, her testimony could not avoid politics.

Analysing these cases collectively within the sociolinguistic landscape of Hong Kong reveals deeper insights into the complexities of language use in legal settings. Sociolinguistic research provides a quantifiable account of Hong Kong's diglossic society (diglossia refers to a situation where two languages occupy different social functions in a society). According to the 2022 census, a vast majority (92.3%) of the population use Cantonese in their homes, with English and Mandarin each used by 2.1% of the population (Use of Language in Hong Kong 2024). Despite this, English maintains a significant presence in law, education, commerce and other professional domains, primarily functioning as a second language in educational institutions and workplaces. A study by Bacon-Shone (2015), which reconciled self-reported language proficiencies from census data with expert evaluations, found that just over a quarter of Hong Kong's population possesses functional proficiency in English. This proficiency is particularly relevant in the workforce, especially in positions that demand reading and writing skills, underscoring English's substantial role in professional contexts. The decision of the expert witness to draft her report in English, her professional language and the defendants' preference to testify in Cantonese thus perfectly align with Hong Kong's functional multilingualism, where English is often associated with professional and workplace settings, while Cantonese is the vernacular for everyday communication. Domain-specific choice of code is highly predictable in a diglossic society. Where a court participant's background provides sufficient grounding for their language choice, the right to testify in one of the two official languages should be respected without undue criticism or speculation about their underlying motives. This principle holds particular importance when such critiques emanate from influential figures like judges or prosecutors, as their comments can carry significant weight.

Until 1974, English was the exclusive language employed by the colonial British administration in Hong Kong. The enactment of the Official Languages Ordinance that year, spurred by public pressure, introduced Chinese as an official language alongside English (see also Ng, this volume). This victory for Hong Kong's official language rights movement was largely seen as a step towards decolonisation and the rectification of historical injustices faced by the majority population under colonial rule. It acknowledged the linguistic and cultural rights of the local Cantonese-speaking majority, aligning with broader efforts to restore equity and dignity to the people of Hong Kong. Official bilingualism and the English common law have been retained after the handover, with the official status of Chinese now reaffirming Chinese sovereignty. Given this historical backdrop, any scepticism or questioning of a defendant's decision to testify in their native language runs counter to the spirit of decolonisation. Such doubts may be reflective of the political paranoia that characterises the current sociopolitical climate in Hong Kong. Drawing parallels with Canadian legal practices, where the emphasis is on the individual's subjective connection to their chosen official language, Hong Kong's approach could similarly benefit from a more inclusive and respectful stance towards language rights. In Canada, the right to use an official language in legal proceedings is upheld without undue scrutiny into the individual's motives, provided there is a genuine connection to that language. Such an approach would not only align with the principles of justice and fairness but also contribute to the ongoing process of decolonisation by affirming the value and status of Chinese in official and legal contexts.

13.6 Discussion: Language Contestation in the Courtroom

The courtroom is an important arena where official language status and rights are not only applied but also negotiated. Historical and ongoing language disputes within judicial settings have played a pivotal role in shaping the landscape of official language recognition and the associated rights. The manner in which legal procedures handle these language contentions carries significant political weight, as judicial rulings in such cases can influence broader language policies and rights. Official language rights are deeply political. They are derived from status recognition, and status seeking in turn tends to be based on identity claims that are politically contested.

From the standpoint of ensuring a fair trial, the rationale behind offering linguistic accommodation based on an individual's proficiency in the court's official language seems justifiable, as such proficiency ostensibly negates any communicative disadvantage. However, this approach to universal language rights is not sensitive to considerations of justice beyond the courtroom's confines. When historical and political contexts are considered, evaluating linguistic accommodation solely based on proficiency rewards state policies that have aimed to assimilate linguistic minorities. Such policies often compel minority groups to learn the dominant language as a means of survival. When individuals from these communities achieve proficiency in the majority language, their proficiency paradoxically becomes a barrier to exercising their right to use their native language in legal settings. The Breton and Irish cases exemplify this type of minority language struggle and double punishment and the continuous efforts for the respective language communities to seek official status recognition. The paradox of universal language rights is that they tend to favour linguistic assimilation rather than protection of linguistic diversity (see Paz 2013 for an analysis based on cases adjudicated by international human rights courts).

In multilingual jurisdictions, constitutions that grant official status are generally vaguely formulated, providing little guidance on the legal implications of such status conferral (see full discussion in Chapter 4 of Leung 2019); implementing legislation may be developed very slowly or be sometimes lacking altogether. Despite status recognition of multiple languages in some jurisdictions, it is common, especially in postcolonial polities, for some official languages to be seen as having practical and instrumental functions while others as having sentimental and symbolic value. Attempts to use the latter in an official setting such as the courtroom challenge such entrenched language ideologies, as demonstrated in the isiXhosa and te reo Māori cases. To change the status quo requires not only the expansion of official language rights but also coordinated efforts in language planning, such as re-evaluating the language requirements for legal training programs and for judicial positions and making legal resources available in different official languages (Docrat 2022).

The final set of cases discussed in the chapter dealt with contestations not about the delineation of official language rights, but about whether the application of established rights is legitimate in particular instances. In Canadian jurisprudence, official language rights are not withheld even if they give bilinguals an advantage over others; rather, they are denied only to an individual who tries to use an official language that is not within their linguistic repertoire. Instances where bilinguals gain a privileged position often highlight broader systemic issues, such as unequal availability of legal practitioners with official language competencies in an area.

While the decision to choose or request a specific language for courtroom use can indeed be a political act and form of advocacy, conjecturing about the motives behind such a choice is generally inappropriate, except in clear cases of procedural abuse – such as when an individual requests to use a language with which they have no genuine connection. Often, assumptions about the reasons behind a language choice say more about the ideological stance of the person making the speculation than about the intentions of the party requesting the language use. This dynamic was particularly evident in the discussed cases from New Zealand and Hong Kong. Engaging in such contestations can be detrimental to the ethos of multilingual jurisdictions and risks undoing legislative and judicial efforts in promoting the status and legitimacy of an official language. The optics are particularly poor when the unmarked official language of the court carries colonial or significant social power, and the contested official language still has a marked presence when used.

The implementation of official language rights does not only bring symbolic benefits to the language communities concerned. The right to be heard in an official language of one's choice, which is only practiced in some multilingual jurisdictions, removes the need to communicate through an interpreter. As Macdonald (1997) highlights, using one's own language in court can allow the participant to fully harness the rhetorical power of language.

Dominant positivist theories view law as the command of a sovereign, a mechanism for dispute resolution or a set of rules that impose social control, all backed by the threat of force. However, akin to language's dual communicative and symbolic functions, law too serves both instrumental and symbolic functions. As posited by Leung (2019), official language laws, for instance, embody symbolic capital with significant political and economic implications. Politically, official multilingualism can be seen as a gesture of power sharing and a means of calming sub-state nationalism by creating a national imaginary that reflects the diversity and values of its populace. Economically, the adoption of certain official languages can also facilitate a country's integration into regional or global markets.

In officially multilingual jurisdictions, status granting through law, which carries immense social and political significance, typically precedes the establishment of rights and obligations. In other words, the symbolic functions come first, and the instrumental functions are derivative. The concept of symbolic jurisprudence, introduced in Leung (2019), elucidates that the mere recognition of a language's official status does not directly equate to the granting of rights. Instead, the process of defining and negotiating these rights involves various forms of contestation, including advocacy by civil society, public demonstrations, interventions by language commissioners and the assertion of rights within legal settings – as discussed in this chapter. These contestations can persist even after rights are formally established, as the establishment of new norms is inherently a gradual process. Consequently, a jurisdiction may retain an ideologically monolingual mindset for an extended period and treat official languages equally only in a formal and shallow manner, despite officially recognising multiple languages.

References

Bacon-Shone, J., Bolton, K. and Luke K. K. (2015). *Language Use, Proficiency and Attitudes in Hong Kong*. Hong Kong: Social Sciences Research Centre, The University of Hong Kong. Available at www.ssrc.hku.hk/files/language_2/HK_lg_survey_Final.pdf

Birdsong, D. (2014). 'Dominance and age in bilingualism'. *Applied Linguistics*, 35(4), 374–392.

Docrat, Z. (2022). 'A review of linguistic qualifications and training for legal professionals and judicial officers: A call for linguistic equality in South Africa's legal profession'. *International Journal for the Semiotics of Law*, 35(5), 1711–1731.

Fuller, J. (2009). 'Hearing between the lines: Style switching in a courtroom setting'. *Pragmatics*, 3(1), 29–43.

Gay, E. (2018). High Court judge asks if interpreter needed following lawyer's comments in te reo. *Stuff*. Available at www.stuff.co.nz/national/108484718/high-court-judge-asks-if-interpreter-needed-following-lawyers-comments-in-te-reo

Inmediahk.net (9 August 2022)【初選47人案】擬認罪劉頴匡申中文聆訊被拒 反問官：大家中國人, 點解講中文唔得? Available at https://www.inmediahk.net/node/社運/擬認罪劉頴匡申中文聆訊被拒-反問官：大家中國人，點解講中文唔得?

Leung, J. H. C. (2019). *Shallow Equality and Symbolic Jurisprudence in Multilingual Legal Orders*. Oxford: Oxford University Press.

Macdonald, R. A. (1997). 'Legal Bilingualism'. *McGill Law Journal*, 42(1), 119–167.

McGovern, E. (2024). 'Irish language used in Belfast courtroom for first time in 300 years'. *Belfast Telegraph*. Available at www.belfasttelegraph.co.uk/news/courts/irish-language-used-in-belfast-courtroom-for-first-time-in-300-years/a1191123085.html

Olsen-Reeder, V. (2019). 'When a judge slaps down a lawyer for a few words of te reo, it's about power'. *The Spinoff*. Available at https://thespinoff.co.nz/atea/05-01-2019/summer-reissue-when-a-judge-slaps-down-a-lawyer-for-a-few-words-of-te-reo-its-about-power

Patten, A. and Kymlicka, W. (2007). 'Introduction. Language rights and political theory: Context, issues, and approaches', in Kymlicka, W. and Patten, A. (eds.) *Language Rights and Political Theory*. Oxford, Oxford University Press, 1–51.

Paz, M. (2013). 'The failed promise of language rights: A critique of the international human rights regime'. *Harvard International Law Journal*, 54(1), 157–218.

Powell, R. and Hashim, A. (2011). 'Language disadvantage in Malaysian litigation and arbitration'. *World Englishes*, 30(1), 92–105.

Standing Committee on Justice and Human Rights (4 March 2014) Evidence, Number 014, 2nd Session, 41st Parliament, House of Commons, Canada. Available at https://publications.gc.ca/collections/collection_2014/parl/xc66-1/XC66-1-2-412-14-eng.pdf

The Judiciary, Republic of South Africa (2017). *Heads of Court Resolution on the Language of Record in South African Courts*. Available at www.judiciary.org.za/images/news/2019/Heads_of_Court_resolution_on_the_language_of_record.pdf

The Witness (6 December 2022). 支聯會拒交資料案｜鄒幸彤呈多份文件反駁 指絕非「外國代理人」控方質疑發表政見. Available at https://thewitnesshk.com/支聯會拒交資料案官准默哀後再開庭-鄒幸彤開始作/

Use of Language in Hong Kong (2024). *Hong Kong Monthly Digest of Statistics, February 2024*. Census and Statistics Department. Available at www.censtatd.gov.hk/en/data/stat_report/product/FA100270/att/B72402FA2024XXXXB0100.pdf (last accessed 9 April 2025).

Vigers, D. (2013). 'Signs of absence: Language and memory in the linguistic landscape of Brittany'. *International Journal of the Sociology of Language*, 2013(223), 171–187.

Wallace, M. (April 2014) 'Statutory Review of Part XVII of the Criminal Code: Report of the Standing Committee on Justice and Human Rights', House of Commons, Canada. Available at www.ourcommons.ca/Content/Committee/412/JUST/Reports/RP6535996/justrp04/justrp04-e.pdf

Cases Cited

AfriForum NPC v. *Chairperson of the Council of the University of South Africa & others* (765/2018) [2020] ZASCA 79 (30 June 2020)

Belende v. *Patel*, 2008 ONCA 148

The Belgian Linguistic case (No. 2) (1968) 1 EHRR 252

Children's Aid Society of Toronto v. *W. F.* [2014] O. J. No. 4338, 2014 ONCJ 480 (CanLII)

Gajecki v. *Surrey School District No. 36* (1989) 11 C.H.R.R. D/326 (B.C. Council of H.R.)

Guesdon v. *France, Communication No. 219/1986*, U.N. Doc. CCPR/C/39/D/219/1986 (1990)

HKSAR v. *Chow Hang Tung and Others* [2024] HKCFI 553

HKSAR v. *Ng Gordon Ching Hang and Others* [2024] HKCFI 1468

HKSAR v. *Tam Tak Chi*, No. DCCC 927, 928 & 930/2020 (2022)

In re the Administration of Justice (Language) Act (Ireland) 1737 [2009] NIQB 66

Mthethwa v. *De Bruin and Another* 1998(3) BCLR 336 (N)

Ontario (Attorney General) v. *Fleet Rent-A-Car Ltd.* [2002] O.J. No. 4693, 2002 CarswellOnt 428629, C.P.C. (5th) 315

R v. *Dubois*, [1935] S.C.R. 378
R v. *Beaulac* [1999] 1 S.C.R. 768
S v. *Damani* (DR224/14) [2014] ZAKZPHC 60; 2016 (1) SACR 80 (KZP) (9 December 2014)
S v. *Gordon* (171298) [2018] ZAWCHC 106 (29 August 2018)
Tagupa v. *Odo*, 843 F. Supp. 630 (D. Haw. 1994)

14 The Co-construction of Witness Statements in a Refugee Family Reunion Case

Judith Reynolds

14.1 Introduction

This chapter focuses on the communicative processes and actors involved in producing witness statements used as evidence in immigration visa applications and appeals. Western legal-institutional ideologies of evidence-gathering and establishing the 'truth' adhere to, and perpetuate, the belief that a witness's narrative statement constitutes that individual's solely authored personal account of an event or experience (Rock 2001). This belief can result in the involvement of others, who act as mediating parties and co-authors in the production of witness statement narratives in immigration cases, being overlooked in ways that linguistic studies of legal evidence-gathering processes find problematic (Smith-Khan 2019; Wadensjö et al. 2023; see also Haworth, this volume).

Drawing from a linguistic ethnographic case study of communication in UK asylum and refugee legal advice, the chapter examines one immigration lawyer's interpreter-mediated interactions with an Arabic-speaking refugee client after family reunion visas for the client's family have been refused by UK Visas and Immigration (the immigration authority for the UK, hereafter 'UKVI'). Across two connected meetings, a witness statement is prepared for use in two legal procedures (an appeal against the visa refusal decision for two individuals, and a new visa application for the others) to counter UKVI's assertion that family relationships have been falsified. The discourse analysis of selected data from these meetings shows how three authorial voices – client, lawyer and interpreter – are involved in the co-construction of this client's statement and how the specialist knowledge and expertise (legal, linguistic and contextual) of each co-author is necessary for building a successful evidential argument. The chapter shows how this co-authorship enhances the credibility and persuasiveness of the client's statement, enabling rather than impeding a more effective presentation of the truth of the client's situation.

Funding statement: This work was supported by the Arts and Humanities Research Council (Grant Number: 1494314).

14.2 Witness Statements in Immigration Legal Practice

In UK asylum and immigration processes, evidence about the personal circumstances of applicants or appellants is often presented through a witness statement. Witness statements in asylum applications, which rest on evaluation of the credibility of the evidence presented about the applicant's experience of persecution or fear of persecution (UK Visas and Immigration 2023; Thomas 2006), present a version of the applicant's experiential narrative. They may supplement or respond to evaluation interviews and statement of evidence forms in the evidence-gathering process (Good 2011). In refugee family reunion visa applications, where the core issue is what relationship exists between the refugee sponsor and the family member applicant(s), witness statements may present an account of the family relationship(s) where other documentary evidence (e.g., birth or marriage certificates) is not available or is doubted to be genuine by the decision-making authority (British Red Cross 2024).

In an appeal process the witness statement serves as one piece in an interconnected chain of evidence and decision-making processes (Rock et al. 2013). The authenticity of the account depends partly on its internal coherence as a convincing explanatory text, and partly on its consistency with other evidence, including past statements made by the applicant at earlier stages of their case (see Good 2011 for a fuller discussion of witness statements and credibility in UK asylum processes). From the procedural perspective, the witness statement performs two roles: standing as 'the totality of the evidence in chief of the person giving that statement' (IAC Practice Direction 2022, Section 5.1), and telling the client's story as it is relevant to the appeal 'in a credible and persuasive manner' (Henderson et al. 2023: 12.13).

Credibility and persuasiveness are two separate but interlinked goals of witness statement drafting in wider legal practice. The core of credibility is that the statement should present the witness's own account of their personal experience and should be believable as such. Formalising this, statements are required to be in the witness's own words, expressed in the first person; represent the witness's own knowledge or beliefs; and conclude with a statement of truth (IAC Practice Direction 2022, section 5). Expert advice to asylum legal practitioners highlights the implicit demands of 'believability' in this context, commenting that the witness statement must contain a relatable story that '"rings true" to the judge when he reads it' (Henderson et al. 2023: 12.20). This advice links to problems associated with cultural bias in credibility decision-making, in that decision-makers are inevitably informed by their own cultural norms and values when deciding what they find credible (Thomas 2006: 84–85). Thus, editing by a legal representative may be needed to present the witness's own account in a believable manner in their statement.

Persuasiveness is a question of rhetorical force, or how language is used by one party to present a preferred version of events or preferred set of meanings, that is taken up by the other party in a situation where events or meanings are contested (Arribas-Ayllon et al. 2011: 57). Rhetoric is central to the development and practice of law (Brooks & Gewirtz 1996) and legal decision-making hinges not only on the presentation of credible evidence but also on the persuasiveness of the explanatory accounts accompanying such evidence. In an immigration or asylum appeal, the applicant must contest a version of facts or events that the immigration authorities have decided is the true version and have used as grounds to refuse an application. An appeal witness statement will need to present an account that persuasively contradicts the version of the facts or events underpinning the refusal decision. This chapter shows how linguistic analysis can uncover the collaborative work done to elicit and suitably present such a narrative.

Applied linguistic research has examined and theorised how statement-taking happens in a range of legal contexts and procedures. In the criminal investigation process, analysis of police-suspect interviews and the resulting written statements highlighted how in the shift from talk to written text, oral accounts can be transformed in form and content to become more detailed, more objective and more coherent stories (Jönsson & Linell 1991). Examination by Rock (2001) of police-witness interviews in England and the resulting statements demonstrated how such transformations are produced through narrative elicitation, focused questioning and drafting and editing of a written account during multiple dialogic exchanges between police officer and witness. The resulting statement is the co-authored product of the evaluation and mediation by the police officer of the witness's words (Rock 2001: 62), yet this is invisible in the form of the statement itself. Further, the evidence elicitation process is contextually framed and guided by institutional texts such as relevant laws and guidelines, police procedural codes and other evidential statements, with the institutional actor directing questioning and text construction in ways that will ensure the resulting narrative 'fits' relevant legal frameworks (Rock 2013). Such research shows witness statements in the criminal investigation context to be co-constructed products of dialogic and deeply intertextual interactions.

Although the legal processes of criminal prosecution and asylum determination differ significantly, studies have observed similar processes of narrative co-construction to those described in the previous paragraph also taking place in the preparation of asylum witness statements. Applicant witness statements may be generated in evaluation interviews between applicants and immigration officers (as in Maryns 2006, Wadensjö et al. 2023) or in preparatory meetings between applicants and their legal representatives before the evaluation interview (as in Jacobs & Maryns 2022, 2023). Studies foreground that in addition to processes of dialogic co-construction, evaluation, mediation, talk-to-text transformation and moulding of the narrative to fit a legal-institutional framework (characterised by Jacobs & Maryns 2023: 167, drawing on Jakobson 1959, as 'intralingual mediation'), the need to work across different languages is a further complexifying factor in asylum-related work. This may happen through using a second language or lingua franca, which can give rise to misunderstandings and misrepresentations that carry through to the written record with damaging consequences (Maryns 2006), or through relying on an interpreter (Grieshofer 2023). Wadensjö (1998) has convincingly shown that interpreters function not only as translators of the primary interlocutors' talk but also as coordinators of the dialogue in consecutively interpreted interactions. Thus, interpreter mediation may significantly impede the degree of control that an applicant and an interviewer have in their communication with each other, for example, over self-corrections, clarifications and making authorship of statements clear (Wadensjö et al. 2023). Jacobs and Maryns describe this combination of inter- and intralingual mediation as 'discursive mediation' (2023: 167), arguing that it is a core, yet hidden, communicative practice in asylum law contexts.

Cultural as well as linguistic mediation can be important in the work of immigration legal representatives (see Smith-Khan, this volume). Through a study examining aspects of family migration advice, Carver (2014) shows how lawyers are active in culturally translating how marital relationships are presented in evidence supporting UK spousal visa applications. This involves working out how relationships that are defined by non-Western cultural frames can be described and depicted as authentic to UK immigration decision-makers approaching the concept of marriage from a Western standpoint. Carver characterises such work, which responds to the legal requirement to demonstrate a 'genuine and subsisting' (Immigration Rules Appendix FM 2016, para. E-ECP.2.6) marital relationship between applicant and UK-based spouse, as a process of 'displaying genuineness' (Carver 2014: 272, drawing on Finch 2007) in marriages. She argues that lawyers are essential to the construction of a marital narrative that will be accepted as suitably authentic by the UK evaluating officers. Her study does not, however, feature interpreters as actors in such processes of cultural translation.

The literature briefly discussed in this section aims to contest legal–institutional conceptualisations of evidential statements as single-authored texts for which their purported authors bear sole responsibility. Smith-Khan (2019) argues that in asylum and immigration contexts, the mismatch between such ideologically grounded conceptualisations, and the reality of how evidence is produced, leads to injustice and should be challenged. She calls for further research 'better to understand and emphasise the impact of third parties in the application and appeals processes' (Smith-Khan 2019: 427), who go unseen by official processes and positionings. The present study contributes to this discussion.

14.3 Data and Methodology

The data presented constitute transcript excerpts from two lawyer–client meetings, both featuring an interpreter, which were audio-recorded and observed. In Meeting One, a client is interviewed to gather information for a resulting witness statement, and in Meeting Two, the finished statement is read back to, and checked by, the client one week later.

The data were collected during a linguistic ethnographic case study of communication in the delivery of asylum and refugee family reunion legal advice. Linguistic ethnography is a qualitative research approach in which ethnographic fieldwork in a research site of interest is combined with close analysis of language use in communicative interactions taking place there. It has been fruitfully used by applied linguists to deepen understanding of communicative processes in different areas of legal practice, including legal advice communication and court hearings (see, e.g., Jacobs & Maryns 2022, 2023; Grieshofer 2024). In this study the researcher engaged in participant observations in an English city-based legal advice service over a period of seven months. Where informed consent of all parties was obtained in advance, advice meetings between one experienced immigration lawyer and a range of her clients were observed and audio recorded. Recordings were transcribed by the author, with transcriptions of Arabic data, and translations of these to English, completed by research assistant and experienced translator Alaa Murad in close consultation with the author.

Two specific discourse analysis techniques, transcontextual analysis (Rock 2013) and rhetorical discourse analysis (Arribas-Ayllon et al. 2011), were used to analyse the data from the two connected meetings. The focus of transcontextual analysis is intertextuality, or the ways that texts are inevitably connected to other texts (Kristeva 1980, drawing on Bakhtin). Thus, texts are 'dialogical and polyvocal, containing many elements of other texts or "voices"' (Arribas-Ayllon et al. 2011: 69). (For a fuller account of the concept of intertextuality and its applicability to legal contexts, see Rock et al. 2013.) Rhetorical discourse analysis focuses on 'accounts', language use that is linked to persuasion, explanation and 'the construction of preferred meanings and the disagreement over descriptions' (Arribas-Ayllon et al. 2011: 57). Aspects of persuasiveness in written and oral texts that have been studied by discourse analysts and are relevant here include the structural coherence of a narrative; the level of detail and richness provided (through, e.g., use of metaphor and contrast devices) in describing individuals and events; the use of framing devices to present information and people in a particular contextualised manner; the provision of explanations or justifications; and the use of intertextual links to other texts and events (Arribas-Ayllon et al. 2011: 70–76). Combining the two analytic approaches permits investigation of the rhetorical transformations occurring between a statement-taking activity and the finished statement.

A copy of the finished witness statement was not obtained by the researcher (see Reynolds 2022 for exploration of related issues of ethics and positionality), and therefore the chapter relies on the linguistically mediated reading back of the statement in Meeting Two as evidence of the content and phrasing of the final statement. This is an imperfect evidence base, but it is nevertheless possible to draw some conclusions about the discursive mediation work (Jacobs & Maryns 2023) engaged in.

14.4 Analysis and Discussion

Meeting One and Meeting Two take place between Julia, the advice service's immigration lawyer, and client Khalid (all names are pseudonyms). Both meetings are attended by the same Arabic–English agency interpreter and the researcher. Khalid, a refugee from an Arabic-speaking country, has a wife and several children all still in their home country. After securing refugee status, Khalid was supported by Julia to prepare and sponsor refugee family reunion visa applications to UKVI by his wife and children. The visa applications were refused, with UKVI arguing that the marriage and birth certificates accompanying the applications (issued by the authorities of the home country) did not appear genuine. Thus, UKVI doubted that the family relationships were legitimate.

Julia has already advised Khalid that the quickest, most cost-effective option for challenging this decision is simply for his wife and youngest children, who are still minors, to apply for visas again with more evidence. However, his two eldest children are now eighteen – legally adults – and therefore under the relevant rules cannot make a new family visa application in the same way as the other family members. They must lodge an appeal with the Tribunal against the visa refusal decision. The witness statement by Khalid will serve as additional evidence in both the appeal and the fresh visa applications.

14.4.1 Metacommunication about the Purpose of the Statement

Example 14.1, taken from Meeting One, shows how metacommunication about the statement's purpose is used to open and frame the statement-taking activity. In the data extracts in the chapter, speakers are denoted as follows: L = lawyer (Julia); Int = interpreter; and Cl = client (Khalid).

Example 14.1 Meeting One, 01:48–03:14

	Speaker	Original language	Translation to English
1	L	okay, so the plan for today … is I thought we could do a, updated statement just to talk about the impact um of the refusal	
2	Int	خطتنا لليوم هي عمل إفادة لك لكي نعرف أثر الرفض عليك	Today, our plan is to make statement for you to tackle the impact of the refusal on you
3	L	okay we had done a previous statement with you um so I'm just gonna use that or part of that as as the basis but I think it's important that they they see, um not just for the appeal but for the fresh applications the impact that the refusals have had on you and your family	
4	Int	أخذنا إفادة سابقة منك، لذا سوف وكما تعلم لقد نأخد منها الأجزاء الضرورية وادرجها في إفادة اليوم لأنه من الهام جداً بيان أثر هذا الرفض عليك وعلى لم شمل عائلتك	As you know, we already took one from you. So, we will take the important details and involve them in today's statement. It is very important to highlight the impact of the refusal on you and the reunion with your family.

Through this opening statement to set up the activity, Julia makes clear that the statement will provide another channel for Khalid to demonstrate that his is a genuine family through describing the emotional distress triggered by the refusal. Julia also highlights that she will draw some information from a previous statement of Khalid's, made for the original visa applications, which (amongst other content) detailed problems of political harassment experienced by the family after Khalid had left the home country. In making explicit the purpose of the resulting witness statement at the start, Julia helps Khalid to understand what the upcoming question and answer exchanges will be oriented towards, exhibiting good metacommunicative practice in asylum-related lawyer-client communication (Jacobs & Maryns 2022: 397).

14.4.2 Asking Questions and Transforming Answers

Julia follows her opening explanation by asking Khalid 'so can you explain in your own words Khalid how you and your wife reacted (.) um when you first found out about the refusal?' (Meeting One, 04:06). Here, Julia signals to Khalid the ideology of statement-taking, that is, that the statement represents the client's own words. After interpretation, Khalid responds (in Example 14.2 and other extracts, (.) denotes a micropause and (…) denotes a longer pause):

Example 14.2 Meeting One, 04:35–06:51

	Speaker	Original language	Translation to English
1	Cl	ردة الفعل كانت صعبة جداً, وبالنسبة للأولاد كانت صعبة أيضاً. كانوا يأملون الإلتحاق بوالدهم والتخلص من المشاكل الناجة عن متابعات الحكومة	The reaction was really difficult, and for the children it was difficult also. They hoped to join me and escape from the troubles resulting from the government's follow-up.
2	Int	Yeah, okay, so (.) er it was really difficult for me and for my husband just to to know that er (.) our case has been refused, but the impact was little bit more difficult on my children (.) especially they were they had a a hope that they will er meet their father and just be together as a family er although er we have to take into consideration the problems that er er follow them in the country from the government from the situation (.) so it was really difficult	
3	Int	حسناً	Alright
4	Cl	بالنسبة لي، لن تتخيلي نفسيتي، كان لدي الأمل	For me, you cannot imagine my psychological state, I had a hope.
5	Int	نعم	Yea
6	Cl	كان لدي أمل بعد تقديم المستندات أني سوف أحضر الأولاد (...) لكن عند إستلام الرفض كنت متعب ومتأثر جداً	I had a hope to bring my children here, especially after submitting the documents (…) however, the refusal was devastating and I am deeply affected.
7	Int	yeah	
8	Cl	لحد الأن أنا لست طبيعياً	Until now, I do not feel well, I am not okay.

	Speaker	Original language	Translation to English
9	Int	yeah	
10	Cl	لست مرتاح	I am not comfortable.
11	Int	Er in the beginning when we just submit er (.) the application for reunion the family I had a big hope that I will see my family in the near future but er when they refuse my case I am disappointed (.) until now I am I feel depressed and I can't be relaxed, stop thinking about this refuse and (.) I don't know what to do	

Here, relevant extracts from the written statement as it is read back to Khalid in Meeting Two are presented (statement extracts are in English translation only, giving both the time stamps from the meeting transcript and the sentence number of the reconstructed statement).

> It was tough on me and on my wife, it was tougher on my children, they had a hope to join me very soon and see their father after that long time. (Statement sentence 9; Meeting Two, 09:48–10:06)
>
> ---
>
> My suffering began after the refusal and I always search for a way to help them as soon as possible. I feel depressed since I had received that decision. (Statement sentences 40-41; Meeting Two, 16.35–16:57)
>
> ---
>
> I wish that my family live with me as they face lots of hurt by the government, particularly after my departure. They left their house in [CITY] and moved to another area just to be safe. I want them with me in order to be secure. All the time, I worry about them … my concerns increase every day. I want them with me to be reunited and live safely in UK. I cannot stay at any place without thinking of them. That is why I am always physically and mentally tired. This mental exhaustion has increased after receiving the refusal. (End of Statement sentences 55-62; Meeting Two, 22:35–24:00)

In the creation of the written statement, the oral account goes through a number of transformations. First, Julia's prompting question from the interview is not included in the statement; Khalid's narrative is presented instead as a first-person monologue. Second, Khalid's wife (who was only implicitly included in Khalid's oral response at turn 1 of Example 14.2, and who was mistakenly referred to as 'my husband' in the interpreter's rendition of his words at turn 2) is explicitly mentioned at sentence 9 of the written statement, reflecting the semantic content of the prompting question. Third, references to Khalid's mental health, only discussed in Meeting One in the opening section shown in Example 14.2, are made multiple times in the statement: at the start, in the middle and at the end. Fourth, the troubles caused by the government, mentioned in the opening part of Meeting One, are incorporated only at the end of the written statement and are combined with other details (originating in the prior statement made for the initial applications) about the risks the family still faces in their home country and their efforts to escape harassment.

As editor/co-author of the final statement, Julia has taken several editorial decisions about how Khalid's narrative is presented. She crafts the phrasing of the narrative to fit the legal requirement of a first-person account, transforming dialogic interpreted question-and-answer sequences into declarative statements. She also builds the coherence and persuasiveness of the story by repeating references to the negative impact of the refusal decision on Khalid's mental health. Repetition of key information is a rhetorical device to emphasise its importance, and changing the order and frequency of this information also builds internal coherence in the statement's narrative. Further, Julia works intertextually to build in a convincing explanation for the family's anxiety and worry – the risks to the family's safety. This repeats, and is thus strengthened by, evidence that was presented in the statement supporting the initial applications. Julia's decision to place this relevant prior information at the end of the statement, directly next to the final mention of Khalid's negative state of mind, is also rhetorically significant: her crafting of the narrative structure creates the intended focus on emotional impact that was discussed in Example 14.1. This brief analysis shows how the lawyer makes use of rhetorical and intertextual strategies to build both the credibility and the persuasiveness of the client's statement, illustrating the impact of the co-authorship on the narrative.

14.4.3 Framing the Desired Content through the Framing of Questions

Like other legal actors from police interviewers to courtroom lawyers (Rock 2001; May et al. 2021), Julia uses different questioning styles to elicit particular answers from witnesses. Example 14.3 shows Julia asking Khalid a leading question, designed to elicit a response that makes a specific point in the statement (in the extracts, (xxx) denotes talk that was unintelligible from the recording).

Example 14.3 Meeting One, 17:50–18:42

	Speaker	Original language	Translation to English
1	L	you mentioned your family a few times during the asylum process um (.) so did you think that the Home Office already knew about your family?	
2	Int	لقد ذكرت عائلتك عدة مرات، فهل تعتقد أن وزارة الداخلية تعرف عن عائلتك؟	You have mentioned your family many times; do you think that the Home Office know about it?
3	Cl	yes	
4	Int	yes	
5	Cl	لأني في أول مقابلة مع الهجرة، (...)	In the first interview with Immigration (…)
6	Int	(xxx)	(xxx)
7	Cl	حدثتهم عن أولادي وسجلت أسمائهم	I told them about my children and I wrote down their names.
8	Int	yeah (.) er since the first interview I had met with the Home Office I had mentioned er, sorry I have mentioned my family and the names and er everything	

The combination of a declarative statement with a closed (yes or no) question (turn 1 of Example 14.3) is a highly directive way of framing a question reminiscent of cross-examination in courtroom discourse (May et al. 2021: 16). Through the declarative statement, Julia draws intertextually on records of Khalid's asylum interviews in his case file, and primes Khalid with the answer she expects to the question that immediately follows. Khalid supplies the hoped-for response at turns 5 and 7, supported by the interpreter's linguistic mediation.

In the statement, this interactional exchange is transformed as follows: 'I have spoken about my family in detail in the interview, and also when I applied for asylum. I mentioned it twice. I thought that the Home Office will understand the situation. I have a wife and children. I want to reunite with them here in UK' (Statement sentences 13–14; Meeting Two, 10:57–11:33).Most of this section of the statement was not uttered by Khalid in exactly this form in Meeting One. The first three sentences are a reformulation of Julia's question in turn 1 of Example 14.3, and Khalid's answer, but extended and elaborated to provide more detail (likely sourced intertextually from Khalid's asylum application documentation, or the previously prepared statement). The final two sentences constitute further repetitions of key information, added by Julia to make the rhetorical point more explicit. This shows how the lawyer's co-authorship is manifest not only in the activity of editing but also in her deliberate elicitation and inclusion of information that will enhance the credibility and persuasiveness of the account.

14.4.4 Co-producing a Narrative of Family Togetherness

Example 14.4 illustrates how the interpreter is also an active party in constructing the statement's narrative. Meeting One continues with Julia asking Khalid to describe an average day with his family. Responding, Khalid spends several minutes describing a typical day, detailing how he took his children to and from school and how they would eat family meals together, ending with the comment that 'I have never left them for such quite long time' (Meeting One, 28:46–28:48). After a lengthy pause while Julia types content into the draft statement, Julia offers an empathetic observation in turn 1, prompting an exchange between Khalid and the interpreter (in the extract, ((xyz)) denotes paralinguistic features and @@ denotes laughter):

Example 14.4 Meeting One, 29:38–30:35

	Speaker	Original language	Translation to English
1	L	so it's safe to say you miss them very much	
2	Int	أنت تشتاق لهم (...)	You miss them (...)
3	--	((sounds of sighing by more than one person))	
4	Cl	كثيراً	A lot
5	Int	جميعهم؟	All of them?
6	Cl	كيف؟	How is that?
7	Int	تشتاق لهم جميعاً أو واحد منهم بالتحديد؟	Do you miss them all or there is someone in particular?
8	Cl	طبعاً البكر له ميزة خاصة سواء كانت بنت أو ولد ولكني أحبهم كلهم بشدة. ولكن عندي إبنتي تحبني بشدة (...)نادياالوسطى	For sure, the eldest child has special advantage whether it is a boy or a girl. Yet, I love them all and my middle daughter Nadia loves me a lot (...)
9	Int	ناديا	Nadia
10	Cl	ناديا (xxx)	Nadia (xxx)
11	Int	er I miss them all of them together but the middle one Nadia she has a special relationship with me (.) er she she is very close to me	
12	L	so everyone has their favourites @@	

In this exchange, the usual participation framework is disrupted and something unusual happens: the interpreter steps out of the role of linguistic intermediary and into the role of question-poser. It is unclear what prompts the interpreter to ask Khalid 'All of them? Do you miss them all or there is someone in particular?' (turns 5 and 7), but the questions trigger a disclosure by Khalid that his daughter Nadia is particularly close to him. Khalid then describes what Nadia does to show her love for him, such as making him juice and wanting to go to sleep beside him, and comments that although for him she is special, he takes care not to show particular affection for her over and above his other children, to avoid the jealousy of the others (Meeting One, 32:57–33:18). Following this disclosure, the parties in the meeting segue away from the statement-taking activity into a lengthy wider conversation about avoiding parental favouritism. Julia and the interpreter, who are both parents, contribute anecdotes about this issue in their own family lives, and Khalid offers observant responses about the impossibility of treating children all the same. This broader conversation is notable for its emotional warmth, characterised by smiling, laughter and supportive remarks, and represents a significant episode of rapport-building between the three interlocutors.

Although it was generated by the unprompted question from the interpreter, perhaps because of its clear authenticity and power to 'display genuineness' (Carver 2014: 272), the exchange in and following Example 14.4 appears in the statement as the final part of a section in which Khalid's family life and relationships are described:

> My relation with my children is so strong, and I have special one with my daughter Nadia, she is unique for me. Many times she falls asleep beside me and then I take her to her bed. I did not show this relation in front of the other children to avoid troubles and jealousy. (Statement sentences 37–39; Meeting Two, 15:54–16:32)

Turns 5, 6 and 7 in Example 14.4 are not translated into English, and so it is possible that Julia does not realise that Khalid's disclosures about his daughter Nadia were prompted by the interpreter's role-transgressing question. To Julia, the exchange could have come across as a simple clarification or repair sequence between client and interpreter. Regardless of whether she understood the interpreter's role in its production or not, the disclosure is retained in the statement as part of Khalid's narrative of authenticity in family relationships. In the context of discussing an interpreter's impact on the written asylum narrative that emerges from interpreted asylum evaluation interviews, Wadensjö et al. (2023: 208–209) note that interpreters' effective control over repair and clarification exchanges within the three-way dialogue can have lasting effects in the written record and can shape asylum stories in unexpected ways. In this case, the dialogic intervention that the interpreter made in the unfolding narrative is significant because it generates this mini-narrative, which is then featured in the statement by the lawyer because of its authenticity and persuasive detail.

14.5 Conclusions

The analysis in this chapter has demonstrated how a witness statement for use in a family migration visa application and related appeal procedure is co-constructed by three co-authors (client, lawyer and interpreter). In this process, the specialist knowledge of each co-author is necessary to build the successful evidential argument. The lawyer, Julia, works intertextually and rhetorically, drawing on her knowledge of client Khalid's situation, earlier stages of the case and previously prepared documents to choose the desired focus of the statement and ask the client carefully framed questions. Khalid supplies the core content for the statement through his answers, and the interpreter provides interlanguage mediation to enable successful communication between the parties, while also in places contributing to the talk in significant, sometimes rapport-building ways. Finally, the lawyer evaluates and mediates what elements of the oral interview's content are included, how it is presented and how to combine it with other information in the statement. Her goal is to build a credible and persuasive written narrative, written authentically so as to present a consistent account from the perspective of the father of a separated family, also ensuring that cultural, legal and procedural aims of the witness statement are met. The final statement must therefore be understood as the result of extensive inter- and intralingual discursive mediation (Jacobs & Maryns 2023) between the three parties.

Metacommunication about what the three of them are working towards in the meeting is a key dimension of the collaboration. Julia regularly makes explicit what she intends the witness statement to convey and how the questions she poses to Khalid are relevant to this goal, such that on the final read-through in Meeting Two, Khalid is satisfied with the statement and requests no changes. This finding supports the conclusions of Jacobs and Maryns (2023: 187) who highlight the importance of metacommunication for establishing trust and mutual understanding in asylum-related legal representation work. The case study also provides further evidence of the need for immigrants from a non-Western background to 'display' (Carver 2014: 272) the authenticity of their family relationships in specific ways to satisfy Western decision-makers, and the crucial role of lawyers and interpreters in effecting this cultural translation work. Finally, the case study illustrates both the substantial impact that legal advisors and interpreters have on the preparation of evidence considered in asylum-related legal procedures and how applied linguistic research can help to deepen understanding of these relatively hidden aspects of legal practice (Smith-Khan 2019, this volume).

References

Arribas-Ayllon, M., Sarangi, S. and Clarke, A. (2011). *Genetic Testing: Accounts of Autonomy, Responsibility and Blame*. London: Routledge.

British Red Cross. (2024). *Applying for refugee family reunion: A guide to the family reunion process*. (1–70). Available at: www.redcross.org.uk/-/media/documents/get-help/get-help-as-a-refugee/british-red-cross-guide-to-family-reunion-2024-v2.pdf

Brooks, P. and Gewirtz, P. (1996). *Law's Stories: Narrative and Rhetoric in the Law*. New Haven: Yale University Press.

Carver, N. (2014). 'Displaying genuineness: cultural translation in the drafting of marriage narratives for immigration applications and appeals'. *Families, Relationships and Societies*, 3(2), 271–286.

Good, A. (2011). 'Witness statements and credibility assessments in the UK asylum courts', in Holden, L. (ed.), *Cultural Expertise and Litigation: Patterns, Conflicts, Narratives*. Abingdon: Routledge, 94–122.

Grieshofer, T. (2023). 'Remote interpreting in immigration tribunals'. *International Journal for the Semiotics of Law*, 36(2), 767–788.

Grieshofer, T. (2024). *Legal-Lay Discourse and Procedural Justice in Family and County Courts*. Cambridge: Cambridge University Press.

Henderson, M., Moffatt, R., Pickup, A. and Nollet, M. (2023). *Best Practice Guide to Asylum and Human Rights Appeals*. Electronic Immigration Network. Available at: www.ein.org.uk/bpg/contents

IAC Practice Direction. (May 2022). Practice Direction of the Immigration and Asylum Chamber of the First-tier Tribunal, Senior President of Tribunals, UK Judiciary. Available at: www.judiciary.uk/wp-content/uploads/2022/09/2022.05.13-Practice-Direction-FtT-IAC-1.pdf

Immigration Rules Appendix FM: family members. (2016). UK Home Office. Available at: www.gov.uk/guidance/immigration-rules/immigration-rules-appendix-fm-family-members

Jacobs, M. and Maryns, K. (2022). 'Managing narratives, managing identities: Language and credibility in legal consultations with asylum seekers'. *Language in Society*, 51(3), 375–402.

Jacobs, M. and Maryns, K. (2023). 'Mediated disclosure in asylum interviews'. *Multilingua*, 42(2), 165–189.

Jönsson, L. and Linell, P. (1991). 'Story generations: From dialogical interviews to written reports in police interrogations'. *Text*, 11(3), 419–440.

Kristeva, J. (1980). *Desire in Language*. New York: Columbia Press.

Maryns, K. (2006). *The Asylum Speaker: Language in the Belgian Asylum Procedure*. Manchester: St Jerome Press.

May, A., Holt, E., Al Saeed, N. and Sani, N.A. (2021). 'Socio-pragmatic aspects of legal questioning: Police Interviews, prosecutorial discourse and trial discourse', in Coulthard, M., May, A. and Sousa-Silva, R. (eds.), *The Routledge Handbook of Forensic Linguistics*. Abingdon: Routledge, 13–31.

Reynolds, J. (2022). '"Making the familiar strange": Reflexivity in linguistic ethnography within a context of former legal professional practice', in Consoli, S. and Ganassin, S. (eds.), *Reflexivity in Applied Linguistics: Opportunities, Challenges, and Suggestions*. New York: Routledge, 35–54.

Rock, F. (2001). 'The genesis of a witness statement'. *Forensic Linguistics*, 8(2), 44–72.

Rock, F. (2013). 'Every link in the chain. The police interview as textual intersection', in Heffer, C., Rock, F., and Conley, J. (eds.), *Legal-Lay Communication: Textual Travels in the Law*. Oxford: Oxford University Press, 78–103.

Rock, F., Heffer, C. and Conley, J. (2013). 'Textual travel in legal-lay communication', in Heffer, C., Rock, F. and Conley, J. (eds.), *Legal-Lay Communication: Textual Travels in the Law*. Oxford: Oxford University Press, 3–32.

Smith-Khan, L. (2019). 'Why refugee visa credibility assessments lack credibility: A critical discourse analysis'. *Griffith Law Review*, 28(4), 406–430.

Thomas, R. (2006). 'Assessing the credibility of asylum claims: EU and UK approaches examined'. *European Journal of Migration and Law*, 8(1), 79–96.

UK Visas and Immigration. (2023, September 28). *Assessing credibility and refugee status: caseworker guidance*. Available at: www.gov.uk/government/publications/considering-asylum-claims-and-assessing-credibility-instruction.

Wadensjö, C. (1998). *Interpreting as Interaction*. London: Routledge.

Wadensjö, C., Rehnberg, H. S. and Nikolaidou, Z. (2023). 'Managing a discourse of reporting: The complex composing of an asylum narrative'. *Multilingua*, 42(2), 191–213.

15 Intercultural Communication in Migration Law Education

Laura Smith-Khan

15.1 Educating Future Migration Practitioners

Intercultural communication is inherent in migration law practice. Those providing immigration advice often have very different linguistic repertoires and social identities from their clients (Jacobs & Maryns 2023; Reynolds 2020). This means extra care is needed during client consultations to successfully obtain complete and accurate information, provide optimal advice and prepare compliant visa applications. However, little is known about how practitioners develop these specialised communication skills during their study.

Therefore, this chapter explores the navigation of (mis)understanding during simulated migration law consultations undertaken as part of students' practical workshops. Examining three examples, the chapter shows how misunderstandings are produced interactively and are affected by both linguistic and extralinguistic factors. The analysis also demonstrates that including contextual data can offer additional insights into participants' discursive choices, perceptions and other factors that may help produce, identify and/or resolve (mis)understanding.

15.2 Lawyer–Client Consultations and Intercultural Communication

Consultations are central to legal practice and producing accurate information during these encounters is crucial. Lawyers must ascertain and understand clients' wishes and all relevant facts; clearly explain legal implications and potential outcomes; and advise a course of action. Ensuring understanding is fundamental: producing accurate, consistent and detailed information is often crucial for clients' credibility and successful legal outcomes (Smith-Khan 2021c; Trinch 2003).

Funding statement: This project was supported by a University of Technology Sydney Chancellor's Research Fellowship (2019–2024).

I thank the research participants for their generous cooperation, Dr Vera Williams Tetteh for research assistance, and the editors and Dr Loy Lising for helpful feedback.

Underlying the production of this information are multiple communicative strategies, observed in both lawyer–client interactions and other investigative contexts (Findling & Heydon 2016; Heffer, Conley & Rock 2013; Oxburgh et al. 2015). These include adequately briefing clients about the purpose(s) and structure of the consultation, asking particular types of questions at particular points in time, providing accessible explanations and allowing clients adequate and timely opportunities to share information, ask questions and raise and clarify any apparent misunderstandings (Reynolds 2020; Reynolds this volume).

While these considerations are relevant to any legal consultation (and indeed other investigative contexts), they deserve particularly close attention in settings where epistemic inequality is common, like many migration law matters, where clients are both legally and often socially outsiders and may also be navigating unfamiliar law in an unfamiliar language (Baynham et al. 2018).

All legal consultations may be considered intercultural encounters, given they involve 'experts trained in the terminology, communicative practices and institutional workings of the law, and these membership statuses are salient within, and impact on, interaction with a lay client outside of this group' (Reynolds 2020: 93). However, some also involve additional forms of linguistic and social diversity (for example, multiple languages and/or ethnic or socioeconomic differences), presenting further challenges and sometimes introducing the need to manage third parties, like interpreters (Jacobs & Maryns 2023; Reynolds, this volume; Xu 2021). However, even in monolingual encounters, participants may use different language varieties and/or have different levels of proficiency, unsurprisingly making misunderstandings more likely (Piller 2017).

In contrast with this perspective, there remains an ongoing tendency across disciplines and professions to characterise intercultural encounters as involving people from different national groups, attributing miscommunication to abstract and essentialised ideas of 'cultural clashes' (Piller 2017). Yet, sociolinguistic and linguistic ethnographic research demonstrates that misunderstandings can have a variety of causes, rooted in both language and/or 'lack of shared contextual knowledge' (Piller 2017: 82). Further, rather than resulting from one participant's lack of proficiency, meaning is 'constructed in interaction, and thus, no meaning or utterance can be construed as the sole products of the narrator' (Trinch 2003: 231). It is also necessary to consider 'situated activity types and participants' roles and power relations' (Tzanne 2000: 7). Critically examining both interactional and other data can therefore provide a useful 'reality check lest we mistake language problems for cultural problems' (Piller 2017: 86). Further, by identifying the specific types of linguistic difficulties that arise, exploring likely causes and situating them within their larger social/institutional context, research is better placed to inform practical improvements (MacLeod & Haworth 2016).

Therefore, this chapter examines how (mis)understanding is produced and navigated in legal education, with a focus on client-consultation role-plays. Section 15.3 provides an overview of the research setting and approach.

15.3 The GDMLP and the Study

In Australia, two groups may provide professional assistance to migration clients applying for a visa or seeking a review of an unsuccessful application – practicing lawyers and Registered Migration Agents (RMAs). The latter are professionals who register with the government regulatory body after completing a legislatively prescribed Graduate Diploma in Migration Law and Practice (GDMLP), passing externally administered oral and written examinations and proving their English proficiency and good character.

Registered Migration Agents play an important role in enhancing access to justice by providing relatively affordable assistance to visa applicants. Application procedures and legal requirements are often complex and demanding, making them difficult to navigate alone. RMAs reduce the number of self-represented applicants, somewhat like lay advisers, or McKenzie Friends, in other legal areas in common law jurisdictions (Grieshofer 2022).

They often also bring to their work valuable linguistic repertoires and lived experience. An estimated majority of RMAs are first-generation migrants, and in this study, teachers reported 43 percent of GDMLP students had English as a second language (L2). Both current practitioners and students report using or intending to use other languages at work (Smith-Khan 2021a), further enhancing accessibility of their services for clients with similar linguistic repertoires (Smith-Khan & Giles, 2025).

However, like other non-lawyer advisors (e.g., those in family law settings, Grieshofer 2022), RMAs have faced ongoing criticism. This has included discourses in which English is presented as the only valued language, and L2 speakers are framed as incompetent, rather than valued for their complete multilingual repertoires, undermining communicative confidence and professional identity development (Smith-Khan 2021b, 2021c, 2023).

This chapter examines data from a digital ethnography of a GDMLP. Digital ethnography follows the long-standing ethnographic tradition, adopting 'a research strategy that prioritises fieldwork-based collection of rich unstructured data through observations and accounts of participants … to make detailed descriptions of what they do and why they do it' (Jensen et al. 2022: 1145). In the present study, this entailed frequent visits to the GDMLP's online learning platform, periodic Zoom qualitative interviews with nine students and two teachers and examining learning materials and relevant law and policy. Following an engaged and active research approach (Maryns & Jacobs 2021), I also conducted a series of sociolinguistics-informed presentations on client interviewing and helped produce and refine other related learning materials, drawing on both existing findings and recommendations developed in investigative interviewing research (e.g., Heydon 2012) and my own ongoing research (Smith-Khan 2020, 2021c; Smith-Khan & Giles 2025).

Finally, I observed and recorded practical workshops conducted on Zoom, across three study periods in 2020–2021. Along with introductory presentations and briefings on relevant law, these workshops involved students role-playing RMA-client consultations. Students took turns playing an RMA, with another student (or occasionally a teacher) as their client, each with a partial set of hypothetical facts. The RMA had multiple explicit goals (set out in a checklist), including developing rapport, eliciting relevant information about their client and explaining their services, duties and law and procedure. The teaching team and I also explained different strategies to help avoid, identify and address misunderstandings. I collected 42 role-plays, involving 26 students and two teachers. Where possible, we also conducted short post-role-play debriefings and/or discussed the role-plays in separate research interviews.

This active and embedded approach is an important part of ethnographic research yet can create apparent tensions and challenges. Like anyone, both my social identities (for example, white, Australian-born, L1 English speaker, law graduate and staff member) and my language practices would have contributed to shaping the interactions (Ensser-Kananen 2024). Likewise, my own experiences, professional affiliation and beliefs shaped every aspect of the research process, from project design, through which lines of enquiry I pursued, to how I interpreted the resulting data.

However, this is a fundamental reality the qualitative paradigm embraces: 'meaning and knowledge are understood as situated and contextual, and research subjectivity is conceptualised as a *resource* for knowledge production, which inevitably sculpts the knowledge produced, rather than a must-be-contained threat to credibility' (Braun & Clarke 2021: 334–335). In line with this approach, analytical rigour was supported through critically reflexive 'immersion in the data, reading, reflecting, questioning, imagining, wondering, writing, retreating and returning' (Braun & Clarke 2021: 332). This was achieved through the long-term and extensive nature of the data collection and analysis, now spanning almost five years; through comparative critical discussions with a research assistant; and through long-term critical research journalling, covering not only evolving ideas about themes but also ongoing meta-reflections on my positionality and how it affected data production and analysis (Braun & Clarke 2021; Jensen et al. 2022).

In line with the existing literature (Baynham et al. 2018; Piller 2017; Reynolds 2020), the study's role-plays constitute intercultural communication in multiple ways. In the hypothetical scenario guiding them, the interaction is intercultural as participants are from two distinct social groups, one an RMA and the other a lay-client, each with their own diverging knowledge, roles and perspectives. In reality, the students were also diverse in terms of previous professional experience (e.g., across marketing, civil service and accountancy), location (living all around Australia and some overseas) and life experiences (migration trajectories, family structures and life stage). Further, most interactions were intercultural even in the narrower sense of involving participants from different pre-migration countries of origin, ethnic and/or linguistic backgrounds.

While the role-plays are obviously not real consultations, they nonetheless constitute authentic examples of student practical activities, providing insights into future RMAs' learning experiences and evolving communicative practices. This also represents a new setting for scholarship on investigative interviewing, which has most commonly focused on police interviews (e.g., Mason & Rock 2020). Integrating recommendations from this existing scholarship into training for migration law students is also novel, and the study offers a first opportunity to critically consider its application in this new setting.

This chapter concentrates specifically on miscommunication arising when RMA students attempt to elicit accurate information from their clients. The examples examined, involving three different pairs of students, are the three most obvious instances where a misunderstanding arose in the RMAs' attempts to collect information from their clients and remained partially or completely unresolved. They thus represent exceptional examples of something going wrong, rather than a broader trend. Indeed, in most role-plays, students apply the advice and follow the structure recommended, and this generally works well, without any apparent misunderstanding, with variation more commonly arising in terms of the *amount* rather than the accuracy of information elicited.

What works well and the variation in information quantity and type both merit their own examinations. However, these three exceptional cases offer the opportunity to explore potential reasons for misunderstandings arising and persisting. Each starts with discourse analysis of transcribed role-play excerpts. The analysis then contextualises these interactions by drawing on additional data – debriefings, learning materials and research interviews – to examine the multiple goals, roles and broader contexts influencing participants' discursive choices and meaning-making (Tzanne 2000). In doing so, the examination aims to demonstrate that rather than resulting from differences in culture or L2 speaker status, these misunderstandings are produced and remain due to a combination of linguistic choices and other context-specific factors.

15.4 Navigating (Mis)understanding in Client Consultations

15.4.1 Reformulation and Agreement

One hypothetical scenario provided in the workshops involved a client in Australia on a Working Holiday Visa. The information provided to those playing the client included these details (among others):

'You moved to Sydney about 8 months ago. You worked for *a family in Mosman* as their au pair, living in their house and helping to care for their youngest child' (my emphasis).

Example 15.1 occurs shortly after the consultation role-play starts and is the first opportunity for the client to share information about themselves. (In the following Examples, C = Client and A = Agent.)

Example 15.1

1 C uhm, currently I'm living in Sydney a:nd I have a Working Holiday visa for
2 about eighteen uhm months now. and I first started working in South
3 Australia, for the first eighteen months of my Working visa,
4 and I work in different vineyards uh harvesting grapes and /????/. uhm, and.
5 just six months ago, I have applied for the second. part of that Working
6 Holiday visa. uhm and I have moved to Sydney eight months ago now and
7 living as an au pair with a Mosman family, but uhm, since-so what happened
8 is six months ago, I've met my girlfriend, Sally, and I've moved in with them.
9 with-with HER sorry, and the Mosman family don't want, someone not living
10 with them working as an au pair, but I still help out once in a while.
11 A ... okay, so my underst-so-so just so I can clarify,
12 so you [spent the first 18 months on your Working=
13 C [Yeah.
14 A =Holiday visa working in vineyards in South Australia?. [and] six months ago
15 you applied for a=
16 C [yes.]
17 A =second Working Holiday visa? uhm, and then you worked as an au pair with
18 a Muslim family?
19 C yes.

One recommendation made to students ahead of the role-plays is to summarise the key facts that clients have provided to confirm the RMA's understanding is correct and/or prompt corrections or additional information and to ask the client to let them know if anything in their summary needs correction. Example 15.1 provides an example of this information-checking activity. However, a potential limitation to the RMA's formulation is also evident. The client provides a particular piece of information: The family the client worked for lives in a place called Mosman. The client structures her phrase 'with a Mosman family' (lines 7–9). The RMA hears this as 'with a Muslim family' and this hearing is made evident (to the researcher) as she verbalises it in her formulation (line 18). However, presumably the client mishears this as identical to her original utterance and therefore, rather than correcting the RMA, confirms her formulation. This means the misunderstanding persists undetected by either participant despite the information-checking activity.

There are potential language-based explanations for the initial misunderstanding. One is that instead of having Mosman positioned after the locative preposition 'in', it appears as a qualifier for 'family'. This makes mishearing it as 'Muslim' plausible. However, another factor is also relevant: a correct hearing depends on specific contextual knowledge. Sydney locals are likely to know of Mosman, a highly affluent suburb on Sydney's North Shore. However, those from other cities or countries are unlikely to know this and therefore less likely to identify it as a place. In contrast, if Mosman had been positioned after the locative preposition 'in' (as in the hypothetical facts), interlocutors would have had the grammatical clue needed to identify it as a place, perhaps prompting them to seek clarification.

However, these reflections offer no immediate assistance to RMAs in this type of situation: these are the client's utterances and therefore are not directly within the RMA's control. Still, crucially, the RMA did have the choice over how they summarised or formulated the information to the client to ensure their understanding of the facts. Here, resembling a problem common in other settings, this summary is 'presented as a statement inviting a simple confirmation, which provides … pressure for agreement' (Oxburgh et al. 2015: 153) and therefore unsurprisingly leads to the client providing a series of simple affirmations.

Fortunately, in this scenario, the family's suburb or religion had no material bearing on the RMA's advice, reflecting the banality of many misunderstandings in everyday interactions (Tzanne 2000). However, it demonstrates that the specific form that the summary and checking take may affect whether misunderstandings are identified and whether clients have genuine opportunities to correct information. For example, rephrasing the information into different grammatical forms may have helped, such as, 'you lived and worked with a family of Muslim faith'.

The RMA's attempted formulation, albeit not completely successful, exemplifies a discursive strategy towards fulfilling one specific goal of the consultation: obtaining accurate information. Example 15.2 demonstrates how misunderstanding can also arise when this strategy is neglected altogether and how competing discursive priorities may influence this choice.

15.4.2 Goal and Role Prioritisation

While the RMA in Example 15.1 attempted to check the accuracy of their understanding of client information, albeit unsuccessfully, it should be obvious that misunderstanding can also persist in situations where RMAs do not actively check important details. The next role-play is a good example of this. Here, the client seeks advice after the breakdown of his relationship with his Australian partner, who is sponsoring his partner visa. Again, the RMA mishears one of the client's utterances and the misunderstanding persists.

The extract shown in Example 15.2 occurs just over seven minutes into the consultation, where the client is explaining his situation.

Example 15.2

C Raquel and I have been together for four years, but last week I found out that uh she's been seeing someone else.[u:h,
A [yep.
C when I confronted her, she said, that uh she's planning, on marrying HIM-
A =yes. [yep.
C [the other guy, and if I interfere,
A yeah,
C she will report me to the department for my deportation.
A uhuh,
C but over the time, we: had some arguments and exchanged heated words which is you know,
A uhuh,
C it's nasty and disgusting. uhm, one of my friends told me that family violence- about the family violence provisions. I was wondering if you could be able to help me of preventing HER,-
A =uhuh-
C =for my deportation. she was pretty aggressive last week,
A uhuh
C but what do you think about my case?
A yep. u:h, I will tell you. u:h. first of all, uh, I should let you know, uh 24 months begins from the granting of your three-oh-NINE subclass visa. doesn't matter whether you're in relationship for, for example, four years before uh with Rachel. if you're granted 309 24 months after THAT, that's second /????/ which means the second stage of the processing of your subclass 100 visa will begin, and if you're in a continuing relationSHIP, you can satisfy the decision-maker at the department of immigration, to grant you a subclass 100 visa. otherwise, uh if you are uh broken down, your family relationship, maybe because of some reasons including the family violence, u:h you can be eligible uh to be granted a subclass 100 visa, provided that, you can PROVE the family violence is happened. it means-
C = but our, but our relationship now is, you know, we broken up. uh is there a way you could try to: uh convince Raquel to tell immigration that we are still together until I've got the permanent visa? is that possible?
A uhuh. u:h your obligation is now just uh let immigration know about the uh relationship uh breaking down, and uh that's the first thing I should tell you. and because everything, in terms of any changes in your relationship should be notified of the uh immigration uh department, and in this case, if you have any evidence of family violence, you can rely on that to ease uh your next step of I

mean, the granting of subclass 100 visa. what happened to you after family violence? did you have any report uh or maybe reported to anybody in terms of police or maybe any official bodies, or not?

The pair go on to explore various other potential visa options, but, unlike in Example 15.1, the RMA does not attempt to summarise or check the information the client provides related to potential family violence, despite it being crucial to his concluding advice regarding next steps. Nor is there any discussion of the (legal) meaning of family violence (e.g., physical vs. non-physical harm), which is far from self-evident for laypeople generally, and even more so in a migration context (Grieshofer 2023; Tambasco et al. 2024). Rather, 'family violence' becomes an accepted fact ('what happened to you after family violence?', lines 39–40) and attention shifts to providing evidence (e.g., 'references to 'report', 'police', 'official bodies' in lines 40–41).

Unlike the first role-play, where a misunderstanding is evident (to the reader/listener) in the interactional data, here, a crucial misunderstanding is only identified afterwards, thanks to additional data. The preparatory materials alerted me to the fact that the client had not experienced physical violence and that, while family violence can be non-physical, relying on 'arguments' is problematic. I raised this during debriefing, uncovering an undetected misunderstanding: the RMA student believed the client said he had been 'hit' by his partner.

Once again, the initial misunderstanding may have resulted from multiple converging factors. One possible factor is the client's pronunciation of 'heated' (line 10), with a relatively short 'ea' sound and an even distribution of stress across the two syllables. An approximate IPA transcription is /hit̬ɛd/, rather than, for example, /ˈhiː.tɪd/ or /ˈhiː.t̬ɪd/, offered as 'standard' UK and US pronunciations (Cambridge University Press 2024). The use of lingua franca English between two L2 speakers who acquired English in very different contexts may have contributed to the RMA's mishearing. It may also have been influenced by its discursive context: immediately afterwards, the client intro duces the topic of family violence provisions (lines 13–14).

However, crucially, the misunderstanding persists because of the RMA's subsequent choices. Rather than probing to clarify the information about the violence, he begins an extensive and detailed explanation about visa categories (e.g. lines 20–30 and 34–41). This reflects more generally the unequal division of talk throughout the encounter, where the RMA spends substantially more time speaking than the client, against teaching advice. It also demonstrates a role reversal that appears to originate at line 19, when the client becomes the questioner, with the RMA switching to providing ad hoc responses.

Again, debriefing provides additional insights, where the RMA student's first utterance is directed at his client counterpart: 'I tried to answer all of your questions but I'm not sure I did or not'. This points to the multiple simultaneous goals and activities within the consultation that influence participants' choices. While collecting information about the client's situation is a crucial goal of the consultation, the RMA foregrounds another key activity: that of providing advice. That he values this role is clear throughout the role-play, in his relatively heavy inclusion of technical explanations, even discussing visas unlikely to apply to his Irish client, like explaining asylum provisions and English language requirements. This is despite being cautioned to limit the use of technical language (see similar in Chow et al. 2023) given its potential to exacerbate epistemic inequality (Baynham et al. 2018; Reynolds 2020).

Further and relatedly, this is a first consultation with a prospective client and the RMA has a clear identity-construction goal. He attempts to perform a professional identity by providing technical legal explanations, reflecting his beliefs expressed during research interviews. There, he constructs his RMA identity and communication practices around technical knowledge, drawing parallels with his previous career as a scientist (Smith-Khan 2025). However, in this particular encounter, prioritising this answering/information-provision role in the way he does comes at the expense of another important activity: gathering and verifying important information about the client.

Therefore, it is insufficient to attribute the misunderstanding to English variety or L2 status. The ongoing misunderstanding results from the RMA's discursive choices throughout the consultation. Contrasting with the consultation in Extract 1 and teaching guidance, this includes not attempting to check important information. Further, the participants' role change from line 19 appears to result in diminished control over the consultation, which becomes unstructured, deviating from the checklist, with the RMA prioritising expansive responses to client questions in an ad hoc manner.

This occurs in the context of a time-limited initial consultation, where, along with demonstrating his competence and 'securing' the prospective client's business, the RMA also needed to establish basic facts and decide suitable next steps. Had the RMA made different choices over the goals to prioritise or how to achieve them, for example, dedicating less time to detailed explanations of visa categories, he would have had more time and cognitive space to explore and confirm the important detail related to family violence. This could have been achieved by explaining the legal meaning of family violence and reclaiming the questioner role to ask probing questions and/or prompt the client to share more about his experiences.

Here, it is clear how meaning-making in consultations is an interactive, multi-participant process, with legal professionals having shared responsibility for the production of clients' narratives (Trinch 2003; Reynolds, this volume). The RMA's overemphasis on technical information shifted the focus away from the client and their experiences, leaving unresolved ambiguity around crucial information.

Example 15.3 raises another, different difficulty related to lexical ambiguity that can arise when legal and lay language (and their speakers) interact.

15.4.3 Lexical Ambiguity

While Examples 15.1 and 15.2 involve misunderstandings arising in the activity of gathering information about clients' life experiences, the next involves another type of information-gathering. Professional conduct rules prohibit RMAs from assisting clients who have already engaged (i.e., contracted the services of) another RMA. Therefore, students are explicitly advised to check this with prospective clients, and this usually occurs during the opening sequences.

Example 15.3 provides an example and demonstrates another way misunderstandings can arise and, once again, remain – at least partially – undetected.

Example 15.3

A okay. so have you- have you already engaged with other migration agent?
C uh yes I did and they referred me to you.
A oh, okay, uhm so I heard about, uhm… your visa has been cancelled. is that right?
C yeah, that's right, it's been cancelled, yep.

Here again the misunderstanding is not clear from the interactional data alone. However, in this case, the RMA does detect a potential miscommunication but chooses not to address it. This becomes clear only through debriefing, set out in Example 15.4.

Example 15.4

A =but, yeah, can I have a question? (CLIENT) said he's ALREADY engaged with another agent, I assume he didn't pay, he just enquiry around, you know?-

The RMA's original intended meaning remained unclear to both me and the client (and is unclear from the transcript alone) until she raised it in the debriefing: she meant to ask whether the prospective client had already entered into a contract with another RMA. Here is an example of a commonly used word that can take on a 'distinct legal meaning' (Grieshofer 2024: 8), which was the RMA's intention. It also somewhat resembles the difficulties police face when providing cautions that replicate formal wording directly from legal and institutional texts, rather than reformulating them into plain language (Heydon 2013). An additional complicating factor is that the RMA, as a student and perhaps as an L2 English speaker, is still in the process of acquiring a specialist legal repertoire. This may explain her use of the phrasal verb 'engage *with*' (a general term) instead of 'engage' (a formal legal term), which likely caused the client's apparent misinterpretation of the question as meaning a general interaction rather than forming a contractual relationship. The RMA's reluctance to address the ambiguity around this term during the interaction is perhaps understood when contextualised within her broader experience and beliefs: she is an L2 English speaker who, throughout the research, expresses her lack of confidence in using spoken English, comparing herself to an imagined ideal native speaker, and intending to use Chinese and avoid English to perform a more professional identity with her (future) clients (Smith-Khan 2025). Therefore, she may have been unsure about her own usage and may have wished to avoid potential loss of face by raising it.

However, despite these potential challenges, the RMA still seems to have adequate confidence in her identification of the client's divergent interpretation, likely aided by the elaborative 'and they referred me to you' (line 2 in Example 15.3). She manages to incorporate this shift in meaning without explicitly flagging the misunderstanding, continuing seamlessly with the interaction while preserving her professional identity. This was only possible due to the form of the client's response. A shorter response, like a simple 'Yes I did', would have required the RMA to take active steps to clarify meaning, if indeed she would have identified a potential misunderstanding at all.

While this was a lucky outcome for the RMA in this situation, the likelihood of initial misunderstanding could have been decreased through different discursive choices. For example, the RMA could have avoided the challenging term, 'engaged', and opted for an alternative, as some other students did, for example, 'Have you actually seen any other migration agents for a consultation or signed up with anybody regarding this matter?'. Alternatively, explaining the purpose behind her question could have helped clarify its intended meaning, helping to avoid any ambiguity that such a term of art may cause for a lay (and possibly L2) interlocutor. Again, this was demonstrated by another student who similarly used the non-standard 'engaged with' but went on to explain the purpose for the question and clarify that they could proceed if the client had not signed an 'engagement document with anyone else'.

This example, where the client's response inadvertently resolves the difficulty, represents a broader trend among many of the interactions; the students playing the RMAs were often assisted by what the RMA in the third example characterised as 'cooperative' clients. Most often this influenced the *amount* of information clients provided, with additional facts being introduced even when the consultation had proceeded in another direction. This is undoubtedly a consequence of this particular social context: these were role-plays involving empathetic classmates playing the clients, who had been given a specific limited set of facts. While it is possible that real clients are often similarly helpful, analysis of authentic consultations with practicing RMAs and genuine clients would help clarify whether similar practices and patterns exist in that context.

15.5 Understanding (Mis)understanding

In her study of miscommunication, Tzanne (2000) posits that if we start our analysis with reference to cultural differences between participants, it should be unsurprising that these come to be identified as the reason for communicative breakdowns (8). Sociolinguistic examinations of interactional data provide a strong basis for dispelling the myth that culture is to blame.

The examples explored in this chapter provide evidence from a new setting of how (mis)understanding is produced and negotiated through dynamic, interactive processes. Even where issues related to language proficiency or diverse language varieties, or lexical ambiguity arise, miscommunication is best understood not with reference to these features alone. Rather, misunderstandings are also produced through participants' ongoing discursive choices, such as whether to reformulate or probe further or to move on to a new topic or activity. In turn, these choices are better understood when participants' multiple goals, roles and beliefs are explored. The second role-play provides particularly persuasive evidence that 'multiplicity of roles' can be pivotal (Tzanne 2000: 91). Likewise, participants' beliefs about themselves and how best to discursively achieve their goals can also help shape interactions and produce (mis)understanding within them.

Naturally, there are limits to what can be learned from simulated encounters. Beyond those already discussed, there are tensions between the highly monolingual nature of RMAs' educational context and their everyday work practices. Their communicative practices in class only represent one limited part of their complete, often multilingual, repertoires, which many (intend to) mobilise in their work (Smith-Khan 2023).

Inclusion of additional data sources beyond the interactions allowed greater insights. Misunderstanding is not always evident on the face of an interaction itself. Preparatory guidance, participant debriefing and research interviews can all help elucidate the occurrence of misunderstandings and the multiple reasons behind them.

Finally, and importantly, the project uncovered the potential benefits of extending the lessons and recommendations from existing scholarship in other investigative interview settings into this novel setting. The examples examined in this chapter constituted not only the most obvious occasions in which RMAs fell short of obtaining accurate information. They also each demonstrate that how much and how well these evidence-based recommendations are implemented has impacts on the production, identification and resolution of misunderstanding. This suggests not only that they are useful in this new setting but also that there remains scope to improve how they are integrated into training.

References

Baynham, M., Callaghan, J., Hanusova, J., Moore, E. and Simpson, J. (2018). 'Translanguaging immigration law: A legal advice drop-in service'. *Working Papers in Translanguaging and Translation*, 33.

Braun, V. and Clarke, V. (2021). 'One size fits all? What counts as quality practice in (reflexive) thematic analysis?'. *Qualitative Research in Psychology*, 18, 328–52.

Cambridge University Press. (2024). 'Pronunciation of "heated"'. *Cambridge Dictionary*, https://dictionary.cambridge.org/us/pronunciation/english/heated

Chow, W. W. S., Wong, K., Hiramoto, M., Wong, A., Ng, M. H. K., and Go, C. (2023). 'Tell me what happened: Pragmatics of affect in legal communication'. *International Journal for the Semiotics of Law*, 36, 561–77.

Ensser-Kananen, J. (2024). '"I almost died": Knowledges of pain in a Finnish school for refugee-background adults'. *Nordisk tidsskrift for pedagogikk og kritikk*, 10, 191–205.

Findling, J. and Heydon, G. (2016). 'Questioning the evidence: A case for best-practice models of interviewing in the Refugee Review Tribunal'. *Journal of Judicial Administration*, 26, 19–30.

Grieshofer, T. (2022). 'Lay advisers in Family Law settings: The role and quality of advice provided on social media'. *Social & Legal Studies*, 31, 941–60.

Grieshofer, T. (2023). 'Courts forms as part of online courts: Elicitation and communication in the early stages of legal proceedings'. *International Journal for the Semiotics of Law*, 36, 1843–81.

Grieshofer, T. (2024). *Legal-Lay Discourse and Procedural Justice in Family and County Courts*. Cambridge: Cambridge University Press. http://doi.org/10.1017/9781009378031

Heffer, C., Conley, J. and Rock, F. (eds.) (2013). *Legal-Lay Communication: Textual Travels in the Law*. New York: Oxford University Press.

Heydon, G. (2012). 'Helping the police with their enquiries: Enhancing the investigative interview with linguistic research'. *The Police Journal*, 85, 101–22.

Heydon, G. (2013). 'From legislation to the courts: Providing safe passage for legal texts through the challenges of a police interview', in Heffer, C., Rock, F. and Conley, J. (eds.), *Legal-Lay Communication: Textual Travels in the Law*. New York: Oxford University Press, 55–77.

Jacobs, M. and Maryns, K. (2023). 'Mediated disclosure in asylum encounters'. *Multilingua*, 42, 165–90.

Jensen, L. X., Bearman, M., Boud, D. and Konradsen, F. (2022). 'Digital ethnography in higher education teaching and learning – a methodological review'. *Higher Education*, 84, 1143–62.

MacLeod, N. and Haworth, K. (2016). 'Developing a linguistically informed approach to police interviewing', in Lawson, R. and Sayers, D. (eds.), *Sociolinguistic Research: Application and Impact*. London: Routledge, 151–70.

Maryns, K. and Jacobs, M. (2021). 'Data constitution and engagement with the field of asylum and migration'. *Journal of Pragmatics*, 178, 146–58.

Mason, M. and Rock, F. (eds.), (2020). *The Discourse of Police Interviews*. Chicago: University of Chicago Press.

Oxburgh, G., Fahsing, I., Haworth, K. and Blair, J.P. (2015). 'Interviewing suspected offenders', in Oxburgh, G., Myklebust, T., Grant, T. and Milne, R. (eds.), *Communication in Investigative and Legal Contexts: Integrated Approaches from Forensic Psychology, Linguistics and Law Enforcement*. Chichester: Wiley-Blackwell, 135–58.

Piller, I. (2017). *Intercultural Communication: A Critical Introduction*. Edinburgh: Edinburgh University Press.

Reynolds, J. T. (2020). 'Stability and hybridity in refugee legal advice meetings: Discursive structure as a resource for lawyer-client intercultural communication'. *Journal of Applied Linguistics and Professional Practice*, 15, 91–115.

Smith-Khan, L. (2020). 'Migration practitioners' roles in communicating credible refugee claims'. *Alternative Law Journal*, 45, 119–24.

Smith-Khan, L. (2021a). '"Common language" and proficiency tests: A critical examination of registration requirements for Australian Registered Migration Agents'. *Griffith Law Review*, 30, 97–121.

Smith-Khan, L. (2021b). 'Deficiencies and loopholes: clashing discourses, problems and solutions in Australian migration advice regulation'. *Discourse & Society*, 32, 598–621.

Smith-Khan, L. (2021c). '"I try not to be dominant, but I'm a lawyer!": Advisor resources, context and refugee credibility'. *Journal of Refugee Studies*, 34, 3710–33.

Smith-Khan, L. (2023). 'Intercultural communication in migration law practice'. 3 July, *Language on the Move*, www.languageonthemove.com/intercultural-communication-in-migration-law-practice/

Smith-Khan, L. (2025). 'Language, culture and professional communication in migration law education'. *Language, Culture and Curriculum*, 38(3), 340–60. https://doi.org/10.1080/07908318.2025.2481051

Smith-Khan, L. and Giles, C. (2025). 'Improving client communication skills in migration law and practice education'. *Alternative Law Journal*, 50, 101–6.

Tambasco, C., Hammond, K., Smith, J., Bottriell, N., McKenna, T., Burdon-Smith, L., and Fahmy, M. (2024). *Barriers to Access: Migrant and Refugee Women's Experiences of the Online Family Violence Intervention Order Process*. Melbourne: Northern CLC and the AMWCHR.

Trinch, S. L. (2003). *Latinas' Narratives of Domestic Abuse: Discrepant Versions of Violence*. Amsterdam: John Benjamins.

Tzanne, A. (2000). *Talking at Cross-Purposes: The Dynamics of Miscommunication*. Amsterdam: John Benjamins.

Xu, H. (2021). 'Roles, ethics and lawyers' reactions: An ethnographic study of interpreters' role performance in lawyer-client interviews'. *Multilingua*, 40, 617–46.

Index

For EU product safety concerns, contact us at Calle de José Abascal, 56–1°, 28003 Madrid, Spain or eugpsr@cambridge.org.

www.ingramcontent.com/pod-product-compliance
Ingram Content Group UK Ltd.
Pitfield, Milton Keynes, MK11 3LW, UK
UKHW020812270926
475880UK00019B/202
* 9 7 8 1 0 0 9 5 4 0 9 5 7 *